A FORGED AFFAIR

A FORGED AFFAIR

LIFE IS A JOURNEY BOOK 2

MARYANN CLARKE

COPYRIGHT

ALL RIGHTS RESERVED. No part of this publication may be reproduced, distributed, or transmitted in any form or by any means, including photocopying, recording, or other electronic or mechanical methods, without the prior permission of the publisher.

Copyright © 2019 by: Mary Ann F Clarke Scott

Ebook ISBN: 978-1-988743-01-1
KDP print book ISBN: 978-1-988743-27-1
Ingram Spark print book ISBN: 978-1-988743-00-4

This is a work of fiction. Any resemblance of characters to actual persons, living or dead, is purely coincidental. MaryAnn Clarke Scott holds exclusive rights to this work. Unauthorized duplication is prohibited.

WANT TO READ THE FIRST BOOK IN THE LIFE IS A JOURNEY SERIES?
BUY THE ART OF ENCHANTMENT NOW getbook.at/Enchantment
WANT TO CONNECT WITH ME?
www.maryannclarkescott.com
maryann@maryannclarkescott.com

If you enjoy reading this book, please rate it and leave a review on Amazon HERE. Your opinion can make or break an author's success, and it means the world to me.
Click here to leave a review: http://mybook.to/Forged

For my Family, who wander with me

"Life's a forge! Yes, and hammer and anvil, too! You'll be roasted, smelted, and pounded, and you'll scarce know what's happening to you."

— LLOYD ALEXANDER

"Those who do not succeed do not believe in their ability to exercise the potential power to forge beyond perceptions of limitations."

— T.F. HODGE

CHAPTER 1

As Niki Ballantyne had told herself many time before, risk was something to manage, not fear.

She squatted on the wooden platform, firmly gripping the zip-line handle in her gloved hands, hoping for a moment of exhilaration. High in the tall pine forest of Aquitaine, in the south of France, she waited for the all-clear signal from Paul, *Parc-en-Ciel*'s owner, before launching.

Once Paul had seen her search and rescue credentials, and her IRATA rope access certification, and she'd signed the release of liability waiver, she was finally good to go. She could ride and climb and jump circles around most people, but her petite build and girlish features threw them off. That could be fun too, though. Catching people off guard with her agility, skill and strength gave her an edge that made up for being small.

She sought *Parc-en-Ciel* because she'd heard about the extreme zip-line runs, but it had taken some effort to persuade Paul that she was up to it. At forty-five meters in height, with a total length of 470 meters, they normally reserved the run for stunt professionals and certified club members. It was this extreme height, speed and relative risk, however, that she found appealing.

"'You may think it's a long way down the road to the chemist.'"

"*Quoi?*"

"Nothing, Aziz."

Paul's assistant Aziz, an agile youth with skin the same rich blue-brown tone as the bark of the pine trees where they perched like tree sprites, mumbled in French and touched his headset. "All set, Niki?" His English wasn't half bad, though strongly accented with his native Moroccan French. Anything was better than her broken French, they'd been quick to inform her.

Lifting her face, she filled her lungs with the fresh tangy air of the evergreen forest. Not quite as majestic as her own North Shore Mountains in British Columbia, it was still a cool refreshing break from the hot summer sun and dust of the winding country roads she'd been cycling this past month.

She nodded, winking, and pushed the play button on her iPod, releasing a blast of EDM into her earbuds. "You bet, Aziz."

He grinned, his white teeth flashing brilliantly against his skin. "*Trois, deux, un, ALLEZ!*"

"Cowabunga!"

She gripped the trolley handles tighter and leapt from the platform into the trees, shutting her eyes and drawing cool forest air through her teeth for the first few moments, feeling the breeze whipping against her face and throat. Her pulse quickened as her speed built, the canopy of green whizzing by in a fifty-five kilometre per hour blur; the high-pitched whine of the cable hummed in her ears as much as into her hands and arms.

Part of the risk involved stopping unassisted at two intermediate platforms high in the trees and re-hooking her gear from one line to the next. As a certified rope access tech, this was something she could manage in her sleep. In the two-and-a half minutes she took to reach the final platform, she had time to acknowledge that, however invigorating a good zip-line run was, the cheap thrills were wearing thin. It fell far below her threshold for true excitement.

As the ride ended, she prepared for her landing. She twisted her body to align with Paul, who braced himself to catch her. Landing with the agility of a flying squirrel, she laughed and gave Paul a kiss on each cheek as he unhooked her harness from the line, and then from her body.

"*Merci* buckets, *mon ami*." Laughing, she let the harness drop to the platform and spun away from Paul, crouching and springing off the edge of the deck into a double back flip, landing on the soft thick layer of needles at its base.

"*Mon Dieu!*" Paul's voice echoed through the forest. "Niki! You could have killed yourself!"

She cussed in French and faced him, grinning, craning her neck to look up the fifteen feet or so to where he bent and peered down at her.

His wry expression told her she'd done it again.

"What?"

"'Shit of the bull?' You cannot keep translating English expressions literally."

She shrugged. "You knew what I meant, right?"

Paul shook is head. "I told you no monkey business on my gear, you crazy girl," he said.

"I thought you were in the monkey business." She laughed. "I'm not on your gear anymore, Paul. I'm on Mother Earth and she gave me a nice soft landing, thank you."

"It's a good thing you have ten times the training I do."

"Admit it. You're impressed. Anyway, if you'd fainted you know I'm qualified to save you."

"You give me hives. Heal that!" He liked to put on a grumpy face, but she knew he was teasing.

Aziz drifted to a stop beside her on his ATV with a spray of dirt and pine needles. Paul snorted and scampered down the ladder to her side. "That's it. No more rides for you. You're trouble." Belying his stern words, his grin stretched wide.

Aziz did a poor job of hiding his amusement, too.

"S'okay, Paul. I gotta go anyway." She'd already spent the better part of the day climbing and riding all over *Parc-en-Ciel* with these guys. She threw her arms around each of them in a quick hug and hoisted her pack onto her shoulders. "Hey, can you tell me the closest village where I can find a bed tonight?"

Paul made a face. "Le Village de Petit Bergeron is a few kilometres to the West, but I don't think you'll find a vacant room. The Medieval Festival starts tonight."

"Thanks, guys. That's where I'm headed then. See you!" she shouted as she leapt onto her bike and careened down the path toward the road, waving with one hand.

"*Adieu* Niki!" called Aziz.

"Good riddance!" she heard Paul tease as she pumped hard on her pedals, riding into the low rays of late afternoon sun. The further west she got, the sooner she'd be home.

She missed the sense of purpose, urgency and involvement that her usual rope access and search and rescue work both provided. The challenge and unpredictability of dealing with real high elevation rope work, and especially HETS rescues, were the only thing that made her feel alive, and could drive the darkest thoughts from her head. Both chief, who'd started all this by forcing a leave of absence on her, and her boss, would be happy that she was well-rested, at least. Thankfully, she was almost at the end of this enforced break, and would fly home from Bordeaux in another couple of weeks.

～

Upon cresting the rise, the vista opened up again, oaks, maples and sweet chestnuts parting like velvet theatre curtains to present an extravaganza of rose, orange sherbet and lavender. Niki placed one foot on the fine gravel verge by the narrow country road and sat back on the saddle to catch her breath. After weeks of cycling, she felt at one with her bike, and at ease in the French countryside.

When Chief Brian had suggested, or rather insisted, she take an overdue break from her search and rescue work, she was really pissed off. She didn't need a break. She loved her work. She lived for the riding and climbing in the pristine Coastal Mountains. The weekly quest of their ground and chopper searches, dropping on a line when they finally had located their target, invariably some inexperienced hiker or skier who'd lost the trail and fallen, the technical challenge of extraction, was hardly work to her. Every day of her search and rescue work brought surprises and thrills and made her feel incredibly useful.

But, she had to admit, she was grateful now that Chief had forced her to take this break. While she could have kept up her rope access work and just stepped away from search and rescue for a while, it was probably best she took a real vacation away from all of it. Brian had been right. She'd been long overdue for a change of pace, and after her weeks of adventure and relaxation, she felt wonderful and alive. She'd made this holiday her own. Despite her fear of excruciating boredom, she'd found enough to entertain and challenge herself traversing the south of France.

First, she'd been able to connect with some of the best parkour *traceurs* in the region, and had some incredible runs. Urban environments in Europe, with their stone lintels, balustrades, arches and classical details provided an exciting and very different world for her to explore, and it was all the better for having met some awesome practitioners in the country that had invented her sport. Between parkour, the challenging long distance cycling itself, and occasional detours, such as galloping on horseback on the Camargue beach, and her side trip to Pamplona to run with the bulls in mid-July–that had been a blast–it wasn't turning out to be such a bad holiday. And now she could add zip-lining to her list of satisfying ventures. Now she had to decide how to fill her final two weeks.

The light had changed again. There were times, cycling along, that the soft, buoyant quality of the light in the south of France made it appear she were floating, carried by an invisible force that rendered the peddling effortless—no, more than that, infused her and her bicycle with extra energy, a part of something larger than herself and infinite—the unnamed something that had inspired both writers and painters through the ages. Sometimes the air seemed to comprise lucid shimmering greens and blues, sometimes hazy almost-grey lilacs.

Now, as she rested at the apex of a small rise, she gazed down across a broad green and gold valley. Across cornrows strongly shadowed in the fading light, the maritime pines, willows, oaks and fruit trees were now swallowed into the dark throat of the gently rolling landscape, bowing out, stepping back to make way for the spectacle in the sky. A sky in which the benign afternoon cumulus clouds bunched, cracked and rolled into violent brushstrokes of vivid cobalt blue and violet shadows. She let her eyes rove over the colours.

In her rope access work, she was always way up in the sky, on a bridge, a tower or tall building, so she'd seen more than her share of spectacular sunsets. But this was something else.

Underlit by the sinking sun, the clouds reflected jarring pink, oriental orange and painful, glowing gold that made her think there was a god. She drew a deep lungful of cooling afternoon air, felt her face crack open in a broad smile of delight, and rubbed her moist hot hands across the cool dry skin of her face, smelling sweat and earth and the ripe peach she ate a while ago, chafing and massaging her skin back to warmth and life.

Music snaked upward, carried on a gentle breeze beyond the valley where a small, typical French hamlet perched on a gentle knoll, shadows gathering in the low light, gold glinting off of glass windows facing the setting sun. The music, however, came from dreams and memories, not modern or expected, but ancient, Medieval music, pipes and lute strings, and the lyrical voices of balladiers.

Intrigued, she pushed onward. It would be good to rest. A festival sounded mildly entertaining. If this were a nice town, maybe she'd even stay a few days and catch up on her beauty sleep.

The village on the mound turned out to have a steep approach, so by the time Niki pedalled partway up, to the outside edge of the ancient town walls of Petite Bergeron, she was breathing hard.

Now she understood what Paul had been saying as she left. It was like arriving during a circus or passing through a time portal. Or both. A bigger production than she'd expected, they'd built makeshift stone piers and a wooden gate and portcullis from plywood and expertly painted, creating a sense of arriving in a Medieval town. Beyond the fake gate though, and the knight in full shiny tin armour being photographed with throngs of tourists, the town was real enough, and Medieval enough, to be convincing. Colourful banners with coats of arms hung from the golden limestone buildings, and yellow and blue pennants flew, competing with the riot of red geraniums that tumbled from window boxes. Dozens, maybe hundreds, of people hiked up a steep cobbled avenue beyond the gate. Building anticipation filled the air. She'd seen many French cities and towns so far this summer, but this was by far the prettiest.

She pressed on up the ramp that wrapped the village walls, following the music. Even as she'd approached the walls, she passed people in costumes. Now she was entering the town, there were more people dressed in Medieval clothing than modern.

Soon, smells joined the sounds, drawing her onward and upward. Winding up a long cobbled street that bent around the walls, between the curving facades of two and three-story stone houses and a wide limestone baluster overlooking the countryside below, were rows of small white tents and market stalls. She pumped her bicycle over the cobbles, past farm produce, averting her eyes from a pile of oranges gleaming under lanterns lit to enhance the sinking sun. Instead, she admired small smelly cheeses and withered *saucisson sec*, and displays of clothing, toys, leatherwork and armour. To her left, narrow twisting cobbled streets lead uphill. A ghost image of the oranges lingered in her mind, but she shoved it away. There was no point in wishing that Sam were here, sharing this adventure with her. But he surely would have loved this Medieval fair. History and circuses always fascinated him, and this felt like a marriage of the two.

Everything had been more fun with Sam. A perpetual child, his excitement had fed her desire to maximize the joy he felt every day and had measurably enhanced her own experience. Despite the hard times, they'd had the best of times together. That old familiar heaviness in her chest hit her. She missed him as much now as ever, and felt a hollow sorrow every time she wished she could share something new with him, and see his sweet face light up.

The best part of doing anything with Sam was that he always had wanted to share. He always cared as much about how she felt as he did for his own pleasure. No one else had ever replaced him in this way.

She paused at the entrance to an even narrower lane that led uphill, past a few shops selling *jambon-beure* sandwiches and ice cream cones, wondering if the town square were up there somewhere. The path teemed with people, some tourists, others locals who were as much a part of the spectacle as participants in it. She'd need to save enough leg strength to hike up there and see what was happening.

"Where shall we have lunch, Sam?"

Winded, she nearly stopped to dismount when another cyclist surged past from behind her, shredded, cut legs driving forward, his lean butt raised from his seat, waggling in the air. Except for the padded crotch of his cycling shorts, he held no secrets. Here was a heart-stopping, beautiful specimen of manhood. And she wasn't going to cack out while he could see her, so she pushed up on her own pedals and strove to keep pace.

Thankfully, in another dozen strokes he stopped and dismounted just ahead of her, so she followed suit, breathing hard, her heart pounding with the extra effort. He tugged off his helmet to expose short dark hair mussed and spiked with perspiration and scratched his scalp roughly with a gloved hand. She knew that feeling, how itchy her head got, after a few hours of cycling, especially in this heat.

She should have pushed her bike past him. She should at least have pretended to ignore him. Instead, her eyes raked the man's lean, ropey cyclist's body, right past his lycra-clad hard-as-rocks buttocks to his sinewy calves. This was without a doubt one perk of cycling, and her pulse quickened at the thought of tangling between the sheets with someone as hard and fit and energetic as she was herself, liquid heat pooling in her belly. He was an excellent match for her, and she was even ripe for a dalliance after weeks on the road. Not that she got any regular action back home. But this was a holiday. His head turned in her direction, and their eyes caught. She slid her gaze away, but he'd seen her checking him out, and his sexy mouth had quirked in amusement, his bright eyes flicking up and down her body in reply. Her overheated face flushed hotter. Damn. She turned away and angled her bike toward the narrow uphill street to escape his knowing stare.

"Are you just arriving in Petit Bergeron?" His voice was as sexy as the rest of him, his caramel-toned tenor wrapping around the French syllables like a magic spell, drawing her in.

She groaned inwardly, stopped and turned. "I'm passaging through."

He tucked his chin and pulled back. "Where're you from?" He switched to unaccented English, surprising her. There'd been no hint in his French he wasn't a native speaker. Not that she was qualified to judge.

"Canada. You?"

"Same. Vancouver." He opened his fanny pack and pulled out an orange.

So not Quebec. "No shit. Me too. Small world." She rolled her eyes at the inane cliché, mentally tripping over the orange. Don't open it. Please don't open it. But he did. Of course he did, spoiling the moment.

A brilliant white grin split the handsome taut planes of his beard-shadowed face, and his intelligent blue eyes conveyed all kinds of naughty, flirtatious thoughts that made her stumble on the rough cobblestones beneath her feet. His teasing smile told her he could read her thoughts. Though he couldn't know all of them.

She swallowed, watching his strong tanned fingers puncture the pitted skin of the orange, breaking the brittle flesh. Frost vaporized into the hot afternoon air and dissipated, carrying the strong scent of citrus to her nose. Her stomach pinched and her head felt light and buzzy.

She recoiled, averting her gaze, suddenly needing to escape. "Uh– can you tell me where the town square is?"

"The *Place des Arcade*s is straight up there." A toss of his chin indicated the narrow street while he pocketed the peel from the orange and slipped a section into his mouth. He even chewed sexily.

Her throat worked, unable to swallow again, and she cleared her throat. "Why put the town square on the top of a hill? Kind of inconvenient, isn't it?"

He nodded. "That was the idea. To make it difficult for the enemy to get to. These small fortified towns were built during the Hundred Years War, nearly six hundred years ago."

"You sound like a teacher."

He lifted one shoulder. "Maybe I am." He offered her a chunk of his orange.

"Humph." She shook her head, no, and blinked at him. She wanted to enjoy a pleasant conversation in English, after a month of struggling in French, but she fidgeted, needing to move along. "Good for you."

His bark of laughter surprised her. "Do you want a hand getting your bike up the hill?"

Her smile faltered. "No. Thank you."

He pointed at her loaded bike. "But… It's no trouble."

"I've got it." She put up her hand, palm out, and moved ahead, shouldering her bike, saddlebags and all, and trudging up the steep slope, her quads burning with every stride.

"All right then. See you 'round."

She tossed one last glance over her shoulder, shaking her head and smiling at his attempted chivalry. Too bad. Delicious as he was, it was a good thing she was moving on so soon. The last thing she needed was a stupid fling with a guy from home, however tempting. She pushed on, feeling his sharp eyes following her progress up the hill, painfully conscious of her own lycra-wrapped butt.

∽

A few minutes later, she emerged into a large open square, surrounded by stone arcades at the ground floor of its framing buildings. The music grew louder, the aromas of delicious foods stronger. Her stomach growled as she anticipated choosing her evening meal from the wonderful choices laid out. Past the throng, in the centre of the square, stood a large roofed and pillared shelter. She'd seen one or two like it before, in other *Plus Beaux Village*, all of which they'd designated heritage resources, and popular tourist destinations. It was easy to see why. They were very picturesque.

She cast her gaze around the perimeter. This one though, had achieved a particular harmony in the balance of two and three-story buildings, in the elegant shapes of the arcades around the square. Painted wooden shutters, overflowing window boxes, and banners accented plainer buildings in just the right places.

Spilling out from under the open-sided roof, folding wooden chairs flanked rows of paper-covered folding tables. People young and old, costumed and not, sat at the tables eating, drinking and talking. It was difficult to navigate through the dense crowd with her bike, so she looked around for a place to tuck it safely away. Under the arcade, she found a railing surrounding a small ice cream shop with tables nestled under the stone vaults. She leaned her bike against it and locked it. Then she exchanged her stiff clip-on cycling shoes for the pair of pliable parkour sneakers she kept in her saddlebag.

Free to move, she plunged into the throng, smiling at the onslaught of stimuli. She still hadn't located the source of the music she heard, but she passed jugglers, a fire-eater with a crowd around him, and a marching procession of Knights Templar in bright white and red tunics, carrying spears. It was a spectacle, spread out through the village.

More booths and tables ringed the square, selling food that people could buy and eat right there. Her nose filled with the scents of roasting meat and spices. She stopped to admire a gigantic forty inch diameter pan of paella, filled with chicken and seafood, the rice glowing vermillion with saffron, and salivated. Soon, she told her twisting belly, soon. There were local wine vendors, too, and people selling gorgeous glazed pastries and breads, soap, textiles, candles and sweets. She walked on, admiring the craftsmanship of wood carvers and silversmiths. The merchants were friendly, to tourists and locals alike.

Admiring a colourful display of melons, tomatoes, strawberries, grapes and other local produce, a gnarled hand darted out and tightly gripped her arm. A tiny old woman, a printed kerchief tied over her grey hair, her face wrinkled and brown like old cowhide, had a hold on her and was pressing an orange toward her face.

"*Orange?*" she croaked in a heavy accent and gravelly voice.

"Ouch!" Niki backed away, trying to escape the claw-like hand that pinched her. "*Non, merci.*" What was it with the oranges today? Her arm slipped out but was grabbed again by the insistent old woman, who peered intently at Niki with black eyes clouded by cataracts.

"*Prenez!*" She insisted. "*Prenez!*"

"No, thank you, Madam. I don't like oranges."

The old woman curled her lips and swayed her head sadly. She set the orange back on its pile and pulled from her dirty apron pocket a bound bundle of twigs and pressed it against Niki's stomach. *"Vous devet vous preparer au changement."*

Prepare for change? What?

"C'est l'heure." It's time.

Reluctantly, Niki accepted the herb charm and smiled tightly, backing away from the annoying crone as she repeated her cryptic warning, which meant absolutely nothing that Niki could decipher.

Slipping into the crowd, she sniffed the twig bundle suspiciously, thinking it was likely infested with bugs. It's smelled nice though, of lavender and sage, so she tucked it into her pack. Who knew? Hopefully, the old Gypsy had given her a good luck charm and not a curse.

Under another of the stone vaults, a small group bent industriously over low benches. She moved closer to discover that people were learning how to carve designs into blocks of buttery limestone from a man with a canvas apron and white beard. The ground was dusted white, as were their skin and hair, making the entire tableau appear carved of stone.

A sudden burst of applause drew her attention, and another song started. Interested in the music, she followed the sound until she came to another small square off of a narrow passageway. People sat under patio umbrellas on a raised platform, overlooking a lower level where five musicians played.

Stone stairs led up to the cafe where people dined, and Niki sat on a stair, leaning against the stone wall, warm from the afternoon sun, to watch and listen.

A woman in a long, green dress with flared sleeves sang a sweet melancholy song. An elegant twist of velvet and satin cloth wrapped her head. Four men in tunics and tights played various instruments, a lute, pipes and percussive things she couldn't name. One guy, short and sturdy, with a couple days' beard and a conical suede cap, played a long oboe, and stamped his feet to the rhythm, the bells tied to his leather, curl-toed boots jingling with every step.

He began to sing with the woman, but appeared as much Shakespearian clown and court jester as he pranced around, bouncing in front of the audience, drawing them into his performance. His band mates jiggled and weaved as they played their instruments. They took turns harmonizing. He continued to tap his bell-trimmed feet, adding complex rhythms to their voices.

She gazed at the musicians and watched them play their instruments. It was uncanny, how authentic their costumes were, and more than that, their manners. The fantasy absorbed them as they smiled and danced, and they clearly loved what they were doing. She tried to imagine a group of twenty-first century friends getting together to practice this early music in someone's living room or garage but just couldn't picture it. They were so much a part of the illusion.

Niki closed her eyes for a moment and luxuriated in the exotic atmosphere. It was music unlike any she'd heard. She caught a hint of cinnamon and bitter orange rind on the warm air, as though flavoured with melancholy. She felt transported back in time to the year 1415. It would have been interesting, although harder, without modern technology and medicine. But in some ways society had evolved little in six hundred years. An image of Sam rose unbidden in her mind, and she wondered what life would have been like for him back then. People would have branded him the village idiot, no doubt, but would they have been kind, or cruel?

CHAPTER 2

M*on Dieu*, she's incredible!
 He deserved an Academy Award. As soon as he'd turned onto the ramp at the base of the hill, her sweet, tight bottom and powerful, pumping legs entranced him. Luc was about to dismount, exhausted, but pushed on to pass her, a part of him fully aware of trying to impress her like a randy teenager. Then he stopped, his heart racing from the effort, and did his darnedest to pretend he hadn't noticed her at all, as he took off his helmet and casually fixed his hair. Apparently he'd got away with it. Or maybe not. Hard to tell. Her expression was sardonic, and flirtatious. At least at first.

What had come over him? He shouldn't care. Each summer, he met hundreds of tourists passing through the village, many from back home. But some mysterious force grabbed him and compelled him to pursue an acquaintance with this one. Where did she came from? Why was she here?

She was gorgeous! It was hard to look good in lycra, a helmet and a layer of sweat and road grime. But she managed it. Small and solid and sexy. Radiating a weird energy and light like she hid a fuel source deep down inside of her, she drew him like a wave to the shore, his brain no longer fully driving the bus.

Though once he'd talked to her, he wasn't sure why he'd done it. No clever witticism had emerged from his mouth. And meeting women was not on his agenda.

But this one… the longer they spoke, the more curious he became. She wasn't immediately impressive. Ignorant, tomboyish, stubborn and aloof, but a sharp intelligence shone in her greenish-gold eyes, which met his directly and confidently. He'd nearly cowered under her challenging gaze. Yet he'd held his own, more intrigued than intimidated.

Her French was atrocious. Abominable. Godawful. And yet somehow, endearing. She got by, obviously. People must make allowances because she was so earnest, sincere and unselfconscious. And so damned cute. No poser there. You got what you saw.

Though perhaps that wasn't quite true. There was something walled off about her. Something defensive.

Something about her made him smile, and made him want to reach out and wrap his arms around her, hold her close, keep her safe. He'd never felt that way about anybody, not even his sisters. All the women in his life were so competent. He grew six inches. And grew lighter. Like he'd floated up off the ground a little. *Phhtt*. What Neanderthal nonsense.

He didn't understand why he found her so interesting. He wasn't exactly interested, anyway, just curious. He'd made his plans. Just because she was from his hometown, and different from any woman he'd ever met, and exuded an entrancing energy, didn't mean he had to drop everything and get to know her. Where did that thought even come from?

When the music stopped, she opened her eyes and watched the musicians put away their instruments. She rose, brushed the dust off her pants and returned to the main square, determined to find something to eat. Just as she approached a row of vendors, the crowd suddenly parted for a troupe of acrobats. A guy dressed in a jester's suit, with striped leggings, did a series of hand vaults in her direction. Her heart soared in recognition of his joyful movement, her arms and legs tingling.

In response to her broad smile, he bounded toward her and took a deep bow, and gracefully back-flipped away again. The acrobats turned the corner toward an open space next to the carving workshop she'd stopped by earlier.

Unable to control the urge to move, Niki loped forward, dropped her pack, cat-leapt over a low pylon and threw herself into a forward roll, landing in the middle of the acrobats.

They froze for a few seconds and then grinned in appreciation and kinship. A beautiful brown-skinned woman dressed in bright satin languidly bent backward like a stretching cat. She flipped her legs overhead and behind, righting herself, her smile wide.

They shuffled back a little to make space for Niki, and she obliged by running at a nearby stone pier. She leapt two meters up the side of it and doing a back flip, planted her feet back where she'd begun. The crowd let out a collective gasp and applauded. Two other acrobats took a turn entertaining the crowd with their antics while the jester guy approached her.

"Welcome stranger," he said in French, offering her his hand to shake.

"Hi," she replied, taking it in a warm grip.

"Hey, you're American!"

"Close. I'm from Vancouver. Canada," she said.

He turned her hand over, took it between both of his and ran his thumbs over the callouses on her palm, and met her eyes with a question.

She smiled. "Parkour."

"Ah. Splendid." He waved his friends over. "I'm Alain." The woman dressed in turban and baggy pants like a Persian dancer, and another man in yellow tights, jogged toward them, curiosity on their faces. "This is Sabine, and Rocco."

To Niki's surprise, Sabine swept her into a warm soft embrace, redolent of vanilla, musk and spice, laughing. "Hello, my friend."

Rocco also shook her hand.

"I'm Niki. It's great to meet you all. Do you live here?"

Alain answered for the group. "Not in Petit Bergeron, no, but in Bordeaux. We are here only for the festival."

"Me too, I guess," she said, looking around. What a fantastic discovery. She'd stay for the entire festival. It would be a blast.

A disturbance swept the crowd, and people pressed back with murmurs and cries of delight to allow a fantastical creature to wade through. He was easily ten feet tall. He'd painted his androgynous face metallic green and brown and purple. It was partially covered by a carved leather mask sprouting a beak and horns, like a demon, and his leather clothing was painted and embroidered with twigs and leaves.

Gauzy fabric trailed down from his arms and legs and wafted on the evening breeze as he waved and gestured to the crowd. The craftsmanship and showmanship was outstanding and again transported her into a magical carnivalesque world.

Glancing down, she confirmed that he walked on stilts, but his clothing draped to the ground and created the illusion of enormous height.

"Bravo!" she cried, but noted that Sabine and the others were rolling their eyes and smirking.

"*Mon Dieu*," murmured Rocco. "*Se crâner.*"

The stilt-walker paused in front of their group and grinned down at them. "*Salut*, Alain! Little jokers."

"Well, if it isn't Jacques, the beanstalk," Alain snarked. In a mumbled aside to Niki, he said, "His name is really Jean, but he thinks he's hot."

Oh, re-ally? She smiled widely and stepped toward Jacques, or Jean, tilting her head back to shout up to him. "Hello there!"

He looked down. "Hello, little one."

She waved. "D'you think I could try your walking sticks?" She didn't know the French word for stilts.

He smirked, shaking his head in disdain.

What an arrogant prick. "Seriously. I really want to try them." She stood with her arms akimbo, grinning.

"It's not as easy as I make it look, *petite*."

She shrugged. "I didn't say it was. I'm up for the challenge if you'll let me." She made eye contact with Alain, lifting her brows a little.

His eyes widened, as if to say, Are you truly able to do this? Then his mouth quirked up at the corners when he saw the confidence in her gaze. "What's the harm, Jean? Let the girl try. She won't fall. We'll hold the bases, eh?" The crowd had figured out what was happening, and gathered round. Niki recognized the musicians, who had sauntered up from the lower terrace, standing nearby, curious.

Sabine and Rocco joined Alain in urging Jean to agree, until he shook his head with a smug smile and said, "*D'accord*. Okay. One moment." Rocco and Alain gripped the stilts, and Jean bent to unsnap his long leggings, which dropped to the ground. Then he bent and loosened the straps that held his shins to the stilts, jumping down with a grunt. Swaggering over to Niki, he doffed his cap and made a bow with a flourish of his arm. "Be my guest, *mademoiselle*." He obviously assumed she would utterly fail in her challenge, making him look even better.

Niki scanned for something to climb onto, relishing the prospect of putting the arrogant fellow in his place.

The oboe player stepped forward and shouted to someone seated by a display nearby. "Oy, Didier. You're needed over here, big guy."

Niki glanced over in time to see an enormous, broad-shouldered blond man behind a table set down a book and turn toward them. She did a double-take, her heart jammed in her throat. Sam! Sam?

She gasped, her hand flying to her mouth. Then released the quickly indrawn breath on a long sigh. Her pulse settled again.

Of course, not Sam. It's only that he'd been on her mind. But her first impression brought a flood of familiar feelings, both joyful and painful.

The blond guy had apparently been following their antics, but feigned disinterest now, glancing with distaste at the musician. He turned away, picking up his book again, the tiny object delicate and out of place in his giant meaty hand. When she'd seen his face, he was nothing like Sam. His colouring was wrong, but something intangible in his profile, his posture, his manner and expression had screamed Sam at her. It shook her down to the soles of her shoes.

"Oh, come on, *Girafeau*. Seriously." The oboe player sneered and swaggered over to the blond man and nudged him. "Make yourself useful."

Niki didn't like the tone or attitude of the musician, and neither did the big blond guy, who obviously didn't want to get involved. But instead of sneering back at the obnoxious little musician, his body collapsed, his shoulders curling over his chest like a sagging scarecrow. He averted his gaze and bent lower over his book. The side of his face blazed with heat, and his Adam's apple bob.

Rather than backing off, the oboe player, and his two sidekicks, too, moved in closer, surrounding him, nudging and egging him on in some age-old schoolyard game. "Don't be a spoiled-sport, *Girafeau*. Come and play."

Now attention was on him, though, he faced them, his mouth grim, his eyes flat. Reluctantly he made to stand up, placing large hands on his knees. Niki couldn't tear her attention from him as he stood. He unfolded in slow motion. He seemed to be standing up forever. That's how long he took to stretch out his full length. She noticed his hands, though clean and neatly groomed, had black ground under his nails as though he worked with paint or grease. She scanned him from his oversized shoes up his incredibly long, thick legs, up, up, up until she could tilt her head back no further. Oh, lordy. Hello, Friendly Giant! She met his blue eyes, in their expression a world of hurt and resignation, with sympathy and understanding, trying to contain her shock.

Moral outrage overcame her. Now she understood why they picked on him. He was different, and that's all a bully needed to target his prey. But he was so huge, he might have swatted the annoying little men away like the despicable fleas they were.

Yet he didn't.

"How can I help you, miss?" His voice matched his size, deep and rumbling, though soft-spoken. She believed he could make the windowpanes rattle should he choose to, but she'd never seen a more diffident person. She doubted this man, Geoffrey or whatever, had raised his voice since he was a baby in his mother's arms, so uncomfortable was he in his own skin.

An image of Sam flashed in her mind. Although they were very different, despite the light thatch and sprinkle of freckles, she now saw what it was about this sad gentle giant that reminded her so much of her little brother. He radiated pain. It rolled off of him, and she knew he had been suffering a long, long time.

Then she caught the eye of someone standing in the crowd. The handsome cyclist from earlier stood with his arms full of boxes. And he wore a mighty scowl on his shadowed face that mirrored her own feelings.

Suddenly, this spectacle was about something else entirely. The giant would not defend himself. Like Sam, he needed champions to stand up for him and protect him. Because despite his powerful size, his spirit had been crushed long ago.

A heavy weight pressed down on Niki's chest. Her breathing slowed and her attention narrowed on the wounded giant. His blue gaze cast down, he scuffed a giant shoe against the pavement. His massive arms hung listlessly at his sides awaiting his latest torture. She tried to swallow, but the tightness in her throat made it impossible. For as long as she could remember, this was her life. Feeling as though she had to take on the entire world in defence of her little brother. What could she say or do to help?

Somehow she had to ease his pain.

CHAPTER 3

Luc Ehrenskjold hefted the large flat of farm produce to the top of the hill, heading towards the market square. His arms and legs felt shaky with fatigue from all the to-and-fro. There was still so much more to prepare for tonight's festivities. His stomach dipped and rolled at the thought. This year, both anticipation and dread warred in his gut.

"Luc! *Un moment!* Wait, *s'il te plait, mon enclume!*"

He paused and turned to the familiar voice of his dear friend. Charles hoofed it up the polished cobbles in his stiff Italian leather shoes, his face red with effort.

"*Salut, mon gros.* What's up?" He laughed at his friend. He'd gotten soft since their youth, his job as an engineer keeping him too long at his desk. When they'd been boys together, Charles had been the faster, stronger one as they tore around the French countryside together. No longer.

Charles approached, panting, and Luc waited for him.

"Are you on your way home from the office?" Luc enquired, giving him time to catch his breath.

"*Oui.* I'll pick up Francine and return later. What are you doing now?"

Luc's arms trembled with the effort of holding up his load. "You have the IQ of an oyster, *Frerot*. What's it look like? I'm taking these vegetables to *Grandmère Bougis.*"

"Ugh. That freaky old crone?" He shuddered. "She scares me."

"Don't be a superstitious fool. She needs help to stock up for tonight. It will be a big crowd this year."

Charles placed his hands on his hips and leaned back, beaming. "It's that time again."

Luc felt it too, the excitement of the festival. It crested just now, on the first evening, after weeks of preparation and anticipation. This year, more than ever. "Patrice will make it in time? I haven't heard from her."

"Ah, I remember why I stopped to talk to you. She left me a message. She's waiting for a later delivery at the shop and she'll be late."

Luc frowned. Why hadn't she texted him? Maybe he missed it? He wanted to check his phone, but his hands were full, and his phone was in his backpack.

Charles grinned. "Don't worry. She'd never miss the start of festival." His eyes narrowed as he peered closely at Luc, scratching the back of his head, his lip curling.

"What?" Luc sometimes wished Charles didn't know him so well. It made his intentions so much more awkward. It was difficult enough proposing marriage to your best friend's sister, someone you'd known since childhood, and considered an old friend.

"Is that what you're wearing tonight?" He cast a critical eye over Luc's biking clothes, now filthy and sweaty with the day's efforts. "You stink."

Luc bulged his eyes and pushed his face forward in faux aggression. "I'm cleaning up at Madeleine's later."

"Ah. Good. My sister wouldn't appreciate that smell."

Patrice.

After years of mixed signals, they'd finally hooked up late last summer during the festival. Charles said he'd always expected it. He'd often said their parents had, too. Although Luc loved and admired Patrice, he'd grown up thinking of her like one of his sisters, so that was, at first, weird.

But it had happened, and though initially awkward, had been nice. They'd spent a few days in bed together, and on long walks, holding hands, kissing, talking. But it was the end of his summer vacation, and they'd not had time to pursue their new relationship. Charles, though, had referred to it often through the winter whenever they emailed or video chatted, his pleasure obvious. "You're already my brother, *mon gros*. This just makes it official, *non*?"

And so that's what Luc had decided to do.

He'd seen her only twice this summer, so far. When he'd first arrived, he briefly stopped in to see her at her shop in Toulouse. But she was preoccupied and busy, so, feeling in the way, he'd left. Then three weeks ago, she'd come to Charles's for the weekend. They'd had a nice family dinner, and there'd been friendly flirting. Plenty of it. He thought she'd end up in his bed, but she'd had too much to drink. After Charles and Francine had retired, there'd been kissing, a little groping. And then she'd passed out. So, yeah. That happened, but he didn't read much into it.

Two weeks ago she'd come for another visit, but Luc had been cycling up at the Dordogne and missed her. She'd left him a cute note and the small gift of an old copy of French poetry. She knew him well.

Now, Luc smirked and replied, "Don't worry. I'll smell fresh as a daisy. I want to mingle, catch up with some regulars. Then I'll catch you all at the restaurant about eight, okay?"

"*Oui, oui.*" Charles spun on his heel and strode back down the hill, waving at Luc as he went. "*Au revoir.*"

Luc continued on with his flat of produce in search of *Grand-Mère Bougis*'s market stall. "*Bonne après-midi, Grand-Mère Bougie,*" he called out as he approached the old Basque woman who sold the biggest melons and the best oranges, her stand piled high with lovingly arranged produce.

"Ah, la, la, Luc," she muttered, waving and gesturing him closer with a stiff, leathery hand. She knew him because he always bought an orange or two for his rides. And sometimes she gave him one in exchange for a favour.

He set the vegetables on the ground and stepped toward her, kissing her cheeks. "*Puis-je vous aider plus?*"

She pinched his shirt and tugged him behind her table, pointing beneath it. "*Là-bas. Prendre ce carton.*" He looked down. She pointed to a flat carton of wilted vegetable leaves, trimmings and discarded bruised fruit. "*Le prendre à la décharge, oui?*"

He squatted to lift it, twisting his nose at the odour of rotting compost that had accumulated all day in the hot sun. As he stood, his face averted, she blessed him with a wrinkly toothless smile.

"*Avez-vous vu qu'elle est arrivée? L'as-tu vu?*"

He frowned his confusion. "Seen whom? Who arrived?"

"*Ta femme, mon fils,*" she tossed her kerchiefed head back and let out an amused cackle of laughter.

His belly rolled over and pinched. "My... I don't have a... wife, *Grand-Mère*. As you know." He narrowed his eyes at her. What was she going on about? Was she just teasing him? Not another soul knew about the ring box in his backpack. It was so freaky when she did that. "Do you mean... Patrice?"

"*Non, non, non.*" She wagged her crooked finger side to side. "*Le nouveau. Le filou.*"

His mind scrambled to translate her word. It wasn't one he'd heard, possibly ever, in modern conversation in all his years in France. But he knew what it meant from his studies of French literature. Trickster.

However, having translated it, he was no wiser. He made his apologies and took the box of stinking compost to the bin outside the wall.

∼

Niki smiled sadly up at the giant and stepped closer. The top of her head came to just inches above his belt. She guessed that made him over seven feet tall.

"Can I talk to you?" She gestured for him to come closer, since she was nowhere near his face.

He nodded and bent, resting his hands on his knees.

She set a palm on his forearm and gave him a comforting squeeze, and a rub along the soft copper hair on his arm. She nodded and held his gaze to show him she would not be one of his tormentors. She spoke in a soothing tone, softly and gently, for his ears only. "Well. First, I'm sorry to draw unwanted attention to you."

He tsked and shrugged. "I am used to it."

She shook her head, determined to turn this around. What he needs is a champion, a catalyst. "Do you want to help me put these losers in their place?"

He shrugged again, and she sensed this was more than a habitual gesture, but to a greater extent an attitude to life in general. How she wished he would stand up for himself and fight back a little. It had been the same with Sam, though Sam was ill-equipped to deal with social pressures. They were both victims of the circumstances of their birth. Sam, too, always stood and took his hard knocks, almost as though he didn't mind. But she knew the truth.

"And so…?" he asked.

"I have a plan and I need to get up there," she pointed at the empty stilts, still held by Rocco and Alain.

"Certainly," the giant said, and gallantly bent to one knee, joining his hands to make a step for her.

The more agreeable he was, the angrier she got. She smiled at him and stepped up onto his hands as if a princess into a grand carriage, placing one hand on his broad shoulder. He stood, lifting her up to his level. She kept her eyes on his face. When he was standing, he met her gaze, and she saw intelligence and a wry humour there, and again that overwhelming sense of resignation to his fate. She immediately liked him. Leaning toward his large but well-proportioned ear, and whispered, "I need you to be a mountain. An oak tree. Be ready for my dismount." His golden brows drew together, but he said nothing, taking one step closer to the stilts that waited. Niki turned her attention to them, grabbing the poles and shifting her feet from the giant's hands to the footrests. He stepped back but stayed close while she twisted to attach the padded shin straps one by one, then stood up. He kept his steady blue gaze on her face, now above his own, and she knew he'd be ready.

Jean and the others, however, backed away, watching the stilts warily. Despite their encouragement, they expected catastrophe. Niki found her balance, shifting her weight from one pole to the other, getting a feel for them. It only took her a moment. Balance was one of her super powers. Then she took small steps forward and back, urging the guys below to give her freedom. Her audience seemed to think she was teetering, possibly falling, and a quiet murmur rose from the crowd. "I'm good!" she hollered down to Alain and Rocco. Reluctantly, they removed their hands from the stilts, but hovered nearby, palms out.

Niki began to stride. The space grew wider. She marched in a little circle to shouts and whistles of appreciation. But she was only getting started. She turned and walked past the crowd toward a booth, bent and grabbed a floppy jester's hat that hung on display and set it on her head, to whoops of laughter and more applause.

This display wasn't true to parkour. It went against the principals, to make a show of her skill. But she'd always secretly fantasized about joining the *Cirque du Soleil* and having her moment in the sun. This was even better. She was doing it for a good cause.

"Hey, hey, take it slow, *ma petite*," said Jean. She smirked down at him. Despite his arrogance, she could see his reluctant admiration. He knew how hard this was.

Tossing the hat back to the blond woman behind the stand, she returned to her starting spot and began a little jig, lifting one stilt up, then the other, holding each one a little longer in the air, testing how long she could stand on one pole. "Play for me Oboe-guy, and I'll dance for you," she said to the astonished musician gaping up at her. At last she found a solid footing and lifted one leg up as high as she could, careful to avoid knocking someone it the head with it as it arced up three or four feet.

The crowd hushed. Alain spoke quietly. "Okay, Niki. You're making me nervous now. I think you made your point."

"All right, Alain," she said, bringing her leg slowly down and standing still while Rocco and Jean leapt forward in relief to grab the stilts. She bent to undo the straps and slowly stood up again, looking down to meet the giant's eye, and she gestured for him to step back instead of closer. She saw him understand, draw a breath, and brace himself. Then, without warning, she crouched to gather momentum and leapt from the footrests into the air. She did an airborne somersault and landed feet first against his solid chest, bending her knees to absorb the shock. He grunted in surprise, but was as immovable as the oak tree she'd requested. She pushed off instantly and did a back flip, landing softly in a *saute du fond* with a squat and shoulder roll on the ground in the centre of the circle, then stood with her arms up. The crowd exploded with gasps, cheers and applause as she stood calmly grinning.

As people dispersed, Sabine embraced her again, kissing both her cheeks. "Brava, Niki. That was an amazing maneuver. What do you call that landing?"

"Ahh," Niki shrugged. "It's called *saute du fond*. Bottom jump doesn't really describe it very well though. I like to think of it as a shock absorber. An... uh... *amortisseur?*"

"You must teach us. You are welcome to come to work with us in Bordeaux, my little friend," said Alain.

"I might do that before the summer ends," she said, wishing them all a goodnight and turning to walk away. If only. Her time in France was nearly over. Another couple of weeks and she'd have to fly home. She looked forward to getting back to work.

But first, she had more to accomplish here.

She turned, located her pack, and looked for the giant. She felt exhilaration, at both her stunts and the goodwill and attention it garnered. The big man, however, sat down behind his booth and picked up his book, done with the whole affair. It made her wonder whether they often picked on him for random stunts. She could just hear them, that musician and his cronies. "Hey, Geoffrey, my kite is stuck in a tree, do you mind?" Growing up running interference for Sam, she knew all too well how mean people could be to someone who was a little unusual. She felt sorry for her part in it and wanted to apologize somehow, without making it worse. She strolled over to him.

"Hey, thanks, Geoffrey," she said, leaning against his table, examining his wares. He displayed various iron objects, like knives, daggers, swords, scissors with scrolled handles and such. There were smaller items, fancy coat hooks, trivets and candle holders. She picked one up and examined its elegant lines and lovely hammered surface. "These are really nice. Did you make them?"

He nodded, a small rough noise coming from his throat.

"I'm sorry if that made you uncomfortable. I didn't know…" she stopped. Was it wrong to convey condolences for his unusual size? "Sorry, I don't mean to imply that there's anything–"

"Not a problem." He shrugged. "It is what it is."

"Well, I'm sorry anyway, for drawing attention to you. I can see you're a very private person. I was having a riot. And taking a shot at that Jean guy."

"A riot? A shot?"

"Humph. I suppose that doesn't translate literally. If only I had a Babel fish."

Screwing up his brows, he shook his head, the hint of a smile turning the corner of his mouth. "Your French is terrible. You're interesting though."

"Not that interesting." She thought a moment. Was she? Her stomach suddenly announced it was done waiting for dinner with a loud growl. She could make it up to him. "You want to get something to eat?"

He glanced up from his book. "Me?"

"There's no one else here, Romeo."

He took a few moments to deliberate, and she prepared for his rejection when he slapped his book shut and said, "Okay," rising to his impressive height. "*De toute façon*, I am called Didier."

CHAPTER 4

Charles and Francine's house, his home away from home, was a mere twenty-five minutes ride outside the *Beaux Village* he'd visited every summer since his twelfth birthday. At first, with his parents and sisters, spending a month each summer with his father's old university friend and his family. Then, as they grew up, on his own. When his own, and then Charles' parents both died several years back, Luc continued to come, though his sisters no longer did.

Contemplating the prospect of a permanent move to France was disconcerting. He'd considered it long and hard.

Despite his reluctance to leave the teaching job he adored at home in Vancouver, and his sisters and their families, it's what would be necessary. Patrice owned two prosperous fashion boutiques in Toulouse and Bordeaux, and he wouldn't ask her to give them up and move to Canada to be with him. They'd known each other here, on her *territoire*, most of their lives. Anyway, he figured she'd be able to support him while he got settled and found teaching work here.

Luc had not yet told Charles of his plan. First, he must talk to Patrice and make sure she would go along with it. He felt strongly that she would. She'd been eager enough to pursue their summer affair these past few years. But still. One must ask the lady first and make it official. And it's not like he required permission or a blessing from Charles. It's only that he was less confident of Patrice's approval than he was of Charles'.

He'd never seen Patrice as the family type. And she wasn't the love of his life, but she'd encouraged him often to settle in France, and he'd resigned himself to this plan. He wondered if she even wanted him to be a stay-at-home father so she could carry on with the career she loved. The French were pragmatic about marriage.

It might not be precisely the dream of an idyllic family life he so badly wanted. That he'd been dreaming of since... well, since his mother, then his father had died too young, and ripped away the supportive, loving atmosphere of his youth. Both his older sisters had married, and Charles had married Francine. They all had kids now and had each in their own way recreated the perfect family they'd all shared growing up.

Except for Luc.

Mentally he shrugged. He loved France. He loved kids. He was a teacher, after all. As he prepared for his thirtieth birthday, he was more than ready. He wanted a family of his own. Even if it meant moving to France, leaving his job, his family, and settling down with a woman who was, in the end, merely a good friend.

~

Didier led Niki around the square, from vendor to vendor. Musicians continued to play, and booths displayed local peaches, tomatoes, courgette and foods such as foie gras, small rounds of soft goat's cheese and crumbling blocks of salty cow cheese. She commented that some of the wrinkled, leathery sausages looked and smelled like mouldy old socks, and Didier laughed and laughed at her.

They stopped to admire other crafts, leather shoes with pointed toes, and pouches embossed with crests, shields, crosses and convincing replicas of Gothic parchments.

He quietly greeted each artisan and merchant by name, and they responded in kind, exchanging friendly words. He affirmed the paella was good, so they bought some. Then he insisted she try the grilled Merguez sausages, and they were so incredibly delicious, she wanted more. He capped it off by buying a bottle of a red wine.

Niki tried to curb her brain from marveling at this giant of a man, his charm and civility. There was no reason in the world he would be otherwise. He was no ignorant mountain man. His size was immaterial; she chastised herself for her narrow thinking. She ought to know better.

And then she began to understand how difficult it must be to be him. To have always to battle people's preconceived notions and expectations, both positive and negative, about what a man over seven feet tall could and should do.

∽

After Luc watched Didier leave his table and walk off toward the food stalls with the strange woman, he carried on with his business as before, his mind stuck in a feedback cycle.

His heavy limbs dragged as thoughts skipped and spun. If she fascinated him after their first meeting, on the strength of only her beauty, energy and eccentricity, how did he feel about her now? Well, he shouldn't be feeling anything at all, but how could anyone ignore a woman like that? Evidently Didier agreed. He'd planned to catch up with Didier later, but now wondered if he'd be intruding. Where did Amélie fit into this scenario?

Seeing the new woman boldly challenge Jean to use his stilts absolutely stunned him. She apparently mastered them in a matter of minutes, and then utterly astonishing everyone with her dramatic dismount. He was gob smacked by her skills and daring. Not merely athletic, she was a wonder of strength, agility and coordination. But her spirit drew Luc like a locomotive.

And if her hypnotic charms so distracted him, he imagined everyone else in the village was equally so, including his friend Didier. Curious, he stopped to chat with Amélie at her clothing booth. She carefully folded garments that shoppers had examined, tidying her display before boxing it for the night. Tomorrow would be the busiest of days.

"Hello, Amélie. *Ca va?*"

"I'm well, Luc. How did your day go?"

He picked up a lace-cuffed shirt and shook it. "Good thanks. Busy with all the setup. Did you see, uh, everything?"

"Of course. Who could miss all that?" She took the shirt from him and folded it gently and expertly.

"What do you think of the newcomer?"

"I think she's cute and funny." Amélie paused and peered at him. "She's very different, *non*? So bold."

"Yeah." Preoccupied, he straightened some embroidered slippers.

"You saw Didier talking to her? They went for dinner I think." He glanced up to catch her reaction.

"Yes. I never miss a thing he does."

He narrowed his eyes, trying to glean some meaning from her placid expression. He knew she and Didier were good friends and had known each other forever. Like Didier, Luc didn't know if Amélie wanted more from Didier or not. She was unfailingly friendly and kind, but hard to read. He'd always assumed Didier's awkward crush embarrassed her a little. He kind of understood Didier's unwillingness to risk their friendship on a miscalculated move. No man wanted pity from the woman he loved.

"Do you mind?" he probed.

She avoided his gaze, peering out over the busy square. "She might be good for him. He never has much to do with tourists. Never makes new friends." She shrugged and gave him a wry smile when she finally glanced back at him.

"Do you want to join us for a drink?"

"*Merci*, but I'm meeting some friends later."

"*D'accord*. See you later."

She waved him off.

His thoughts drifted back to the stunt woman. How long was she planning to stay? Was she going to make a scene everywhere? It was a concern, he told himself, if she would disrupt or distract from all the carefully planned exhibits and performances that local acrobats, artists, artisans and businesses had prepared for the week. This festival was a big deal for Petit Bergeron and the region, a major draw for tourists, and a significant boon for business and employment locally.

He ground his teeth and scratched his beard, mulling over the problem as he hiked downhill to the large parking lot to retrieve another case of wine for Victor from his truck. One of the jobs he regularly helped his friends with was as a runner. They were typically family businesses or very small producers and didn't have people to help if their supplies ran low during a busy summer day. So Luc checked in with them, and he ran up and down the hill, and back and forth across the *Plàce* for a part of each day. He didn't mind. It kept him occupied. And he loved the Medieval festival and had loved it ever since it had got started. Being a part of it was a highlight of his summer vacation. And if he were handsomely rewarded with free dinners, bottles of local wine, the occasional dried sausage or linen shirt, he couldn't complain.

"Here you go, Victor." He set the case behind his table.

"*Merci*, Luc. You are a Godsend. Would you like some Monbazillac for your evening?"

"Ah, yes. *Merci*. I'd love that. But can I pick it up later? I have to shower and change at Madeleine's before dinner."

"*Bien sûr*. Come by whenever you want." Victor turned to serve a customer and Luc sauntered away.

The square was filling up with diners and revelers for the evening, the atmosphere buzzing with excitement. Opening night of the festival was a favourite, especially with the locals. On the way to Madeleine's he passed several stalls of food and produce. The aromas of cooked food roused his appetite.

Finally he made it to Madeleine's toy shop just as she was locking up. "*Salut*, Luc. Come on upstairs."

He followed her through a narrow stone doorway, up to her small apartment above her shop. Years ago, when she'd noticed him trying to change his clothes in the public washroom between the sweaty work of the day and the dinner hour, she'd offered her guest bath for his use anytime he needed it to freshen up. Her place had become like a second home, a place he could stop in for a moment's respite if he hadn't the time or energy to cycle back to Charles's place. And Madeleine had become like a favourite aunt, always happy to chat.

"Cup of tea?" she offered.

"No thanks, Madeleine. Perhaps a glass of water?"

She handed it to him and he drank, gazing out the second-story window, past the tumbling geraniums and colourful Medieval banners, to the crowd below. From this perspective, it was simple to pick Didier out. Sure enough, there she was by his side as they strolled the perimeter of the market square. An idea pushed itself forward.

Madeleine stood beside him. "You seem preoccupied. You all right?"

"Yes. Just tired. Busy day."

She inclined her chin out the window. "Did you see the young *Canadienne* on stilts?"

"*Oui*. Everyone did. How do you know she's Canadian?"

"People talk. Interesting day, *non*?"

He agreed, sighing heavily. As he feared, her antics were distracting everyone from the festival celebrations.

"Didier's made friends with her, it seems," Luc mumbled, to explain his staring. He tugged at his sweaty shirt, eager to get in the shower.

"Hm. I'd say she was more suited to you than to Didier."

He turned to her, rubbing the back of his damp neck. "What? Just because she's Canadian?"

She smirked. "She intrigues you. Admit it."

"Don't be ridic–," he scoffed and shook his head, turning away. "She's not my type. Anyway, sorry, I've gotta–"

He showered and changed his clothes for the evening. He had to meet Charles, Francine, Patrice, and some other friends at *Le Bistrôt du Prince Noir* after his planned drink with Didier. He ought to put the distracting *Canadienne* out of his mind. He had other, more pressing things to worry about, such as exactly where, when and how he would propose to Patrice. But instead of being nervous and excited, the scenario agitated him, and he couldn't help wondering if the newcomer would still be there when he found the giant.

CHAPTER 5

Niki and Didier carried their food and wine to an empty spot at a long, paper-covered table under the market roof. Didier smiled and shyly greeted several people on the way. He poured wine into plastic cups, and they sat down. When seated, it was easy enough to forget that he was so tall. He was large in every way, but well-proportioned and good-looking, with unruly strawberry-blond hair, a strong chin with a cleft, and bright blue eyes that seemed to miss nothing. He held his plastic cup of wine in oversized, grime-stained fingertips and closed his eyes as he took his first sip.

"Tell me about yourself," she said. "Why are your fingernails stained?"

He shrugged, lifting a sandy brow at her bluntness.

Niki again had to temper her own biases when he ate what she deemed a normal amount of food for an extra large man, but nothing out of the ordinary. Given her own athletic activity level, she knew she ate much more than most women her size.

"Your family. Have you lived around here long?"

"Yes. My family have been hereabouts for generations. I'm a fourth generation blacksmith," he added, with a wiggle of his black-creased fingers, to answer her earlier question.

"So you were born with dirty fingernails?" They shared a laugh. "Not much demand for that these days, I guess?"

"More than you'd think. But mostly now I'm an artisan, as you see.

My father could not quite make a living, but I'm doing better because of the modern romance with the past. This festival, for example. If I were to expand my market, I would do even better."

"You learned the ropes from your father, I guess?"

"Ropes?"

She groaned. "Your... craft."

"Ah." He made a face at her. "Is it that your French is so bad, or that you are willful?"

Meeting the teasing twinkle in his light blue eyes, she deigned not to respond, or perhaps not knowing the answer, she asked instead, "How would you expand your market, then?"

Pulling a face, a look of resignation settled over him. He twitched a little, though. His docility and mien of fatalism looked painfully familiar to her.

"You're not happy. What do you dream of?"

After a rather long moment, he replied. "It's my fault, I suppose. There are people I'd like to meet in Carcassonne, Avignon, where the Medieval tourist trade is strong, but I... delay going there." He shrugged, his jaw jutting.

Her chest tightened. He'd never ventured even halfway across his own country. "Have you travelled much?"

His mouth twisted. She knew he understood the question, and the answer was obviously no.

"Why, dude?" She flung out an arm. "Because of that A-hole with the flute?"

Didier's face hardened, and she dropped the subject, digging into her meal.

"This is the best paella I've ever eaten," she said, instead.

"Have you never been to Spain?"

"Oh, yeah. I was in Pamplona last month."

"To see the bull run?"

She grinned. "To run with the bulls." She relished the long silence that followed as he processed that fact, his blue eyes closely assessing her.

"You are insane, Niki. Have you a *désir de mort*?" A death wish.

She laughed, and said, "That seems to be what my coworkers think. That's why I'm here."

At his quizzical expression, she told him about her job and enforced holiday.

Chief Brian's words still haunted her. *I know you're good at the job, Niki. I trained you myself.* Niki recalled how uncomfortable he'd been delivering the news. *Look, no-one here is questioning your skill or commitment. I love you like a daughter. Everyone on the team loves you.*

I've got an excellent track record–

And yet, too many close calls. Tired people make mistakes, Niki. And so her six-week sabbatical had begun. But that was boring, and so she focussed on telling Didier about all her European adventures and the entertainments she'd been engaging in all month.

"You really are an extraordinary woman." Didier glanced over her shoulder and inclined his head. "*Bonsoir*, Luc."

"*Bonsoir*, Didier" said a man behind her chair, and the hairs on the back of her neck stood up. Niki turned toward the familiar voice to see the cyclist from earlier approaching as he carried two bottles of wine above the heads of the seated diners. He was clean and well-groomed. He'd changed into jeans and a linen jacket over a white dress-shirt, and though his lycra was more revealing, she admired the way they clung to his lean, muscled form, and the way he moved toward her like a cat.

Niki blinked.

There was no mistaking the man standing at their table now. One light strung from cords above them flared in the shadows, momentarily casting a soft blue glow on his chest. She looked away, then a moment later, glanced back at him. He was unabashedly staring at her. Rather than cower, she turned to face him and met his eyes straight on in challenge.

His eyes, unwavering, were intensely blue, and hooded, suggestive, and she squirmed and looked away again, her pulse hammering. No-one deserved to be that handsome!

Instead of looking away embarrassed at being caught, he stepped towards her, tilted his head and quirked his perfect features into a smile that melted her knickers.

"Mind if I join you?" He set down the wine bottles. "Courtesy of Victor."

"Suit yourself," she replied, letting her gaze scan the wine labels he'd brought, as though she were only half as interested as she really was.

"This local winery is just on the wrong side of the border to the official Bordeaux region, as good as the expensive stuff."

Didier said, "*Bienvenue*, Luc. *Merci*. How are you, *mon ami*?"

Niki's gaze darted back and forth between the two men. They were friends?

"*Superb, merci*. Introduce me to your friend?"

"*Oui, oui*," said Didier. "This is Niki."

"We've met, actually," Niki said.

"Yes, but I didn't know your name, nor you mine."

His voice, a warm tenor, mocked her. He sounded like anybody from home. Any guy she'd gone to school with, or worked with, or the barista at her local Starbucks. Except he slid into smooth French like a native and had the most amazing, sexy voice she'd ever heard. It filled her with tingles and the urge to climb onto him, lick him all over, and follow him home like a hungry puppy.

His hand appeared in front of her. "Luc. Luc Ehrenskjold."

She ignored the hand, looked up at him, and instantly knew he felt the chemical surge of attraction too. They were like two mating lions circling each other in the wild. The pheromones were a-jumping between them. She took a shaky breath. "You don't sound Scandinavian."

This prompted a gust of warm laughter from both Luc and Didier.

He sat down beside her and she swallowed, unsure why he made her so nervous.

"My grandparents were Danish."

"Luc is *Canadien*, like you," said Didier.

She scowled at him. "I knew that."

"When did you meet?" Didier asked.

Without glancing at the new guy, she murmured, "Just in passing."

"How did you enjoy the paella?"

She frowned. "How do you know what I ate for dinner?"

He smiled, his eyes sparkling with humour, and pointed at her chest, where two bright orange grains of rice clung tenaciously to her t-shirt.

"Tsk." She rolled her eyes, brushing them off. Observant. She liked that. And that he respected her personal space and didn't use that as an excuse to touch her like some jerk at a bar. "It was the best."

"Hey Luc, listen to this. Niki ran with the bulls last month."

His brows lifted. His warm, broad smile revealed teeth that were white and straight, except for one charmingly overlapped incisor. A ripple of heat emerged in her throat and set off a chain reaction, warming her chest, her belly, her lady parts. No one so unassuming ought to be this hot, with features so ideal. He could have been a catalogue model. Too perfect. Even his skin was perfectly smooth and tanned on his brow and above his neatly groomed beard.

He smelled good, too. Like pine trees and fresh air and fruit, like the mountains back home. She felt a powerful urge to touch him. Her eyes roamed across his chest, the dress-shirt stretched smoothly across his toned pecs, down to the faded denim that curved over his lean thigh. She swallowed and tore her gaze away.

"I won't bite." His voice held the tenor of amusement.

She knew he'd seen her stunt earlier. Seemed to know Didier well. She hummed her skepticism.

"Nice to meet you, Niki." He lingered over her name, tasting it, trying it on for size.

"Are you meeting Patrice and Charles for dinner?" Didier asked, and the two men exchanged an amused glance that puzzled Niki.

Luc nodded slowly. "In a little while, yes."

Didier hummed, then looked up suddenly, his jaw jutting forward.

Something ruffled the crowd seated at the tables near them. She and Luc both turned to look. The trio of musicians, led by Didier's nemesis, swaggered toward them with expressions that spelled trouble.

"It's that time again, my friends," bellowed Rosaire, who Luc knew played the oboe with a local trio during the festival, with an exaggerated bow. "I humbly interrupt your dinners and conversations to command your presence at the spectacular and modest puppet show. You will gasp! You will laugh! You will cry! It begins in fifteen minutes! Get your seats now."

What an idiot.

Niki laughed, but the sound was tight. "They reminded me of the three stooges," she said in an aside to Luc, who smiled at the image.

Or Shakespearean buffoons, with their pointed caps and pantaloons. They always got laughs though. Luc peered at Didier. Only they didn't make Didier laugh because he was always the butt of their stupid jokes. Didier kept his gaze cast lowered, his face tight. Luc frowned. An undercurrent of ill will rippled between him and his tormentor.

Rosaire and his cronies paused before them. "Are you coming, *Girafeau*?"

Didier sighed and collapsed into himself. "Perhaps not, Rosaire."

"And you, *Petit Polisson*?"

Piss off.

Niki glanced at Luc for help. "*Polisson?*"

"He calls you ah... scamp... a little monkey," Didier answered in English.

The monkey and the giraffe. How apt. Luc smirked at her and earned a scowl in response. She pulled a face and eyed the little man warily. "Yeah, thanks Rosaire. I'll think about it."

Luc rose to his feet, levelling a warning glare at Rosaire to back off and after a theatric bow, Rosaire and his friends moved along, weaving between tables, urging others to attend the performance.

"Puppets!" she said. "That sounds like fun. Right? Let's take our wine and go."

Didier demurred. "I must pack up my booth and load the truck."

"Aw, c'mon, Didier. It'll be fun."

Luc met Didier's stony eye. Yeah, tons of fun. "I'll go with you if you want company. You'll need a translator," Luc said, and received a narrow-eyed glare from Niki.

She hummed and turned back to Didier. "Will you be here afterwards? How long will it last?"

"Long enough," murmured Didier. His large shoulders slumped and Luc felt his fists clench, and the back of his neck tighten. Rosaire's antics frustrated him, but so did Didier's complacency. He could humble the runt with one look, and yet he never retaliated. Never defended himself. Despite wishing to help, it was Luc's opinion he needed to fight his own battles.

"I'd like to say good night before you leave."

He lifted one shoulder. "Where do you stay?"

"I don't know. I haven't found a room yet."

"What?" Luc and Didier said together, both gawking at her. "You won't find a room now. The village is complete," Didier added.

She made a face. "I haven't tried yet. I'm sure I'll find something. I'm not fussy."

Luc and Didier shared a frown of concern. Perhaps Luc could speak to Charles about offering her the couch.

Niki remained oblivious and focused on Didier. "Thank you for dinner. Maybe I'll see you tomorrow?"

"Hm. Perhaps."

Luc led her away then, and they strolled away in the wake of Rosaire and his sidekicks, in search of the puppet show.

Luc led Niki to the far corner of the square where the puppet theatre sat. Some vendors had already packed up and left for the evening, and organizers had moved a few aside to make space for the theatre booth. A plywood box, painted with whimsical curlicues, and draped with velvet curtains in the deepest shade of blue, sat at an angle to the steps leading down to the central square, creating a small amphitheater. Behind it was deep shadow, allowing the puppeteers to move around invisibly.

As they sauntered through the crowded square, she felt his eyes on her, her skin tingling with awareness. On the way, she watched as several people nodded and smiled at him as he passed through. Many greeted him by name. "Hey Luc," and "*Bonsoir*, Luc."

"How do you know everyone here?"

"I've spent every summer here since I was eleven." He shrugged, and she raised her brows, wondering what it would have been like to grow up with so much freedom and adventure. Keeping Sam both safe and entertained while her mother worked had consumed all of her summers growing up.

Niki scanned the front of the puppet stage, where a crowd of people already filled the stone pavement. Children sat closest, cross-legged on the ground. Behind them, some adults also sat on the limestone pavers. Many people used the steps like stadium seating. Further back, she found a narrow gap on a low planter wall that encircled a plane maple tree just wide enough for one, and squeezed in, waiting for the show to begin.

She lifted her chin and blinked with exaggerated innocence at him, as if to say, so sorry. There's no room for you. His sexy lips curled up on one side and she squirmed, unsure what he found so amusing. After another thousand heartbeats of staring at the closed velvet curtain, and pretending to scan the crowd of children, she stole another glance.

Still, he stared at her. This time, when she widened her eyes and lifted her chin in challenge at his nerve, his soft mouth split into a flashing white grin, his chest shaking with laughter. Taking her eye contact as an invitation, he stepped toward her.

"Mind if I squeeze in beside you?"

No! That's not what she wanted. Was it? Yet she made room for him as he thanked the person on his other side and wiggle his tight butt into a few inches of space on her wall. *I am not thinking about his ass.* She kept her face averted, feigning disinterest while painfully conscious of the feel of his broad shoulder and hard hip and thigh as he slid in beside her. Their bodies pressed together from shoulder to knee, creating heat and sending awareness of him zinging through her bloodstream.

"Why was Didier was so reluctant to join us?"

Luc made a vague face. "Doubtless he's seen the same performance a trillion times before."

A commotion from the stage drew their attention. Someone dressed in black stood to the side with a mic, and introduced the show, but they spoke so rapidly Niki's French failed her. Something about a maiden?

"Did you catch that?" she said, turning to Luc. "Your French seems quite good."

"Not bad," he said, his handsome mouth quirking up at one corner. "The play's about a young seamstress who lived in this village years ago, who was the object of much admiration from the local gentlemen."

"Oh." The furling curtains caught Niki's attention. With a fanfare of music, the show began.

CHAPTER 6

After the narrator's introduction, a skit began. Despite her inadequate French, Niki became rapt in the tale being told with whispered translations from Luc now and then. The stage set and puppets were vividly colourful and exciting.

Three little elf-musician puppets came onto the stage and pranced around playing tiny toy instruments. Children giggled and squealed. A piped jig from a boom box below the puppet stage filled the air, the tune itself a sprightly caricature of a Medieval tun. One or another of the musicians, added a flourish from time to time.

Niki scanned the crowd to the side of the stage, and sure enough the three actual musicians stood nearby with friends, drinking and laughing at their own likenesses. It was some kind of roast, and they were enjoying it.

Niki noted that Rosaire, though not tall, was the tallest of the trio, with a prominent Roman nose and wiry hair. His two sidekicks were slightly rotund. All three had thatched dark hair, the widest one with the fullest beard. She squinted at the stage. One puppet had the same exaggerated dark brows over sad sack eyes and a five o'clock shadow as the man it mimicked. The others had prominent pointed ears to match the silicone one's Rosaire's friends wore as part of their costumes. There was no mistaking their identity.

"It feels as though this is what it would have been like in the Middle

Ages, doesn't it?" Luc murmured in her ear. "The open air minstrels and travelling theatre troupes for the common folk."

She nodded, certain he saw or sensed her quiet movement in the gloom. "It seems a little more current than that," she replied dryly.

She heard him sucking thoughtfully on his teeth. "Just wait."

There was a burst of fanfare, and the three puppets put their heads together and whispered secrets, looking over their shoulders, off stage. Shortly, a little pigtailed blonde girl puppet, like a Heidi character in a white apron, skipped onto the stage. She demurely sat on a stool and began overblown "stitching" motions. The seamstress Luc had mentioned.

Niki's attention oscillated between the spectacle in front of her eyes, and the cascade of sensation beside her. Luc explained and translated, and she liked the sound of his amazing voice soft in her ear, the whisper of warm breath against her cheek and the vibration from his chest crossing the boundary of their touching skin. As heat built between them, she noticed his scent. The freshness of forest and fruit mingled now with a musky manliness that caused a coil of heat to pool in her abdomen.

A moment later, a fifth puppet stumbled into the limelight. He was twice the size of all the other puppets, and grotesque, with overlarge hands and feet, and a great box of a head that wobbled and made him look like a simpleton. Niki's chest tightened, and her smile slid from her face as she gasped in recognition. Her hand shot out to clutch Luc's arm, and then realizing what she'd done, released him just as abruptly.

The giant puppet hovered around the seamstress making clumsy flirtatious gestures, while she blushed and hid her face. Niki's heart skipped a beat and then raced forward in the cage of her ribs. This was no harmless fairy tale about long ago residents of Petit Bergeron!

"Who is that supposed to be?" she asked.

Niki whipped her head around, scanning the crowd. Most people, especially the children, were laughing, innocently unaware. A few faces appeared uncomfortable, and some heads bent together whispering and smirking. "This is cruel!" she hissed. "Where's Didier? He obviously knew this was happening." Or maybe it had happened before, and he expected it. The events of the day, the uncomfortable exchanges and unspoken tension, shifted and slotted into place in her mind.

She met the glint of Luc's eye, querying him with a frown, and met his sad, knowing expression. Niki felt blood rush to her ears with a roar as her heart rate escalated in outrage.

"Is that why Rosaire made a point of inviting Didier to see the show?"

"Many of the residents of this village have grown up together. They've known each other all their lives," he said.

"Is that supposed to be an excuse?" Niki's face and ears tingled. "Does this happen all the time?"

Luc dipped his chin slightly and pulled his lips between his teeth. "As long as I've been coming here, they've been stoking the fire of intolerance. They think they are being clever."

"Why doesn't someone do something? How can you–"

"Ét voila, here you are, Cheri." An elegant blonde woman with her hair up in a careless chignon approached Luc suddenly and grabbed onto his arm. Niki recoiled, unable to finish her thought. The accumulated heat in her body drained away like an ice water bath.

"What are you doing over here? Charles said you'd be coming to the restaurant." She fluttered an elegant, manicured hand and cast a dismissive glance at Niki, scanning her body critically. "*Viens*. Everyone is at *Le Bistrôt*." She not only looked but also sounded very French. She tugged, forcing him to stand, his jaw set firmly as though annoyed at the interruption.

The space beside Niki left her even more chilled.

"*Oui*, Patrice." He took her hand, kissing her knuckles while resisting her pull, turning back to Niki with a wry grin. "I must go join my friends now. It's been a pleasure meeting you, Niki. I'll–" The woman tugged again, insistent. "Please find me if you have nowhere to stay, okay?"

Niki lifted her brows at him, her mouth open. How was she supposed to do that? She had more questions. And she wanted answers. What was going on in this weird little village?

Luc met her gaze frankly and laughed, flashing his beautiful white teeth again. "*Bon soir, Petit Polisson*," he said with a headshake and turned to leave.

"Hey!" Why was everyone in this town calling her a monkey? But he disappeared into the crowd at the behest of his… whatever she was, she seemed the boss of him. He didn't spare her another glance.

Fine.

Niki stood up and scanned the back of the audience, and around the square by the booths, though there was scant light now, except a few small bulbs and lanterns dimmed, and the glow of a white half moon above in the indigo summer sky. She couldn't see any dark silhouettes that might have been Didier. If he watched, he was well out of sight.

But why would he watch this abomination? Why had Luc brought her here? Did he want her to understand? She had to know.

A collective flutter of laughter from the audience drew her attention back to the melodrama unfolding on the puppet stage and she watched with horror as the 'Didier' puppet tripped and fell, got up and stumbled by, his love-struck eyes glued to the little seamstress, his tongue lolling like an idiot. The seamstress puppet by turns buried her face in her hands, shuddering, and glanced off stage as though searching for someone, or seeking escape. It was horrible.

Stomach tight with crushing hurt on behalf of the ridiculed couple, Niki stepped to the side, hands fisting, nostrils flaring, and scanned the crowd again, for a woman who might be the seamstress. This time she was luckier. At a table on the outer edge of the roofed market square where a few lingering diners sat in small groups drinking wine, a lovely woman sat, her light blond hair pulled back in a tail, reflecting the faint light. She wore no white apron, in fact she wore jeans and a blouse like an ordinary woman, nor did she offer any obvious clues to her identity. But she was neither paying attention to the conversation at her table, nor watching the show, but staring down at the tablecloth, turning her drink around and around. Niki didn't know how, but she felt in her gut that this woman's life, too, had been ridiculed tonight.

Was it true that she was the object of Didier's affections?

The musician-puppets reappeared, pompously heroic, and taunted the giant. Words rushed by in a blur, but their actions spoke loud enough. They threw miniature cloth stones and vegetables at him, and chased him offstage with a broomstick to giggles and guffaws from the audience, but especially from Rosaire and the other two, bent over laughing, slapping each other on the back.

Niki felt her blood boil. Those little shit-heads. What she wouldn't like to do to them. She had to do something.

∾

Luc followed Patrice toward the restaurant where they were meeting Charles, his wife Francine and the rest of their friends, and away from the puppet show and that intriguing woman. Niki.

Now he knew her name.

Why was that so important to him? Only that since the moment he'd first seen her, he'd found her fascinating. Confusing. Disturbing. But fascinating.

"*Bonsoir*, Luc," shouted his friends as they joined the group and took their seats. "So Patrice found you, eh? Did you lose your way?"

"I found him watching that stupid puppet show," said Patrice, drawing a few odd looks, which Luc ignored. Patrice didn't mention Niki, and he let it go, accepting a glass of wine.

Earlier, he'd watched her befriend Didier after her performance on the stilts, and somehow convinced his shy friend to join her for dinner. That was quite an accomplishment. There were few men less likely to befriend a stranger than Didier. He worried about his giant friend. And he wasn't sure he trusted this foreign invader.

What was her motivation? Not that he cared what she did. He didn't know her. Still, Didier was… vulnerable, in his way. Which, he supposed, she now understood more about, having seen the puppet show.

But my God, if he thought she was unique upon first meeting her, his fascination had grown when he'd witnessed her astonishing acrobatics and bold challenge of that pompous stilt-walker. The guy was a newcomer here for the festival, but he saw how Alain and the others regarded him. And she, Niki, seemed to pick up on that, throwing herself into cutting him down a notch. She was a bold soul. Her physical confidence, agility and skill were amazing to see. She could be a star in the Cirque du Soleil. He had to learn more about her.

But afterwards she didn't even take a bow. She just wandered over to Didier and, apparently, asked him to join her for dinner. Because off they went. Like she'd cast a spell on him. Maybe she had. That's exactly how Luc felt, like he couldn't purge her from his head.

She was really something. She stirred some fierce and primitive need in his belly, as though she'd awakened a sleeping beast. As though he'd been waiting for exactly this all his life.

Charles kicked his shin beneath the table. "What's the matter with you?"

He shook his head. "Tired, I guess." He tried to shake off this new obsession with the stranger. It wasn't at all like him to moon over someone, especially someone new. Not someone like her.

Yet he couldn't help but contrast her with Patrice, beside him, so elegant and perhaps in her case, exactly what she seemed to be. The quintessential Frenchwoman. She was everything he should want. It was why he was planning to propose later tonight. How could any man top this? Even if... he hated to admit it even to himself. Even if she left him cold.

Affection, certainly. Pride? Contentment, perhaps. Was that such a bad thing?

That was nothing new. The truth was he needed something more. He desperately wanted to feel something more.

One reason he returned every summer, especially after his parents died and his sisters had married and had kids, was this sense he was missing something never let up, like an insatiable craving. Returning to France always seemed a good strategy for someone in search of romance, passion and excitement. He loved his home, his job, his sisters. He liked their husbands. He adored his nieces and nephew and wanted kids of his own.

But he returned to France every summer seeking something to fill the hole in his soul. He'd hung on so long to the idea of true love because he'd seen it in action. He'd grown up in the cocoon of his parents' special loving relationship, but none of the women he'd ever dated came close to inspiring such feelings in him. His relationship with Patrice had arisen out of loneliness, boredom, habit... and hopelessness.

On the cusp of his thirtieth birthday, Luc was content with his life, happy even, but nothing had ever shaken him up. Not irritated, agitated, bothered, intrigued or especially aroused him.

Until now.

Suddenly he realized he was no longer bored. And neither was he feeling content. He accepted a refill of his glass and tried to pay attention to the banter and fragments of conversation, but his mind wouldn't focus. What was he doing?

He fingered the small velvet box now in his jacket pocket and bit his cheek. Then he picked up the menu, determined to enjoy his evening despite his misgivings.

CHAPTER 7

Niki rose and backed away from the amphitheater, working her way around the perimeter of the square in search of Didier. No luck. He must have had enough sense to go home. She didn't blame him.

Another lap of the square brought her by Didier's booth. He'd packed away his goods and draped a cloth over the table for the night. No sign of him.

She understood the dynamic between Didier and the pipsqueaks who made a habit of tormenting him. Didier had lived in Petit Bergeron his entire life, and if she'd understood him correctly, had hardly been anywhere else. Likely those guys, and maybe the seamstress, had grown up with him, been his classmates, his tormentors, from an early age. How uncomfortable it must have been for him, to grow so extraordinarily tall, and to keep growing long after his friends had stopped.

Her heart squeezed, and her throat thickened thinking of the gentle giant who shared the same rosy cheeks and thatch of light hair that Sam had, though he was lighter. Shackled by a lifetime of conditioning. Living amid his own jailers, gazing daily on the woman he loved and feeling incapable of acting on it.

She would figure something out. There must be a way to help. She'd find Luc tomorrow and ask him about it.

But first, she needed a place to sleep.

"Excuse me," she said, stopping a waiter who was clearing tables at one of the outdoor restaurants on the edge of the square. "Can you tell me where the local inns are, or a bed-and-breakfast?"

The tired waiter, weighed down with a tray laden with dirty glassware, was terse. "We are closed now," he barked and turned away. "Come back tomorrow."

"No. No. Just tell me where I can sleep tonight," she tried again.

The man stopped, made a show of rolling his eyes and drawled. "Wherever you wish, *mademoiselle*."

"Is there a hotel? An inn?"

"Ah." At last his features showed comprehension. "*Oui*. There." He set down his heavy tray with a long-suffering sigh and pointed diagonally across the square. "And also there." He pointed over his shoulder where a small street abutted the corner of the square. "A small *gîte* with a few rooms. But you will not find–"

"Thanks!" Niki, relieved to at last have have directions, hitched her pack onto her shoulder and bounded away.

Trying the elegant old inn that fronted the square, with its small and subtle sign hanging within the vaults of the arcade, Niki entered a simple wooden doorway. Who knew what function this building originally had, five or six hundred years before, or over the intervening centuries? Perhaps it had always been an inn.

Niki cast her gaze over the low, beamed ceiling in the ancient foyer. Across the hushed but brightly lit space, a tiny birdlike older woman stood behind a small desk, reading glasses perched on her nose, shuffling through some cards.

"Good evening," Niki said, approaching.

The woman looked up. "*Oui?*"

"Do you have any rooms available?"

The woman tilted her head. "For which dates, *Mademoiselle?*"

Niki blinked. "For tonight."

A titter of laughter escaped before the woman caught herself and arranged her features. "*Mais non*. It is the festival. We have been fully booked for years."

"Years?" Niki swallowed.

The woman raised her groomed brows and tilted her head a little more. "Years. The festival is the same week every year, year after year. Many people come."

Niki took a shaky breath and turned toward the door. "Thank you."

Outside, she recalled the words of Didier, the waiter, Luc, even Paul at *Parc-en-Ciel*. She hadn't been listening, so confident she could saunter up and take a room whenever she was ready. How naïve. How arrogant.

She loped around the square, cat-leaping over bollards. At first she saw nothing resembling a hotel of any kind. Just a row of stone town houses with wooden shutters and potted geraniums. Then a small illuminated sign hanging in a window, backed by a lace curtain, caught her eye. It read '*Gîte Armande - complet.*' Above the word '*complet*' the word '*chambre*' was dark. The interior was dim as a church at midnight. Her shoulders fell. Now what?

"Are you ready to go home?" a soft gravelly voice said behind her.

She spun, searching the shadows for the shape of the giant.

Relief flooded her chest. "Where've you been? I was looking for you after the show."

He chuckled. "Sometimes I prefer to shave the walls."

She squinted at him in the dark. "I don't understand."

His mouth twitched to the side. "We too have idioms that don't translate so well. I mean, 'keep a low profile,'" he said in heavily accented English.

"Oh, I see."

"You'd better come and stay at my house."

"That's kind, but surely there's something else here."

He shook his head with a tight-lipped smile.

I guess that means I'm crashing with the giant. Lucky I met him.

He turned to walk down the street. "Coming?"

"Wait. I have to get my bike from the square. Assuming it's still there."

He spun on his heel and walked the other way, and they fell in step side by side. He paced himself to her shorter stride, though she knew he could step right over her. Despite her fading energy after a long and eventful day, she bounced on the balls of her feet and dashed forward, leaping up onto a railing post and executing a forward long jump.

It took four of his long steps to catch up to her. "My God. It exhausts me to watch you."

She laughed. "Yeah, well. I can't stand you mincing along beside me like a ballerina. You walk your speed and I'll keep up."

He looked down, studying her. "I don't know what to think of you, little monkey."

"Oh, don't you start, *Girafeau*."

They both laughed and continued on to the centre of town.

As they paused so she could unlock her bike from the railing, more and more people trickled past them on the way downhill from the square, in a general, low key exodus. The puppet show was over, restaurants were closed, the DJ had stopped playing dance music, and only a few die-hard revellers drank at tables here and there. Only a few lights in the square remained lit.

"Can I carry the bicycle for you?" Didier asked as she hoisted her pack onto her shoulder again.

"Don't even ask, Didier."

Niki whipped around to see Luc among his group of friends as they trouped past. Luc, too, pushed his bike along, still wearing his dinner jacket, and approached them ahead of his group.

"*Allo*, Luc," said Didier.

Luc grinned at her narrowed expression. "*Le Polisson*'s too independent to permit anyone to help her," he continued, laughing at her.

She noticed the others had paused and stared at her curiously.

"Luc! *Viens*. Come on. I'm tired," said the blond woman.

Luc frowned, pensive. "*Un moment*, Patrice." To Niki he said, "Did you enjoy your evening?"

Under her breath, Niki whispered. "I have to talk to you about the show."

His eyes flashed, and he nodded.

"Why do the villagers allow it?" she hissed.

He shrugged. "It's a small community with a lot of history, and many traditions."

"That's no excuse. It was horrible. I'm... I'm livid."

"You haven't seen anything yet."

"Lu-uc," called Patrice.

"Oui, oui." With a head shake he continued. "I must go. How did you make out with your search for a bed?"

"Wouldn't you like to know?" Despite her exhaustion, her skin tingled at his suggestive tone. Or was she imagining it.

"She's coming to my place," Didier replied, stepping closer.

Luc's eyebrows lifted. He lifted his head to look quizzically at Didier, who just shrugged his massive shoulders. Luc shifted his assessing gaze to Niki.

"What?" she challenged him, in English.

"I don't know." Luc replied. "I don't know."

"So, you want I should carry your bike or no?" Didier asked.

Her eyes on Luc, Niki said, "Sure, Didier. That would be great. Thanks."

He hoisted it up, saddlebags and all, and strode downhill toward the gate, away from them.

Niki followed him at a jaunty pace, but not before glancing over her shoulder to see Luc's astonished face, to which she responded by sticking out her tongue.

CHAPTER 8

Waking in the morning in a strange room, Niki took a moment to absorb her surroundings, and ponder how she'd got here. Delicious smells wafted into her room. Despite being stranded last night, she'd landed on her feet again.

Didier had been a gracious host, carrying her bike to his truck as if it were a coat hanger, and making pleasant small talk along the winding dark road to the outskirts of Petit Bergeron where he lived, just as if he hadn't been the butt of the night's entertainment. She didn't see much in the dark except a low fence bounding the long bumpy lane, and the dark silhouette of a house with some outbuildings.

Once inside his mid-century stucco cottage, he'd shown her to this room, a cozy guest bedroom on the main floor beside the sitting room, with a small cot covered in a lovely handmade quilt, and a charming antique dresser. Niki examined the faces in the vintage photographs hung in frames on the walls, seeing some resemblances between them and Didier, though none came close to his size. The room was feminine and neat as a pin.

After minimal washing up, she'd climbed into bed and listened to the creaking of beams overhead as Didier prepared himself for bed above her. Very few minutes had passed before she fell into a deep peaceful sleep.

Now rested she was eager to explore both Didier's home and the village of Petit Bergeron in daylight. She jumped out of bed and straight into the adjacent shower. Digging for fresh clothes in her bag, she found the tied bundle of dried herbs the old woman had pressed on her at the market. She brought it to her nose and sniffed, inhaling the exotic blend, earthy and aromatic. Smiling to herself, she set it on the dresser. Her chest filled with warmth for Chief Brian, for forcing her to travel outside her comfort zone. Something like that would never have happened in Vancouver.

When she emerged into the great room, with its vaulted beamed ceiling, she stood and watched Didier putter in his kitchen for a few minutes. Today he wore some kind of subdued period costume. He was master in his own domain, and at ease here. He was stirring something on the stove, and muttering in a soft lilting voice, as though having a conversation.

Bending, he picked up something off the floor and brought it to his face.

Curious, Niki stepped forward. "Good morning, Didier."

He turned, and she saw he held a tiny cat in his hand, tucked against his chin. "Ah. Good. You're awake. Do you like eggs?"

"Who's that?"

He smiled and held the ball of grey fur out to her. In his huge hand she was like a tiny ball of dryer lint "This is Minou."

Niki took the cat. It was barely bigger than an eight-month-old kitten, but she could tell from its proportions it was full grown. "Aren't you a sweet thing?" She nuzzled it and kissed its small head. "How do you keep from stepping on her? You can barely see her she's so small."

"She has survival strategies. And she has a way of making her presence known. Not unlike you, little monkey, she is always jumping and climbing on places where she should not be."

"Humph. Cats are nature's first *traceurs*."

"What does this mean to you, *traceur*? To trace." He inscribed a curlicue in the air with his large index finger.

"It's what you call someone who practices parkour. It means, to map, to follow a path. But the path is my own. A way of experiencing my environment intimately and fluidly."

"Interesting. It is cat-like, the way you move."

"We even have a kind of maneuver that's referred to as a cat leap."

He carried two plates to the oak table and set out cutlery. He brought two steaming mugs. "*Cafe au lait?*" His own chair was an interesting, large frame made of twisted iron bars.

"Thank you. Yum. You made that chair for yourself?"

He nodded, lifting a fork to his mouth. He looked almost regal sitting in his high-backed chair with its whimsical scrolls of black metal. Because he'd scaled it to fit him, he seemed less awkward, less uncomfortable than he did in a world made for average men.

"Do you make those to sell, too?"

"Yes. I make many things. Whether they sell..." He stretched his face and shrugged.

She smiled at his manner. So accepting. So tolerant. "It's beautiful. You're very creative."

He looked up. "*Merci*."

"You keep a very nice home, for a single guy."

He shrugged. "I like a comfortable home as much as anyone."

"How old are you, can I ask?"

"I will have thirty years on the six of October."

"Do you dream of having a family of your own? Of sharing your home with... someone special?"

He grunted. "*Oui*." He dug into his eggs while avoiding her gaze.

She thought of the puppet show last night, and the blond seamstress that was the object of puppet Didier's adoration. As she ate, Niki wondered about him, whether his unusual circumstances had formed his character, or whether this was simply Didier, who also had gargantuan proportions. So unlike herself, not only smaller than average, but determined to conquer everything in her path. She'd always considered herself a fighter, but there was something kind of appealing about his way of flowing through life, around obstructions, like water in a stream. Something more true to the philosophy of parkour, in fact.

Despite their differences, she knew the one thing they had in common was a permanent core of sadness. She recognized it in him, and thought, if he were more willing to fight, he might be happier. Perhaps they could learn something from one another. She decided then that this is how she would spend her last days in France.

༄

"Are you kidding me?"

Didier stopped in the grassy patch between the house and the shop and turned toward her. "Pardon?"

Niki gestured to the large metal words that made up the sign on the stone wall of Didier's work building, a long rectangular shed beside his house. It read: LeGrand Forge.

Didier's eyes scanned over the sign as though searching for a spelling error and back at her, uncomprehending.

"Is it supposed to be a joke? Don't you think you're opening yourself up to even more teasing?"

A slow smile spread on Didier's face. "What is your family name?"

She hesitated. Why was he changing the subject? "Uh. Ballantyne, why?"

"Mine is LeGrand. My grand-père forged that sign."

It took a long moment before the penny dropped. His name was LeGrand. Didier LeGrand. That was as bad as being called 'Big Al' or 'Andre the Giant.' "Jesus, Didier. I'm sorry."

"I am not." He shrugged. "C'est ma famille ancienne." His chin lifted and she could see it gave him pride. Another thing he could not change. There was nothing to do but laugh about it, and they did.

Recalling the family photos in her room, she asked, "Were any of your ancestors as big as you?"

"Perhaps not quite, but I don't believe they were ever small men. And I suppose they married larger women, too, judging from my family portraits."

An air of melancholy stole across his features, so she spun and strode in the open doorway.

Inside the forge, equipment crowded the dark barn-like space, its ceiling the vaulted timber frame, terracotta roof tiles exposed on the underside. Birds chirped from the rafters. Streams of bright sunlight flooded in from large arched windows on the opposite wall, blinding her and making it more difficult to understand the visual chaos.

At first, all she could see was a large iron stove against the stone wall, with a small window through which glowed a bright white light with a few blue and red flames licking, inviting her closer. Once her eyes adjusted, the dominant object was a tall blackish-green machine with pulleys and pistons, with an assortment of smaller machines arrayed around it, one with large iron wheels that seemed to connect to a shaft protruding through the wall.

"What's that?" She pointed.

"The water wheel at the creek outside provides some power. My great-grandfather built it." He led her into the space and rested his hand on the shoulder of a huge iron arch. "This is the press that my grandfather built, and his bellows."

In the centre of the space, a round concrete bench and a giant iron anvil perched, awaiting their master. Benches and racks and shelves, of metal, some made of battered, greasy oak planks that looked like they had been harvested from the forests of King Henry II himself, lined the walls. A large rack held what looked like hundreds of hand tools, hammers and axes and mallets and pliers and pincers, of all shapes and sizes. There were also innumerable things that Niki could not name.

"Awesome, Didier. Can I see the water wheel?"

"Okay. Come on." He led the way through a door at the back.

On the back side of the forge, a narrow but deep creek with fast moving water burbled between vertical stone walls. In it a large oaken water wheel slowly spun, waterfalls spilling from each of its mossy fins as they rose. A hush fell as they came under the spell of the burbling water.

"It's beautiful," she said.

"Yes. I used to play here as a child, and my mother would worry I'd be hurt by the wheel. She would call out for me and pretend she didn't know where I was. Papa used to say, nothing can hurt Didier. He's as solid as an oak tree."

"Your family sounds lovely. Are they still alive?"

"*Non*. No, both are gone."

"Do you want a family of your own Didier?"

He let a moment pass before answering. "I used to imagine that, but…" His big shoulders lifted a little, in a jerky movement.

"You'll make someone a wonderful husband and father." She watched him carefully, searching for hints of his desire, not sure if she could say anything about what she suspected.

Didier kept his eyes trained on the moving water wheel. "The years pass quickly. I'm not sure I will now. I've gotten used to living alone, just Minou and me."

"Is there… anyone special?"

His breath hitched. "I have to get going. I must set up my booth before the day is burned away, and the festival is over. What will you do today?"

He strode back toward the house and she followed him, addressing his back.

"Didier. Tell me about the blond woman. The seamstress."

Without turning he muttered, "Don't believe everything you see in the movies."

"I saw her last night."

He stopped in his tracks and turned. "Amélie?"

"Is that her name?"

He grunted and lifted a hand to his brow, pinching the bridge of his nose with a deep sigh. "Why do you want to involve yourself in my affairs, Niki? Don't you have your own life to live? Problems to solve?"

"I like yours better. I can actually do something about your problems."

"Humph. Unlikely."

They entered the house. Didier pulled together his jacket and wallet and stood in the middle of the living room, staring at the floor. "What do I forget?"

"Why are you acting like I didn't say anything?"

He frowned. "There is nothing you can do about my problems."

"I disagree. I have a brilliant idea."

"Do you want a ride into town? You can tell me on the way."

"As long as we can take my bike. I need to get out for a ride later."

Didier again lifted her bike into the back of his truck and they left. As they bumped down the driveway, she thought about what she would say. He was silent, his eyes on the road.

"So. Would you say your problem is partly your lack of confidence?"

He said nothing, and they drove along in silence until the conviction grew that she'd been too blunt. The eggs in her stomach took a turn. Insensitive. She always was too blunt.

"I put my foot in it, didn't I?"

"Where did you put your foot?" He glanced over to the footwell, confused.

She groaned. "I mean, I'm sorry. I didn't mean to offend you."

His head shook a little, but his eyes returned to the road ahead. "That's not it. I'm just thinking about what you said. Confidence is part of the problem. But there's more."

"Wait. I'm not finished."

He clicked his tongue but said nothing. She watched his golden brows lift in invitation, his tongue tucked into one cheek.

"Okay. Well, I haven't met this Amélie–"

"I will introduce you."

"Oh. So you can actually talk to her."

He scoffed. "I'm not a complete crétin. We have known each other our entire lives. We are friends."

"Aha. This is good. Great, actually. What pretence will you have to introduce me?"

He flipped a hand. "I need none. You are famous already. We will walk by her booth. You could ask about her clothing. Perhaps you want to buy something?"

"Hmm. Yes. She sells clothing at the fair? Good."

"So. Your analysis of my problems. I believe–"

"Yes. So, I think the other problem, though not related to the first, is those shit-for-brains friends of yours."

"I don't understand shit for head–"

"Didier! Will you go with the flow here? Read between the lines. Cut me some slack!"

He laughed. "Lucky for you my English is not terrible. I have a snowball chance in hell of understanding you."

"You speak English so well!" She groaned. "Why am I killing myself speaking French?"

"Because you are in France, chere. Also, because you need much practice." His big frame shook with silent laughter.

She punched his arm. "What about the 'three stooges?'"

"They are no friends of mine."

"And yet I'll venture a guess you've known them all your life, too."

His chest lifted, held a beat, and fell. "Yes."

"So, unless you move away, you can't escape the image they have created for you over so many years. Neither in the village, nor inside your own head. Is that fair?"

His head bobbed side to side, pulling a face. "That's quite good."

She let that sit awhile. They had reached the parking lot at the edge of the village and got out of his truck. He passed her bike down, then lifted a wooden box that was so big and heavy she was sure not another man could have handled it, hoisting it onto his shoulder, heading off up the steep street into the central square. She pushed her bike along beside him.

When they reached his booth, he set the box down and unpacked it, laying out his iron wares in attractive rows. An older man in a Medieval costume walked past, and greeted him, and Didier waved in reply.

"Not everyone laughs at you."

"No. Friends of my parents are kind. People who respect my work."

"Right. So change everyone else's mind about you."

He faced her and placed his fisted hands on his hips. In his own period pants and tunic, he looked like the jolly green giant on the frozen peas. Only not green. She smiled at the image.

"How do you suggest I do that, little monkey?"

She gestured at him to bend down. He did. "Lift me up. Like yesterday."

With skepticism in his eye, he made a step for her, and lifted her up. As soon was she was off the ground, she crouched low and grabbed him around the neck for balance. They were face to face, and couldn't help grinning at each other.

"We make a good team, *Girafeau*," she said. "All we have to do is convince everyone else that we are more than that."

His smile fell, and he pulled his chin back, his brows knit together while he thought about that. "You're crazy."

She lowered her voice to a whisper. "Think about it. If everyone believes you and the girl from Canada are having a romantic summer fling, then suddenly, all the women will think, huh, if she can do it, so could I. Am I right?"

"No. Because there are not women lined up to date me."

"We're only concerned about one."

"What would she think of me? That's not good for my reputation."

"I disagree. What's holding you back now?"

"My size."

"Aaaand, your lack of experience?"

His eyes darted to the right. "Perhaps."

"What if you not only had experience, but could show you made me happy? That we had fun. A little romance."

"Non." He set her down. "It's a bad idea. You want to create a spectacle. Another excuse for ridicule."

She pouted, glaring up at him. "You're missing the point. A little spectacle is precisely what's needed. Take control of the situation. Spin it in your favour. This is a win-win proposal. I get to date my first giant, and you get to win the heart of Amélie."

Oblivious to her teasing, he gestured between them. "You don't want… we are not… like that."

She knew what he meant. As much as she liked Didier, and they were fast becoming friends, there wasn't that spark of chemistry between them that signaled a potential mate, or at least a fleeting hookup. Unlike Luc last night. If it weren't for that classy French blonde who whisked him away, Niki might spend more time with him.

No. Forget that. She brushed the thought aside.

"We'll pretend. Why not? You're an intelligent, pleasant man, and very handsome too. Why wouldn't I?"

Pink shot up Didier's ears and cheeks, and he diligently rearranged his tools.

"Has no one ever said that to you, Didier?"

He harrumphed.

Her heart broke for him. "Well, it's true."

"Someone will get hurt."

"We won't. Like you said, we're not like that. And I'm leaving soon. That goes without saying. There isn't time for anything serious to develop, not that I'm looking, anyway. And your heart is already taken, isn't it?"

"Yes. But I still think–"

"It'll work. We have one week. How would you like to begin?"

He blinked down at her, baffled.

"Good grief. You don't have a clue."

She watched his Adam's apple slide up and down his neck.

"Flirt with me a little. Squat down." She gestured.

He did, and again they could see eye to eye. She wrapped one arm around his tree trunk of a neck and perched against his knee, leaning in to whisper in his ear.

"What if I were to kiss you?"

Again the vivid colour ran up his cheeks. Niki placed her hand on his strong jaw and stroked it, planting a kiss on his other cheek. He drew in a breath and held it.

"That wasn't so hard, was it?" She wondered whether anyone had touched him at all since he was a child.

He turned toward her, and their eyes locked. He looked troubled. "It is harder than you imagine, little monkey."

She touched her forehead to his for a moment. In that instant, Sam's face flashed in her mind, his innocence and vulnerability, and her heart bled a little.

They both jerked at the sound of someone clearing his throat beside them.

"That, is a terrible idea," said Luc, standing close with his arms crossed over his chest.

"How much did you hear?" Niki's heart thumped in her chest. He wasn't the first person she wanted to see this morning.

"Enough to get the gist of your plan." Luc scowled at her and twisted his brow up at Didier with implied judgment. "What do you hope to accomplish?"

"Well, if you don't blow it, I'm sure everyone in the town square has the general idea, and also knows I'm staying with Didier, so…" She placed a hand flat on Didier's broad chest, meeting his skeptical eye. "You can read whatever you want into that."

Luc continued to scowl.

She shrugged. "I'm going to take a spin on my bike for two hours while you work. How about lunch later? And maybe we can look at some clothing." She dipped her chin and smiled at Didier, plucking his tunic. "I'm thinking I'd like a Medieval costume for myself."

"Didier. *Mon ami*, we need to talk," said Luc, glaring at her until she grinned and pushed her bike along, walking away.

CHAPTER 9

Together they watched her disappear into one of the small lanes heading downhill from the square.

"You're out of your mind. She's a bad influence on you if you think an affair with a stranger will change your life."

"It's make believe," Didier said, and Luc heard the mix of skepticism and curiosity in his tone.

"Is it?" Luc tilted his head back to look up into Didier's eyes. "And how is this supposed to make Amélie feel? Jealous? Is that what you think?"

Didier heaved his wide shoulders and sighed. "I'm pretty tired of the status quo, Luc."

"We talked about that. You know what you're supposed to do."

Didier's head shook minutely. "I don't know. Even if I could suddenly behave out of character, it's not likely to turn around this stale old situation. The little one has a point."

Luc groaned, his teeth grinding. No! "I have a very uncomfortable feeling in my stomach, dude." If he were honest, a small part of his sudden unease stemmed from his own not insignificant curiosity and attraction for the fiery little woman. And he had no more business feeling anything for her than Didier, who had, only a few weeks ago, declared he could take it no longer, and determined to change his fate.

And now here was Niki, like an omen, stirring the pot of discontent in Petit Bergeron. But of good or evil? Time would tell.

After bidding Didier goodbye, Luc, too, headed out for his daily bike ride, despite a slight hangover. Why had he drunk so much last night? Perhaps, a voice in his head said, because he'd already vacillated on his plan to propose to Patrice, and was berating himself on his cowardice.

He cycled the long way around to Villeneuve-sur-Lot and have a strong cafe. He needed to get some miles in, and he needed the time to think.

He'd slept poorly, tossing and turning, his mind spinning with thoughts of Patrice and the fact he'd chickened out last night. The ring box burned away in his pocket all evening, and he couldn't find the right moment to pull her aside, to offer the ring, to say the words. Despite Charles's encouragement, Luc worried this was an ill-conceived, even a strange thing to do. Suddenly his confidence that Patrice would like the idea faltered. Or maybe it was his own resolve that had floundered. What if he were making a mistake? Either way, he'd drunk too much to do a proper job, and put it off for another day.

All night his mind kept jumping back to Grand-Mère Bougie's weird words about his wife, and the trickster. She couldn't mean what he thought she might have meant, but the notion ate away at him.

The other thing that kept him awake was Niki. Why did she bother him so much? Everything she did disturbed him. Since he'd met her, she'd insinuated herself into his thoughts. Last night again, going home with Didier. What was that about? They'd got to know each other quickly. Did she have an ulterior motive? Why should anyone trust her?

He shouldn't care, though. He didn't care what she did. What was she to him? But Didier was his friend. What was she doing with him?

After her comments, he was certain she'd stayed for the entire puppet show. She got the connection. She must understand how complicated the situation in Petit Bergeron was. Luc hoped that she'd also gleaned enough information to deduce that Didier had a serious crush on Amélie, even if she couldn't know the details. Unless Didier told her? Nah. Not likely.

But she and Didier together… even if it were an act… was a terrible idea. Did she see Didier as an easy target? Was she attracted to his unusual size? Was she a sociopath? They didn't know her.

If she messed with his friend, Didier would get hurt, and Luc couldn't allow that to happen. He'd have to keep an eye on her. On them.

Did it cross his mind he would like to get to know her better himself? Was that a slithery snake of jealousy that slid through his gut, at the thought of her staying with Didier, getting to know him, touching him, even if it were fake? He pushed those thoughts down and buried them. That was ridiculous. He couldn't feel possessive about a woman he'd just met, that he knew nothing about, that he didn't even want. Even if she made his blood simmer with unease and visceral excitement.

He shouldn't even be having these thoughts while he contemplated his own happily ever-after with Patrice. He was off limits. He'd already worked this out. He knew what he wanted. On that much he was clear.

Luc was no longer a young man. He always saw himself in his thirties, settled, happy, raising a family of his own. He was tired of feeling alone and uncertain about his future. He wanted the intimacy and security of a forever kind of love. He wanted to experience the connection, belonging and trust that his parents had sustained their entire lives, to carry forward his own version of their kind of happiness.

That's what he wanted.

Patrice was the perfect woman with whom to have all of that.

Thinking about Niki was a waste of time. A woman like that, so impulsive, independent, and so annoyingly stubborn, could never be a part of his dream. She wouldn't want the same things anyway, with her daredevil ways and adventurous spirit, but more than that, she'd disrupt and disturb and distract him from realizing his dream.

In fact she seemed determined to interfere with exactly that dream of Didier's, too.

He'd better keep a close eye on her, anyway. For Didier's sake.

Niki pointed her bike downhill and pushed off, coasting down the slope and picking up speed. Roads fanned out in all directions from the village, like the spokes of a wheel. She headed out of town in the opposite direction from Didier's place, and took a different spoke from the one she'd arrived on, trusting her handle-mounted GPS to guide her back. This route took her past an area of newer houses, with a commercial strip flanking the road. It was obviously the modern working centre of the region, with a large grocery store, a gas station, a car wash, a hardware and building supply store. This took some charm away from the illusion the village presented, especially dressed up in its Medieval finery at the moment, but she supposed the French needed modern conveniences, too.

To escape the banality of the suburban environment, she took a quick turn when a fork in the road presented itself, and glided past a community pool, where the squeals of children echoed through poplar trees lining the road, though it was still mid-morning. The heat built quickly this time of the year, in this part of the world, which made riding difficult in the afternoon.

Soon she was racing through farmland again, the peach-scented breeze in her face, with only occasional country lanes and drives leading to unseen estates. The road narrowed, and she crossed a small bridge over a creek where a willow tree grew close to the road, its long weeping branches veiling the bank, casting a cooling green shadow onto the road. She paused for a moment in its shade, breathing the fresh moist air rising off the small brook, listening to its burbling music, and took a long drink of water from her bottle.

That's when she noticed a stately brick manor house at the end of a straight narrow drive, with beautifully proportioned windows and shutters painted glossy black, with tidy flower beds circling the gravel forecourt. A shiny white Renault sat in the drive. It seemed a fine, sophisticated way of life, as different from her own as any could be, and she wondered what those people did for a living. Something boring, undoubtedly.

A few kilometers further along, between the sunflowers and the vineyards, she began to notice the roughness of the road. Pulling aside, she checked her tires and discovered that her rear was losing air. Examining it didn't reveal any obvious punctures, so she pumped it up and continued.

When she at last pulled into another small village, she had filled her tire three times. Now she'd have to change the tube before she could continue on. Dismounting, she pushed on into the central square, smaller and more intimate but not unlike the one in Petit Bergeron, circled by shops and restaurants, with a tall town hall at one end flying a bright crested pennant from its tower.

There was delicious shade under the small market shelter, which in this case, was a charming relic too small to serve any purpose now. Hanging baskets spilling pink geraniums and petunias hung from its beams overhead and ivy growing from cracks in the paving climbed the ancient stone pillars. It was a sweet reprieve from the hot sun and dust of the road. Gulping down some water, she flipped her bike upside down and set to work repairing her tire.

That's when everything started to go wrong. For some reason, she was all thumbs. She got tangled in the chain which got a kink in it she couldn't work out, until she was covered in black grease up to her elbows. Swearing, she finally got the tire off the rim, and dug out her spare tube. It was one of those days when everything that should have been easy and routine just wouldn't go right. After struggling another fifteen minutes, she discovered that her spare tube also had a leak.

"What the fuck!" She tossed her tire down onto the ground and let out a frustrated growl.

"Not going well?" a familiar sexy tenor drifted across to her.

Niki looked up with a gasp. Not ten feet from her, seated at a small outside table at a cafe with his sneaker'd feet up on a chair, sat Luc. He wore his biking lycra, and she averted her eyes from his long, lean tanned legs.

Had he watched her entire struggle? "You're quite the voyeur."

"Your French improves day by day." He smiled and took a sip of his coffee, utterly relaxed and enjoying the show.

She grunted and stood gazing down at the useless tire, her hands on her hips.

"Do you need some assistance? You seem to have trouble."

Niki bristled at the suggestion she couldn't fix her tire herself. As though he knew more about bike repair than she did. Typical guy. She'd bruised his ego last night, by allowing Didier to carry her bike, when earlier she'd rejected his help. Now he was bent on revenge. "No thanks. Got it covered."

"Looks like maybe not. I don't mind helping."

"Thank you, but I'm set up here."

He let a few minutes pass while she took apart her tire yet again, feeling his gaze on her every awkward moment. For some inexplicable reason, the whole process was doomed, and she fumbled and swallowed her curses. She refused to appear less than competent in front of this smug guy.

When their gazes met, he flashed a wide smile. "Can I buy you a coffee? An ice cream?"

"Don't you have somewhere to be?"

"Nope." Even from a distance she could discern the twitch in his mouth, suppressing his grin.

"Hey, take a break. Please? I'll buy you a coffee and help you with the tire afterwards. I want to talk to you about something."

She stood upright and glared at him, hands on her hips. Evidently, she would not get out of here without talking to him, though she knew she wouldn't like what he had to say. Shoving her tools into the kit bag, she stomped over to him.

"Fine."

"Have a seat. You're filthy."

She sat, huffing.

"Café?"

"No, thanks. Just water."

"You sure you don't want a pastis?"

"Water's fine." He gestured to the waiter and ordered in French so fast and smooth she could barely make out individual words. She studied his profile. His nose was straight, with finely chiselled nostrils. His jaw cut a sharp line, the dark stubble of his beard accentuating the shape. Why did he have to be so good-looking?

Sighing she asked, "Why are you here, anyway?"

He paused before answering. "Drinking coffee. Cycling, just like you."

"In France I mean."

"It's my second home. This is how I spend every summer. Cycling. Visiting friends."

"Like that woman with you last night? Patrice?" Oh, stupid Niki. Why did you ask that?

A shadow passed across his eyes. Not what she'd expected to see. "Yup."

She propped her feet on the chair next to his, crossing her feet. "You take every summer off? All of it?"

He shrugged, letting his gaze slide from her shoes up her legs to her tight lycra shorts before darting away with a sharp exhale. "One perk of being a teacher."

In retaliation, her gaze wandered lazily over his sexy limbs, hair damp with sweat. Damn, he was delicious. Too bad he lived in Vancouver. That broke all her rules for an anonymous summer fling.

Her stomach rumbled. She really could use a snack right now.

His eyes twinkled. "Can I order you something to eat?"

She shook her head. No. That would be altogether too friendly. "Why is your French so good, anyway? Is it really from spending summers here?"

His beautiful lips pressed together and tipped up to the left, carving a crescent into his smooth lean cheek that her fingers itched to touch. "I teach French immersion high school. In North Van. It's kind of my life."

A bark of shocked laughter escaped before she could stop it. "You live on the North Shore."

He nodded slowly. "I suppose you do too."

Their gazes met, and she glanced away, a flutter rising in her belly at the thought they were probably neighbours. Worse and worse.

Luc sipped his coffee, his forehead pinching, and set the empty cup down with a click against the porcelain saucer, his tongue sweeping out across his lower lip.

Niki felt her own tongue touch her lip, pulling it in when she noticed his narrowed gaze following its path. She swallowed as his gaze darkened, dropping to scan her throat.

"So. I only caught the tail end of your scheme with Didier earlier. But I wanted to talk to you about it. You don't know what you're messing with."

So he would go there. She pursed her lips and scanned the square, following the path of a mother with two kids orbiting her like moons. "I think I do. I have a good plan."

"You'll cause him trouble. You know that little seamstress in the puppet show?"

She lifted her chin. "Amélie." She took pleasure in his barely concealed surprise.

"You move fast." His eyes narrowed. "What's your game?"

She jerked. "Huh?"

"What do you want from him?"

Her lip curled, and she leaned back. "Where do you get off? I'm trying to help him. I owe him."

The waiter set down a fresh coffee, a glass and a green bottle shaped like a bowling pin, opening it and pouring for her. Then he handed Niki a stack of damp paper towels.

She accepted them and attempted to clean the dust and grease off other hands, silently cursing his thoughtfulness. Luc held his tongue until the waiter stepped away.

"*Merci*. I don't think you're helping him. It's complicated."

"He's stuck. He needs to do something to... get out of this rut he's in."

"I know that. I'm his friend! But you can't fix it for him. He's a man. He needs to figure this out on his own."

"Oh," she said in a sing-song. "He's a man. Well, then." She snorted. "Don't be an idiot. He needs help or he wouldn't be a thirty-year-old v–"

"What are you planning to do?" His eyes darkened. "Anyway, that's pretty patronizing, don't you think?"

She spun the green bottle around to read the label, wiping condensation off of it. "That's not what's going on here. I only want to help him learn to relax. To play. He's afraid of his own shadow."

"We already have a plan. You're interfering."

"What a hypocrite! I thought he needed to figure it out on his own? What are you doing?"

Luc's fine dark brows lowered into a straight line over his blue eyes, which shifted to the side. "I'm... I'm coaching him and... talking to Amélie, too."

She scoffed, suppressing a full on smile. "Who are you? Cyrano de Bergerac?"

He frowned into his untouched coffee. "Don't be stupid. I'm not... I'm just... trying to find out how she feels about him."

"A go-between? Like middle school? But I guess you'd know all about teenage romance, being a teacher and all. So how's that going, detective?"

He sighed, his gaze wandering across the square. "They're friendly. But she's very circumspect. I've figured out very little."

Niki guzzled her fancy water, blinking at him while she suppressed a belch. She wasn't surprised.

"Didier's introducing me to her later. Maybe I'll talk to her. She might confide in another woman."

He leaned in, and the whiff of his pine scent she caught made her swoon a little, reminding her of their nearness at the puppet show, skin touching skin. "That's not a bad idea. Maybe you could learn something to give Didier some hope. It's better than your ridiculous plan."

Niki lifted her chin, her gaze flicking up to the canopy overhead. She wanted to wrap her hands around his pretty neck and squeeze some sense into him. Leaning in, meeting his gaze straight on, she challenged him.

"While you coach Didier on Medieval courtly love, I suppose." Niki put air quotes around coach. That was ridiculous. Her face heated, and her breath quickened. Her plan would work, she was sure it would. They were nearly nose to nose, and she watched his eyes darken to indigo as his gaze traced a path around her features as she spoke.

"Do you honestly think these quiet negotiations will help? They won't change his reputation in this weird little town. And it won't help build his confidence to have two old women matchmaking for him!"

His jaw jutted to the side for a moment, a muscle ticking in his cheek. He was too stubborn to concede that he agreed with her. "But you think coming between Didier and Amélie by staging a public affair will? That'll go over well, making friends with Amélie while you pretend to screw her boyfriend. You're nuts, lady."

"I guess he's not her boyfriend yet, is he? That's the problem."

Lips pressed into a thin line, nostrils flared, his eyelid twitching, he stared at her for a long moment, then breathed, "I don't want him to get hurt. I don't want anyone to get hurt."

"They're hurting now, aren't they? Or at least Didier is. Look, I may have only met him yesterday, but I'm sensitive and I have some insight here. Believe it or not, I'm his friend too. I want to help him. And I'll do it my way."

Luc raked his fingers through his short damp hair, drawing her eyes to the lovely shape of his skull. Even that was too pretty, damn him. "I don't know."

"Yeah. So you said. You don't trust me."

His hands flared. "Trust you? I don't even know you!"

"Well, that's all right then. I have to patch my tube. Thanks for the drink." She dropped her feet to the floor and stood up, staring at her cycling shoes. Her feet had gone a little numb.

"I have a spare tube. You can have it if you'd like."

She looked up and glared at him. He wasn't very tall, but his tire was at least two inches larger than hers. "It wouldn't fit."

"I suppose you're right. You want a hand?"

She raised a palm and thrust it out. "Hey. Take a hint. I can do it myself, okay?"

Their gazes met and his twinkled with scorn. She knew she'd just contradicted herself. But Didier's situation was different. After a moment he said, with a shaking laugh that riled her, "Okay, then. Bye."

She squatted on the stone pavers next to her bike and pulled out her patch kit, examining the spare tube, testing it with spit until she located the tiny factory tear. Then she set about drying and adhering the patch. While she waited for it to dry, she gazed around. With her peripheral vision, she saw Luc still sat where he was, watching her every move.

She harrumphed and turned her back on him, tidying up and putting away her repair kit.

Enough time had passed, so she pumped a little air into her tube to test it. It seemed to hold, so she assembled the tire and pumped it full. She bounced it and tested it under pressure. Seemed okay. Putting it back on the bike, she tightened the nuts, mounted and took off without looking back, even though she could feel his eyes burning a hole in the back of her head. Annoying man.

When, twenty minutes later, she was pumping up the still-leaking tire yet again on the side of the road, and he cruised by on his bike without stopping or even glancing at her, she decided she hated him, and he was the last man on a bike she'd ever get involved with.

Sadly, she was out of luck with her bike. A few minutes later, she was thinking about hitching a ride when a shiny white Renault slowed beside her. When she glanced up to explain her need to the kind driver, her stomach dropped to her shoes when she saw who was driving.

Luc!

He grinned, stepped out and wordlessly lifted her bike to the roof rack, lashing it with straps. "Get in. I'll take you to the shop."

With a huff of defeat, she dropped into the passenger seat when he held the door open for her.

"Whose car?"

"Francine. Charles's wife. Lucky for you she's home today."

She sighed, and they drove in tense silence the rest of the way to a little bike shop in the suburban mall she'd passed on her way out here.

"Thanks," she forced herself to mutter as he unloaded her bike.

"It was my pleasure, Niki. I'm always happy to help you." She wanted to wipe the smirk off of his handsome face with the back of her hand. Bastard.

CHAPTER 10

By the time Niki had got her tire fixed and pushed it back up to the main parking lot, she was drained, very grumpy and no longer in the mood to enjoy the festival nor get embroiled in the personal life of the local giant. The entire encounter with Luc had left her on edge, with the distinct feeling he'd come out ahead in their battle of wills. She found Didier's truck and lifted her bike into the back, changed her shoes and trudged uphill to the square. She found him sitting behind his table, chatting with tourists about his wares. Once they moved along, she approached.

After one look at her he asked, "What happened, little monkey?" He put out his hand, palm up.

She set her grease blackened hand in his. She wanted him to wrap her in a big giant bear hug and smooth all her irritation away with his unflappable calm. Instead, she stood up taller, pasted a smile on her face and said, "What did Medieval women wear, anyway?"

He laughed, his pale blue eyes sparkling, and stood up, unfolding his long limbs. "Let's see."

They strolled across the square to where Amélie stood within a small tent draped with samples of her clothing. There were ruffled shirts, tunics, floppy caps and heavy long dresses with embroidered yolks, some in dull colors and plain fabrics, and others bright and satiny rich. Niki strolled right into the tent and began to browse before she realized she'd lost Didier. Stepping out again, she saw he wouldn't fit into the diminutive tent.

"Sorry."

"Go ahead and look at the dresses. I'll wait here."

Maybe he was avoiding close contact with Amélie? She was busy with a customer fitting, helping to choose a headdress to go with a dress that a young woman had chosen.

"These aren't for me, anyway. I can't move in these long things."

Just then, Amélie finished and walked back toward her. "Can I help you find something?"

Niki tilted her head and considered the young woman. She was of average height and weight, taller by a few inches than Niki, and while not plump, had a softness and roundness about her that Niki's athletic frame lacked. She wore her pale blond hair pulled back in a twist. Up close, she had a delicate beauty. Her full pink mouth was her most striking feature.

"I don't know. I'd like something to wear for the festival, but I'm not comfortable in a dress."

"Oh. You want to dress as a man?"

"No, I–"

"Good day, Amélie," Didier said, his deep voice soft and tentative.

She spun to face him. "Didier! I didn't notice you there."

That seemed far-fetched.

"Would you like to sit down?" She pulled a stool out and set it down just at the edge of the tent. She smiled warmly as she passed him the stool, but Niki couldn't tell if she was partial to Didier or not.

"Many thanks," Didier said and lowered himself onto it, so he could see into the tent. His big hands clasped together between his large knees, dangling. "Can you help my friend Niki find something to suit her?"

Amélie did a double take, her head spinning to re-examine Niki. "Oh! You are the acrobat from yesterday!"

Niki smiled. Proof that nothing happened in this little village that went unnoticed. "That's me. Niki Ballantyne." She put out her hand.

Amélie took it. In Amélie's smooth grip, Niki was even more conscious of her hard, calloused palm, and her grease-grimed fingers. Amélie didn't flinch at the feel, even though Niki's rough skin scraped at the seamstress's soft skin. "Amélie Laurent. I'm pleased to meet you, Niki. You are already something of a celebrity in Petit Bergeron." Her smile was genuine, but her blue eyes darted to Didier and back a few times, as though she was trying to figure something out.

Niki laughed. "Well, that happens when I'm not hanging with other *traceurs*."

At Amélie's furrowed brow, Didier spoke up. "That's what people like Niki call themselves," he said. "She does parkour, not acrobatics like those others." He gestured over his shoulder.

Amélie drew a finger across her pursed lips, pondering Niki. "I believe I have something for you, Niki, but not here. Can you come by my shop this evening?" She turned. "You can show her where it is, Didier, can't you?"

He nodded, his eyes drinking her in. "*Oui*."

Niki's heart swelled at the way he looked at her, his adoration and devotion obvious. In some ways it was no wonder those buffoons teased him about his crush. No one could miss how he felt. Certainly not Amélie. Niki studied Amélie's response, and decided she liked him quite well herself. Her reserve and polite manners made it hard to see, so she could understand why the men were uncertain.

"I'd appreciate that Amélie," she said with maximum eye contact and her warmest smile. Lifting her chin, she determined to help these star-crossed lovers if it was within her power. The question was, would one week be enough?

∼

Niki was torn between wanting to have dinner with Didier, to make a proper show of their "budding" affair, and hurrying over to meet Amélie at her shop after the festival booths were closed for the night. Both would advance Didier's aim, but dinner first would lay the groundwork, if she played it right–and the reticent Didier would play along.

It was difficult to be playful with him physically because of their difference in size, but it would warm him up for the flirting she had planned over their meal in the market square. Despite being tired from her ride this afternoon, she thought a little parkour might ease the way.

"Hey, Girafeau," she teased, glancing up at him, as they walked toward the food booths. "D'you want to work up an appetite?"

"That's not a problem for me, little monkey."

"Yeah. I wondered about that. You don't seem to eat all that much for a big fella. Aren't you starving?"

"I eat more frequently," he said. "Nevertheless, I am still always hungry."

"You really don't like the limelight, do you?"

His step hitched. "Something tells me you are not talking about citrus fruit." There was teasing laughter in his deep voice.

A warm flush bloomed on her cheeks making her appreciate the fading light of evening. "That doesn't work in French?"

"Ah. *Non*. We say, the light of the projector or the rack."

"Hm. Doesn't have the same ring to it."

"That is the way of idioms, my friend. Light of the lime sounds stupid in translation."

She threw up her hands. "I'll never get it."

"They say if you want to learn a language, you must fall in love with a native."

"Say what?"

"Take a lover who speaks the language you wish to immerse yourself in. Then it comes without effort."

They took a few steps in silence while she pondered that.

"About that–"

"Non. I know what you'll say. I have thought it over, and it's a bad idea. First, it's all a pretence, and second, I don't even know how to behave in the case it is real love. Something is bound to backfire. Then you will ride your little bicycle toward the sleeping sun and leave me here, a bigger turkey of the farce than I am already."

"Oh, now you're just egging me on. Turkey of the what?"

He chuckled. "Laughingstock, *ma petite*," he translated.

She preferred it when he called her 'my little' than 'little monkey'. It felt more intimate. Reaching up, she slipped her hand in his. He flinched and glanced down, frowning.

She grinned. "Relax, *mon grand*."

This time, her effort to express herself rendered him hysterical, and when Didier was laughed, the entire village could hear it. He laughed a deep belly laugh that brought to mind a small thunder storm, echoing off the stone facades framing the square.

Beyond embarrassment she dared to ask, "What now?"

"Let's just say it makes me want to call you 'little mother.'"

"I give up!" She laughed and released his hand, free-running away from him toward the stone arcade. She ran straight up the thick inside face of one Gothic arch and threw herself backward into a flip, reversing it and repeating the move up the other side of the arch. Then she front flipped toward the low concrete walls that edged the central plaza, flanking the broad banks of steps top and bottom, and cat leapt along between a series of handstands, hand walking and flips. When she got to the end of the row, she ran at the pillar of a broad arch and flung her body up to grip the stone lintel, some fifteen feet up. After hanging there for a moment or two, catching her breath, she swung her body, building momentum for a flip back down to the ground, when Didier grabbed her around her middle like a wayward child with his huge muscular arm.

"Hey!" She spun around in Didier's grip and grinned at him. "What's the matter?"

"It's time for dinner, little monkey. You can play afterwards."

Niki wrapped her arms around his thick neck and planted a kiss on his mouth. He froze, their eyes locked, his expression half bewilderment, half warning. She grinned and climbed up to sit astride his shoulders.

She raised one fist in the air. "Onward, *Girafeau*. Take me to my dinner."

Didier shook his head and walked off, unconcerned with her hanging on his shoulders, although a hundred pairs of eyes burned her skin.

CHAPTER 11

Instead of choosing their food from the vendors around the market hall, Didier strode toward a nice-looking restaurants nestled under the stone arcade in a corner of the square, the sign reading *La Grappe de* —something. At the entrance, a *maitre-d'* in a white apron approached.

"Good evening, Didier."

"Marcel. How are you?"

He sent Didier a warning message with his eyes. "Excellent. But we are full tonight, because of the festival."

"You can find a small table for an old friend, no?"

The fellow rolled his eyes, suppressing a smirk. "Just a moment. I'll see."

Didier guided Niki down, and she slid slowly off of his arm to the ground, enjoying his strength and the firmness of his body against hers. This man might belong to Amélie, but it was no hardship to be close to him.

"I'm perfectly happy at the—"

He took her chin between his large fingers and tilted her face up, his eyes sparkling with mischief. "Shh. My treat."

A grin stretched her face in response and she met his eye with a teasing look of her own. If they could keep up this playful banter, no one would question the sincerity of their mutual attraction, or that a romantic encounter was blooming on top of their friendship and rapport.

The sound of Marcel clearing his throat broke into their spell. "Come along. I have something for you." He led the way back out onto the restaurant's wooden deck, weaving between the packed tables, toward the gap in the railing. As they followed, she turned and met Didier's eye. He shrugged at her unspoken question.

"This is the best we can do." Marcel waved one arm toward a small table draped in white linen he'd tucked around the corner, under in the arcade's shadow, not in the restaurant at all, but beside a passageway between the restaurant and an adjacent sweets shop. A wooden doorway stood ajar in the dark passageway, bleeding a band of golden light onto the paving stones, dispersing the gloom and casting a soft light. A single candle flickered in the centre of the table, along with a small vase with a single small red carnation.

"We will serve you from the kitchen, okay?" said Marcel, gesturing to the open door.

"It's perfect!" Niki said. "Romantic. Thank you, Marcel."

Didier, she was sure, was blushing, but he pulled out her chair, and guided it in as she sat down, the perfect gentleman. He may not have any experience courting women, but his mother had raised him well. She wished for their first 'date' she was wearing something nicer than a tank top and a pair of baggy sweats over her cycling shorts. "*Merci*, Marcel," he murmured.

Left alone, Didier sobered and said, "Well I don't know how this will end, little one, but we have begun something here tonight."

She felt it too. But instead of dwelling on the attention they generated amongst the villagers, both friend and foe, the genuine affection that grew between them gave her a warm glow. Although Didier initially reminded her of her little brother Sam, and her sympathy for his predicament was heartfelt, she liked him more with each hour they spent together. He was growing into a true friend. And as a result, she was even more determined to facilitate his happiness.

Emerging from the back doorway, instead of a menu, Marcel brought plates and dishes of vegetables in cream sauce and roasted meat for them to share, like a family meal. It made the occasion even more special, somehow. More than an hour flew by as they enjoyed the delicious meal and talked more about their families. Kind and uncorrupted as he was, Didier would make the best of husbands and fathers. Amélie was a very lucky woman.

Luc reflected on their afternoon exchange, laughing to himself. Niki was so stubborn. She exasperated him. But he couldn't seem to get enough of her, either. She drew him like a siren, compelling him to return and smash his ship on her shores repeatedly.

He'd tried so hard to be friendly and helpful, and she'd thrown it back in his face until she'd had no choice. What was wrong with the woman? He'd laughed all the way home after passing her on the road, thinking if she were too stubborn to accept his help, then she could figure out how to get home on a flat tire without him.

She'd looked so frustrated!

By the time he'd pulled in the driveway five minutes later, he'd felt guilty, and recognized that it was his bruised male ego that had made him so unkind. He'd immediately gone to Francine to borrow her car keys.

He hadn't meant to teach Niki a lesson in humility, but he couldn't say he was unhappy with the way it turned out. How did someone get close to a woman like that? How had Didier befriended her in such a short time? Did Luc have to develop a hardship to lure her in?

"Luc!"

His hand slipped, nearly slicing his finger as his head jerked up and he dropped the knife onto the countertop with a clatter. "Merde! What?"

Francine snapped her fingers. "What's on your mind? You've been making weird faces all afternoon." She stared at him from across the kitchen bar.

He blinked. "How long have you been sitting there?"

She laughed and shook her head. "Patrice got a call."

Patrice sat on the patio just beyond the open glass doors, sipping rosé and talking on her cell phone, frowning. She was always on her phone.

"Are you thinking about Patrice? Is that why you're grinning like a fool?"

"Uh–" Luc felt his face flush with heat. Patrice. If only. He shook himself. What was he thinking? Getting Niki's attention! What would he do with it if he got it?

Francine jerked her chin at him. "I like that look on you. What inspired it?"

"Mm." He ran his hand over his bristled scalp. "My costume."

"Non! That is unacceptable. Can I not leave for two days without calamity?"

Luc and Francine both glanced over at Patrice's raised voice.

Francine snickered. "Don't worry. I won't spill your secret." Sipping her own wine, she said, "What happened to your friend with the broken tire this afternoon? I didn't see when you returned the car."

"Oh!" His pulse jumped. Had she read his mind? "Nothing. I helped her take her bike to the shop. Then I rode in and moved things around for Victor and *Grand-Mère*. Gathered ingredients for dinner…" He tapered off, resuming his preparations.

He had promised to make dinner tonight, before Patrice returned to Toulouse for the week. He'd stocked up on vegetables and wine from the market, deciding what to cook after helping *Grand-Mère Bougie* late in the day.

Before he'd left the village, however, he'd spotted Niki with Didier again. She seemed bubbling with energy despite her difficult afternoon, jumping and flipping across the square. The last thing he saw was her hanging off of Didier like King Kong on the Empire State Building.

Every time he saw them together, they were touching, more and more. His stomach burned and his teeth clenched at the memory. He'd had a powerful urge to stomp over and rip her off of him. They were heading for disaster, yet there was nothing he could do to stop them from pursuing this ill-advised scheme. His conversation with Niki this afternoon had shown him how determined she was. Even that his open opposition egged her on.

He wasn't curious about what Niki had got up to after repairing her bike tire. He didn't ask the villagers for details when he heard them gossip at the butcher shop they had seen her and Didier together and were right now having a romantic dinner together under the arch at *Les Grappe des Raisin*. Some observed that this was unusual behaviour for their Didier, but he'd made no comment, ordering his steaks with the patience of a saint.

Her plan was well and truly underway.

Meanwhile, his plan to propose to Patrice was not going well. Sensing his intent stare, she glanced up from examining her nails while listening to her caller. She smiled softly and fluttered her fingertips at him. He returned her smile, but it felt forced, as did their entire relationship. Acid roiled his stomach, worrying now about the expectations he'd encouraged in both Patrice and Charles. Even Francine seemed to consider their partnership a *fâit accomplis*.

He was having serious doubts. He couldn't hurt these people who were every bit as much his family as his own sisters.

He bent his head to resume his work chopping vegetables for dinner. Whatever he did, he must do it gently and with diplomacy. He would never wish to damage his relationships, or make himself unwelcome here in their home.

"*Cheri.*" He looked up again as Patrice walked towards him, her elegant features marred by a small scowl, and braced himself for bad news. "*Désolé*, Luc. I cannot stay for dinner. There was a problem with a shipment that my assistant cannot seem to sort out without my help. And we have a big sale starting tomorrow."

"You're leaving?" He'd planned dinner!

"*Oui*. I must return immediately."

Wiping moisture from his fingers, he stepped up to exchange les bises and bid her farewell, until the following weekend. Perhaps, she muttered as she threw her bags together and he carried them out to her car. Just then, Charles's black sedan pulled into the gravel drive. He emerged, kissed his sister, and she pulled onto the road. As Luc stood in the open doorway, Francine's hand on his shoulder in commiseration, he could not identify any emotion in his chest beyond relief.

The crowd had thinned, and the vendors had long since packed up their booths for the night once they finished their dinner. Didier insisted on doing the same with his own, though it had been unattended the past couple of hours, and would delay them. Niki sensed he was stalling. Carrying his box to the truck, he left Niki to sit in the dark square and absorb the ambiance of the charming village as its inhabitants dispersed for the night. She was too full from her dinner to practice parkour, though the quiet empty spaces called out to her.

She hoped Amélie was still waiting for them, as she'd promised.

At last Didier returned, standing a few feet away from her, his hands shoved deep into his pockets. He looked grim.

She met his eye and said, "What's eating you?"

He shrugged. "Perhaps it's too late. Amélie is probably gone to bed."

She studied him. His large feet shuffled in the grit on the stone pavement as he shifted his weight from leg to leg.

"What are you worried about?"

"What am I not worried about? This charade you've orchestrated can't go well." He shook his head as though to dislodge bees. "What happens now? If Amélie has heard rumours about us, perhaps she will be hurt. Or mad. Or perhaps she will not care. Either way, it makes me feel ill." He rubbed his large hand over his gut, as though he felt the symptoms of his imagined illness already. "If she has heard nothing, then what? How do we behave in front of her? What do we…"

"You're overthinking it. We don't have to playact in front of her. Just be yourself. These things move slowly, and we've just begun. Nothing is irreversible."

He scowled. "Nothing has changed around here for many years, Niki. I'm not sure I can handle it."

"Are you happy with the way things are, Didier?"

His blue eyes scanned back and forth across the edge of the square, though the last bit of daylight was fading into dusk. That made it close to ten o'clock. "Humph."

"What have you got to lose? Let's go."

He heaved a deep sigh and led the way across the square and into one of the narrow lanes leading down the hill. The adjacent walls of this tiny street were so close together, Niki couldn't resist. She took off running and leapt up one side, spun like a horizontal top and leapt across to the other side, repeating this move over and over so she was running along the walls without touching the ground, like Spiderman. There were no spaces like this in modern cities back home. It was exhilarating, and she forgot herself in the movement.

"Hey, monkey!"

Didier's voice cut through her concentration, and she pushed off, flipping to the ground. "What?"

"You passed it." She saw that he was standing under a small, wall-mounted wooden sign. Light flooded out of an open doorway beside him. Amélie's shop.

"Oh. Sorry." She hiked back up the lane until she reached him.

Didier stooped to enter the small doorway, into a narrow passageway, and Niki followed.

"*Bon soir*, Didier! You're here," Niki heard Amélie's welcome though she could not see past Didier's bulk. She wondered if there would be space for them to fit, until they emerged into a generous beamed room and Didier could stand up. Amélie came forward to greet them and took Niki's hand in her warm grasp. "I'm so glad you made it. Are you ready to find a costume?"

"Yes. Do you have something?"

Amélie was grinning. "I do. I have suggestions for you. Come in." She turned. "Please take a seat, Didier. Niki, come with me to the dressing room." She led Niki by the arm and turned back to Didier. "Would you like something to drink while you wait?"

"Uh. Uh... no, *merci*. I'm fine."

Being so close to Amélie was messing with him. He avoided looking directly at her while he lowered himself into a chair, his hands dangling between his knees and twitching nervously.

Amélie led her first to a small toilet room under the stairs. She picked up a small oval bar of soap and set it in Niki's hand. "A friend of mine makes this. It has pumice, and will remove the grease from your skin before you must touch the clothing." She smiled in apology. "Also, it has a lovely orange fragrance. It will make you feel so fresh and clean. Enjoy!"

Left alone for a moment, Niki stared at her reflection in the tiny mirror hanging above the sink. Her brown irises were tiny rings around huge dilated pupils. Nothing about this brief sojourn in Petit Bergeron had met her expectations so far. Everything was unraveling, as though the strands of her own life were loosening and becoming interwoven with the people she met. She steadied her breathing and turned the old-fashioned tap, letting warm water soften the soap and release its weighted scent.

When she emerged, clean and reluctantly smelling of the vile citrus, Amélie beckoned her behind a curtain and pulled out items of clothing and handed them to her. "Try these. My idea is that, these items will allow you freedom of movement, and still come together into a distinctive look for the festival. Or this. Here is another idea, but... I don't know. The fabric has elastic. What do you think?"

The options came at Niki too quickly to understand or respond. But once she tried on the garments, it made sense.

"My you are so small, but so strong, like a wire spring," Amélie said, admiring Niki's lean bare legs and torso.

The first outfit Amélie suggested was a kind of Persian genie type of thing in a bright orangey-red. A harem concubine or something, with long satin baggy trousers with a low-hanging crotch. Niki lifted her leg, did a squat, jumped, and decided that it would allow her to do parkour despite appearing elegant. It came with a little embroidered vest.

"That looks wonderful," Amélie declared. "The persimmon suits you. Try the other now."

Niki complied. The second outfit was more standard. Something like a typical boy's suit, a tunic and patterned tights with a touch of the jester to it. "What about shoes?"

"Well, many of the people around here wear the handmade leather boots of our friend Léo. They are exquisite, and comfortable, but take time to break in. For you to do your jumping, I suggest a soft slipper with a strap on top of the foot."

Niki removed her Merrell trail gloves and tried them on, flexing her feet, testing the grip of the slippers against the floor. She wouldn't want to wear them all the time, they wouldn't last, but they'd do. She nodded. "These feel good. I think they suit the first costume better though, don't you?"

"Yes, you are right." She lifted a worn pair of boots. "If you prefer the jester suit, I could lend you these boots of mine. They are old and soft, and I think our feet are a similar size, but I don't know if they will allow you to…" she gestured with her hand to indicate Niki's flips.

"Hmm." Niki turned back and forth and studied herself in the tall mirror, tilting her head. She liked it too. It was fun, but not so special. "Is this very expensive?"

"Depends what you call expensive. Will you ever wear these again?"

Niki shrugged. "I don't care. I'm here now. I just want–I want to feel as though I'm part of this."

Amélie nodded and gave her a spontaneous hug. "*Oui*. It has bitten you, non?"

Niki laughed, squeezing back. "I guess so."

"When do I get to see?" Didier's slightly irritated voice came from beyond the curtain.

"Soon. Soon. Patience," Amélie said, smiling conspiratorially at Niki, making her like the woman even more. She continued, whispering, "Which do you think he will prefer?"

Niki hesitated. There was something about Amélie's tone and manner that gave her pause. She seemed to suggest she understood there was something special about their relationship. But perhaps Niki was reading way too much into her sparkling eyes and impish smiles. It seemed, God she hoped she was mistaken, as though Amélie was subtly cheering on Didier's success in his new relationship with Niki. She'd have to do more research.

"Um. We haven't known each other long, you know. I'm only here for a week." She stretched her face in a self-conscious smile. "I doubt he cares."

Amélie winked and whispered. "Well, I have known him all my life, and..." she nodded, "Didier cares about all of his friends. I think this one is better." She held up the genie costume Niki had just removed.

"Er. Yeah. I agree. It's more interesting, for sure." She fingered the bright satin.

Amelie tilted her head. "Also, more feminine. Yes?"

"You bet." She paused, feeling a twinge of guilt. "We're just friends, you know."

"*Bien sûr*, but he's very handsome, no?"

Huh. "You think so," Niki ventured.

Amélie nodded with an arch smile. "Don't be alarmed by his size. Didier is a very gentle man. A very good man."

Confused, Niki stripped off the jester suit and put on the genie suit again. No wonder Luc had a hard time understanding how she felt. "Perhaps he's more your type than mine?"

Deigning to reply, Amélie pulled together a few more accessories to embellish the look now she had made a choice. A snug, elasticized turban that would cover her shoulder-length brown hair if she tucked it in, and not fall off during flips. The soft ballet slippers with pointed toes, and elastic straps. A shiny sky-blue sash the colour of... well the colour of Luc's eyes.

Niki surveyed the effect in the long mirror and decided she liked it. Exotic and alluring, and also *sportif*. The acrobat Sabine had worn something similar, with eastern influences. Cultures had been mixing in the Mediterranean for centuries. It gave her pause. The Middle Ages were likely a far more interesting time than she had previously considered. Perhaps more tolerant than she'd assumed.

More tolerant than suburban bullies raised on fast food and video games. Maybe Sam would have had a better life then. She tried to imagine him in a fun costume. Something like the tunic and tights. He'd have liked that very much.

A soft nudge brought her back to the present. "You're smiling. Go. Show him." Amélie gently pushed Niki through the curtain.

Didier jerked upright as she emerged, as though he'd dozed off. "*Belle! Mythique!*" he exclaimed. "Amélie is a genius. Do you like it?"

Niki felt heat flushing her cheeks. "I love it, actually." She took a step forward and spun to show him the full effect, her pantaloons billowing. The translation of 'genius' confused and amused her. "But it's me that's a *génie*." She put her hands together and made a deep bow. "What wish may I grant you, master *Girafeau*?"

Didier's smile faltered though he forced a laugh at her joke, and he covered his discomfort with another one-sided grin.

"Do a little flip," Amélie suggested, with a limp hand gesture, saving the awkward moment.

Niki complied, though there was little space in Amélie's workshop. She did a slow motion front flip, and then a handstand. Everything stayed in place, including the turban, though the satin flowed in interesting ways. She righted herself.

Amélie gave her a spontaneous hug. "You are a marvel!"

Niki smiled, a little self-conscious. She wasn't a circus performer. "So are you. How much do I owe you?"

"Well, for a friend of Didier's…" she cast a shy glance in his direction, and for the first time since yesterday Niki sensed that there was genuine affection and, perhaps longing there. Amélie named a modest price. Not cheap, by any means, but Niki's chest filled with a sense of well-being and accomplishment. She pulled her credit card out of her bag. If this ruse worked, and she could help free Didier from his prison and achieve his dreams, it was worth every penny.

CHAPTER 12

Back at Didier's house that evening, relaxing over a glass of red wine, Niki felt they had accomplished quite a lot in twenty-four hours. "Are you okay?"

Didier's eyes rolled to the rafters, and he took a deep breath and released it in a long sigh. "It still seems wrong to be playing such games. I feel a sense of doom."

Niki laughed. "I think you are far too used to reacting to the behavior of others, instead of taking the lead in the events of your own life."

He shifted his weight and his head wobbled, considering. "Perhaps."

"You're friendly with each other." She nudged him. "That's great! I thought you were too shy to speak to her," she observed. "Though you were awkward at Amélie's shop."

Didier rose from his oversized timber-framed sofa to refill their glasses. When he sat again, she thought he wouldn't respond to her comment at all. Perhaps she had offended him.

"It reminds me of other times." He kept his eyes down, studying his wine, swirling it around.

"Other times? You've… what, you've hung out there before?"

Obviously reluctant to share, he began slowly. "Erm. Amélie makes my clothing."

Niki sat up, wide eyed. "What! All of them?"

"Not my... er... undergarments. These I can wear in the extra large size. But someone must make my shirts, trousers, and coats for me."

Niki let out a low whistle, trying to imagine what this entailed. "So. Let me get this right. You go there for measurements and fittings?"

"*Exactement.*" His booming voice came out strangled.

"Is there no other source of tailoring?"

He shrugged, his expression pained. "Not here."

"Oh. Em. Gee! Didier, you're a masochist."

"That is the truth."

She gestured with her hand in a "gimme more" sign.

His blue eyes met hers in a prolonged, considered gaze. "*D'accord.* It began years ago. She offered, and I naively thought it was a good idea. I thought, how can I pass up such a special time, just Amélie and me. But it was much, uh... harder than I imagined." Niki watched a flush of colour rise, beginning at his neck and fanning out until his ears were pink. "The first time, we were about... seventeen, perhaps. I stood there in my... he gestured to his middle... well only jockeys and socks, while she measured me all over." He gulped, sending his giant size Adam's apple sliding up and down his thick neck. "It was painful and delicious. I almost passed out. And I..." again he gestured to his groin. "It showed. I think I shocked her. It mortified me."

"Whoa dude." She pinched the bridge of her nose.

"I am too much a fool in love to stop." He tilted his head and met her gaze, his soul bared for her to see.

Niki's eyes filled with unshed tears. His love and longing was so great, and still he felt powerless to act on his desire.

"How can you put up with it? When you want her so much?"

"My love is greater than my desire, I suppose. I'm afraid that if I act on it, I will get into a situation far worse."

"How's that?"

"What if..." Didier's eyes were glassy, and he looked up at the ceiling, blinking. "She may reject me. But what if she returns my love, and by some miracle we are together? Then I'd have to..." he grimaced. "What if I hurt her?"

Niki wore her new costume to town the following day, thinking she would search for Alain and the other acrobats for a little fun and games. Throngs of tourists mobbed the village, children marching in knights templar tunics, duelling with wooden swords in the few open spaces, and being led around the perimeter on pony rides. An extraordinary number of monks wandered around, with real or fake tonsures. She felt more like a local, and less like a tourist today, in her new clothes. She loitered while Didier set up his booth for the day.

"How much of your business comes from these types of fairs?"

He shrugged. "They are significant. About a quarter of my annual income from a dozen events around the region, and regular tourist trade from Thursday and Saturday markets." He paused, gesturing with a hammered Medieval helmet in one hand.

"Then there are more mundane contracts. Fixtures for houses and shops. Railings. Better money for simpler work. I could expand my market for the small, handcrafted items if I could promote them. I have a website, but it's not good. And shipping iron is expensive."

"How else can you find more customers?"

He said nothing for a while, arranging his wares in neat rows, pensive.

"For a long time, I have had an idea."

She nodded, listening.

"There is a shop within the walls in old Carcassonne. Quite a large one. Thousands of tourists pass every day, all summer, and into the shoulder seasons. I know they have several artisanal suppliers."

"Go on."

He stood up, his hands mobile, his gaze unfocussed. "It has long been my dream to take samples of my work there and try to get a supply contract. Wholesale. But the volume would keep me busy all year round, and I would work more on the things I love to make." He picked up a beautiful sample of a long dagger from his display, with a straight gleaming blade and an intricate handle ringed with polished steel and gleaming black oiled iron. Something the Chevalier de Bayard himself might have carried in his belt. "And I would have enough money."

Enough. Enough for what?

"So why don't you go? See what you can line up? Maybe there are other contracts you could get for the old buildings, too."

He shrugged, setting down the blade.

"Didier?"

"I've never been that far from Petit Bergeron."

She assumed that he was self-conscious and shy. "Are you kidding me? Your attributes are a plus. Who wouldn't want to do business with a giant blacksmith called LeGrand?" She screwed up her face. "You need a lesson in marketing, my friend."

He gave her shoulder a gentle shove. "Go see the festival and leave me alone. It will end soon and the giant blacksmith will be the only spectacle you will have seen."

"Fine, fine. I'm going to see the stone carvers and have a look around for Alain and Sabine."

He grunted and sat down behind his table as she wandered off.

Well, more food for thought. Maybe he also felt he didn't earn enough to support a wife and family, if he was traditional that way. Or at least, to tempt one with luxuries. Though Amélie didn't seem the sort to care.

Niki blew out an exasperated sigh and sauntered over to the area under the arcade where two stone masons were demonstrating stone carving and giving lessons to tourists and kids who were bashing on big blocks of limestone. Stone chips and snow white dust littered the ground. A long white-haired and bearded man, in all white clothing demonstrated. You couldn't tell he was coated in limestone dust. He was intent on his work, and she watched, mesmerized, for several minutes while images of doves and vines emerged from the plain block of stone.

"Hello again."

The hairs on the back of her neck stood up at the sound of a familiar voice, so close she felt his warm breath on her skin.

Luc stood behind her. The warmth of his body radiated into hers in the cool morning air. She suppressed a shiver and spun to face him as he spoke.

"You fit right in around here. Thinking of joining the acrobat troupe?" It was as if he'd read her thoughts. Her pulse raced at the transformation his own costume rendered. The lacings at the throat of his fine linen shirt lay opened, and cinched the ballooned fabric down each sleeve, ending in ties. A colourful green sash hugged his narrow hips. Below that, fitted green pants showcased his lean, muscular cyclist's thighs, ending in soft black boots. He reminded her of a dashing Robin Hood, and her skin tingled with unwelcomed excitement. The best-looking Robin Hood she'd ever seen.

Even more striking, he'd shaved his beautiful head, the stubble forming a dark shadow, and his beard was untrimmed. It gave him a dangerous, sexy edge that rocked her down to her pointy slippers. All she could think about was the smattering of dark chest hairs exposed at his open neck and exploring the fine contours of his chest and… lower.

Unable to conjure a witty reply through her suddenly dry throat, she forced out, "Oh, it's you." Remembering their last encounter, she feigned more disinterest than she felt. "I guess I owe you thanks for your help yesterday."

"You're welcome." His sexy mouth bit back a smile, but amusement shone in his blue eyes, along with a hint of apology.

She tsked. It was her own fault, and he'd bested her. She met his gaze in acknowledgment. "Thanks so much for that."

He shrugged, his expression saying, You asked for it, and let his eyes wander over her, his soft lips curling in a fond smile. His tongue slowly stroked his bottom lip, and she felt liquid heat coil between her legs. Why did he stare at her like that? Why was she having this wild, carnal response to a little eye contact? Where was his elegant blond Frenchwoman?

"That colour suits you," he murmured. "Fiery."

She swallowed. "You look like you need one of Didier's daggers to complement that look."

He chuckled. "But it's a ruse. I'm a pacifist at heart."

"Nothing wrong with self-defense." Why did she feel she needed protection from the dark and dangerous predator standing inches from her? When had he transformed from a witty and mild-mannered good guy into a ravaging pirate?

"When required," he drawled, pulling her attention back to his face. "Where are your friends today?"

"I'm just setting out to look for them. Where are yours?"

He turned, flipping a lazy hand over. "Oh, most of them are at work. May I join you in your search? I enjoy watching the acrobatic displays." His bright eyes crinkled as he looked into hers, intense and blue, and she was certain he was referring more to her own antics than those of the professionals.

"Come along then," she turned and wove her way through the crowd, his eyes boring holes in her back as he followed her.

CHAPTER 13

Luc's mind churned as he followed Niki through the crowd. With a moment's reprieve from her burning gaze, he took several deep breaths to dissipate the overwhelming haze of lust that had overcome him when he saw her in that freaking incredible costume. In these close-fitting pants, he couldn't afford to walk around town with a raging boner jutting out.

She was one hot tamale. Instead of her usual basic, sporty tank and baggy sweatpants, which were sexy enough, she looked more like a genie. I dream of genie, he thought, and I have to stop!

What had come over him?

Why couldn't he stop fantasizing about this eccentric, wild little woman whom he hardly knew? He had to stop. It was just the novelty. She was fascinating to watch, the way she moved. The way she bounced on the balls of her feet, and touched walls, columns, posts, almost as though she were blind and taking her bearings with her fingertips. He couldn't recall ever being so turned on by another human being.

She was such a contrast to the serene Patrice, with her perfect blond hair and flowing white silks, which he loved and found exquisite. Whom he knew well.

Niki was so unlike Patrice, who was good for him. A stabilizing influence. He shushed the voice in his head that told him he was already stable enough. Patrice was hard-working, respectable, elegant.

She was a wonderful hostess, a charming travel and dinner companion, an erudite conversationalist. All things he admired. But, he realized, left him feeling flat.

Why would he trade that for… for an erratic, Fun! adolescent, Bold! semi-articulate, Exciting! Reckless Adventurous!… his contradictory thoughts sputtered to a halt. He wouldn't. That was all. It wasn't in his best interest.

Yet as he'd dressed in his costume this morning, his only thoughts were, what would she think? And he didn't mean Patrice. Would he see her? Would she notice him? Perversely, he'd made himself look tougher and meaner by shaving his head and leaving his beard longer, trimming it a little more severely than usual. He refused to be another rescue project for her. His inner cave man compelled him to shed his nice guy image in favour of something darker.

Instinct told him to go against the pattern.

What had made her so determined to accept no help from anyone? As it is thoughts of her–good warring with bad–had distracted him the rest of the day and half the night.

So what was happening with this stranger? Magic?

Well. He'd ignore it and the spell would wear off. Just a ridiculous infatuation with the new. Nothing that was good for him or fit his plans, uncomfortable dreams notwithstanding.

This interest in Niki could lead to no good and was really messing with his head. How could someone who annoyed him, whose morals and behavior were suspect, who could cause him nothing but discomfort and trouble, and threaten his security attract him?

She stopped and turned to face him, trading his view of her lean shoulders and swaying hips in that beacon of a silky thing she wore for her flashing eyes, like the sun in the trees, narrowed in concern. "You okay?"

Sexy! She was so damn sexy.

Shut up! He groaned.

"Mm. Yeah. Sure," he croaked, placing an arm across his groin, and holding her questioning gaze to distract her.

She shrugged and looked around, searching for the acrobats in the thickening crowd of tourists as he watched her.

He sighed, telling himself it was from frustration and not longing.

"Sabine! Alain!" Niki called out in relief, darting ahead of him. Luc had been trailing her for ten minutes, and she thought she'd vaporize under his burning gaze before she ever found them.

"Niki! How are you?" Sabine gave her a warm embrace. "Hel-lo. Who's this handsome pirate?"

"Um." Niki turned as Luc sidled up beside her, as though he belonged there. A perfect fit. "Luc Ehre... something."

Luc offered his hand to Sabine. "Ehrenskjold. Nice to meet you, Sabine."

"You're from Canada also?"

He nodded.

"You're traveling together? I didn't know, Niki. I thought you stayed with Didier."

"I am. Luc and I just met. I'm traveling alone."

"I see. I heard that you and Didier have become close." Sabine's smile and wink came loaded with innuendo. Luc stiffened beside her, and she darted a warning glance his way.

Niki swallowed, her face heating. It seemed the late morning sun was especially hot today. This was the first time anyone had openly acknowledged what she and Didier had staged. She didn't expect to feel so self-conscious, and she wasn't sure it was because she was carrying her own share of the stigma that Didier carried every day, or something else. She didn't mind the whole town watching. That was the point, wasn't it? But she was painfully aware of Luc's hot gaze on her. If he wasn't observing her so carefully, it wouldn't be so bad. She could immerse herself in the charade.

She pushed a cheerful smile onto her face. "You know how it is when you stay with someone, talking through the evenings and sharing meals. It doesn't take long to get to know them pretty well." She felt the weight of Luc's eyes. Why should she care what he thought? Turning to him, she lifted her chin in challenge, although it was difficult to make eye contact, and her gaze quickly skipped back to Sabine. "What have you got planned for today?"

"General monkey business." She grinned. "Perhaps you can help us."

"Are Jean and his partner around today?"

Sabine shrugged. "The other side of town, somewhere."

"Too bad. I wanted to try stilt-walking again." Didier had taught her the proper word for stilts.

They approached Rocco, and Alain, who smiled when he saw her.

"*Salut*, Niki!"

Sabine said, "How does a human pyramid sound?"

That had definite potential. "There are only four of us. Not much of a pyramid."

"I can help," Luc said.

She peered at him.

"What?" he tossed at her, his brows raised in challenge.

She shrugged. Whatever.

Rocco shrugged. "Five. Okay not so much a pyramid as a totem pole. How would you like to be on top?"

She brightened, envisioning the series of jumps that would get her there.

"You like that, do you?" Luc murmured.

Did he mean that the way it sounded? A quick glance revealed flashing heat and teasing in his eyes. He did! The sound of her heart beating filled her ears, rising like a flood tide, drowning out the other sounds around her. Quiet, quiet. She focussed on her breathing to calm the noise.

What was this guy doing? Why was he here, confusing her and her purpose?

Niki studied him surreptitiously. She rarely attached to people easily. Even the guys she worked with in rope access, and her search and rescue crew, they went through a lot together, and yet it took a long time, or a gruelling rescue, for her to bond with someone new. Over the years, she'd developed close friendships with several of the guys on the crew, but that intimacy was hard-earned. What was it about this stranger, Luc, that affected her so much?

"If we had a sixth, we could set it up better," she suggested.

They looked at each other, questioning, waiting for a solution to present itself.

"A sixth what?" Just then, the trio of musicians sauntered up and asked what was going on. Rosaire offered to be their sixth body.

"Okay, let's go." Alain assigned everyone their places, and they counted it out. Rosaire's sidekicks, Izar and Sylvan, pulled out their instruments and started up a regular beat on the drum, with a suspenseful trilling on the flute to add a little tension and gather an audience. They decided that given Luc's size and lack of experience, he would do better in the middle tier.

As the rhythm and tension of the music built, Alain, Rocco and Rosaire aligned in a three-pronged foundation, and between the rest, they tossed Sabine up to straddle their strong shoulders, spanning Rocco and Rosaire with her legs, as agile as a mountain goat. By this time the crowd understood what they were doing, and had made a clear space, their collective eyes focussed on the acrobats, providing moral support with their vocal sound effects.

So far so good. Now Luc's turn. She didn't have much confidence he could get up there. And a jump wasn't in his repertoire, but, with a chorus of hoots and cheers, and a few shoves, he did a fine job of climbing the trio of bodies and getting himself balanced on Rocco and Alain's shoulders, locking arms with Sabine. Niki admired how adaptable and naturally athletic he was, while worrying he couldn't handle it and would collapse just when she depended on him to catch her landing.

"Okay, you guys. Are you gonna do right by me?" she hollered.

The rest of her team cheered.

Niki considered how best to mount the pyramid. They weren't close enough to a wall to run up and jump over. Coming at them from the front was a bad idea, and would throw off their carefully achieved balance. There was no other way than to use their bodies to run up to the top, but how to do it with style? She tried to imagine them as a rocky wall, or the side of a building, testing the mass of limbs in search of foot and handholds, places to shift her weight.

"Okay guys, I need some knees!"

There were murmurs while they figured out what she meant, and communicated it to each other, especially to Rosaire and Luc. She saw them all squat slightly and bend their legs more, to create a series of steps for her to choose from. The first level was a snap. She could rely on Alain and Rocco, without adding undue stress to Rosaire, who was holding his own for a stocky little guy with little fitness. The second level wasn't so easy. Although Sabine was fit, experienced and knew what to expect, Niki knew the force she would impose would challenge her in terms of physical strength. She studied Luc. He was strong but inexperienced.

He broke in mid-thought by catching her eye and giving her a tiny nod to let her know he understood and was ready. But was he? She could easily land on her head on the pavement. The nice thing about parkour was that you seldom relied on other traceurs. Your relationship was with the environment, the walls. For a moment, the relationship between trapeze artists filled her mind. It gave her a whole new appreciation of acrobats, and their mutual dependency and unquestioned trust.

Niki planned her route, one-two across Alain and Rocco's knees, using Rocco's hands to lever up to the next level.

"Okay everybody tight and springy, and hold super still. Rocco, cross your arms over your chest. Luc, I'm leveling up on you, so make a shelf for me by joining your arms together, like... like you're going to bump a volleyball, but stiff. Got it?"

"I can do still," he smirked.

Rolling her eyes, she showed him, and he imitated.

She met his eye, and he nodded again. She waited, watching his body, making sure he was alert and prepared. It was up to her to add the something extra to the show. Then it was up to Luc to keep his balance. The two remaining musicians had a knack for building tension with their drumming and lilting flute riff.

She backed away to give herself some room to free-run up and build momentum.

"One! Two! Here I come, ready or not!"

Niki had a loose idea of her steps, but with parkour, you couldn't plan too much. So much depended upon being in the moment. She had to trust herself to solve it as she went. She pushed energy into the run-up and leapt onto Alain's knee, sprang from there into a flip onto Rocco's knee.

This was the hardest part. It took all her strength to twist upward from Rocco's knee to bounce onto the platform he created with his folded arms, lifting her up high enough to spring off. Slowing it down, she placed her hand on Luc's knee, grabbing the branch he'd created with his arms for balance. She pushed her body upside down, arcing backwards so her legs flipped over his shoulders, grabbed him around the neck with her shins, then slowly levered her torso until they were face to face, more or less.

As she took her bearings, she discovered that his head was between her thighs. It was a strangely erotic juxtaposition, yet made absurd by what they were doing, and that they were about ten feet off the ground with every muscle clenched tight. His now free arms came up to support her from behind, his hands splayed over her butt cheeks.

He was holding it together, sweat beading on his brow, but his expression just about caused her to lose her concentration.

She let out a small snort of laughter. "Not what you were expecting?"

He didn't hesitate with his reply. Through his gritted teeth he ground out, "I'd like to say... I'm thrilled at your offer, monkey... but perhaps another time."

"Don't flatter yourself, I don't think you've got the stamina."

"Wouldn't you like to find out," he growled.

Laughing, she grabbed his beautiful shaved head, noticing that he had a tiny arrow of a scar above his right eyebrow, secretly pleased that he had an imperfection, and twisted around so she was riding his shoulders. "Hold steady now, don't wobble."

"Right. Doin' my best here. Ow! Watch the ears, hey, I'll be needing them. Your hands are like freaking sandpaper, lady."

"You're doing great, both of you," murmured Sabine, encouraging, just a hint of worry in her tone.

Niki's face was close to Luc's head as her body wrapped around his. He was solid, and her nostrils filled with his warm masculine scent, a hint of cologne and his soap as her face grazed his soft fuzzy shaven head, an undertone of musk no doubt brought on by their daredevil maneuver. She couldn't stop the impulse. She kissed the top of his head.

"Steady now." Then, holding his head for support, she shifted her limbs, placing first one foot then the other on his shoulders, keeping herself compact, trying not to lever too much out into space and throw off the balance of the troupe. A slight tremor in her feet transferred down into Luc's shoulders, and through his body into Rocco's. She had an innate sense that an inch up here was worth two feet on the ground. She would have liked to grab a handful of his hair for stability.

"You picked a fine day to shave your head," she said.

"It's true I did not plan for this," he said, laughter in his voice.

"Stop jiggling already, damn you!"

"Right. Right. Sorry."

Niki, squatting on Luc's shoulders, shifted one foot to Sabine's left shoulder, then moved her left foot from Luc's left shoulder to his right, to centre herself on the pyramid. Feeling for the stability of the bodies beneath her, she slowly stood up, to a wave of cautious, respectful applause from the crowd down below.

"Hold. Hold everyone. I'm not done."

Niki bent at the hips, placing one hand on each of Sabine and Luc's shoulders, next to her own feet. "Steady now." She shifted her weight from feet to hands, balancing her body mass so it stayed centred over her friends. She'd done nothing like this on a living, shifting base, but she had done it on a roof parapet, with a twenty-five foot drop to the ground. At least if she screwed this up, she wouldn't have so far to fall, even if she took a few bodies with her.

Once she was fully up into a handstand, the crowd seemed to release its collective breath, while expressions of wonder floated up. She held, not wanting to give anyone the impression they could release just yet.

"Okay, Niki. You call the dismount," shouted Alain from the bottom. She supposed this kind of communication was normal and critical among acrobats.

Niki was almost afraid to dismount. In some ways it was harder to plan. She could do another saute du fond but she didn't have much room to roll. She just wanted to get the hell out of there. Just then, she noticed a large presence separate the crowd. Didier stood hesitantly at the edge of the space.

"*Mon Dieu,*" she heard him say under his breath. "*Quoi ensuite!*"

"Don't worry, Didier. Just catch me!" And with that, she sprang off into an airborne somersault, hoping and praying that Didier would step up to the plate and catch her before she landed in a heap on the pavement. A second later, he gripped her firmly in his arms, and she released her breath. "*Merci, mon cher,*" she whispered. She couldn't have planned it better.

He grunted and rolled his eyes.

In thanks, she took his big handsome face between her palms and planted a giant-size kiss on his lips.

The crowd cheered as the pyramid disintegrated and everyone jumped down and huddled, back-slapping and laughing at their success.

As Didier set her down on the ground, she turned to congratulate and thank Luc, but he was gone.

CHAPTER 14

Later that evening, Niki and Didier sat at a long table with Alain, Sabine, Rocco and a few other performers in the market hall, drinking wine and laughing, sharing stories of their various escapades. Luc sat with a few others she didn't know, except for Amélie, and she wondered if he was attempting to advance their cause in his own way.

Saturday evening was the grand social gathering of the summer, and a big opportunity for locals, visiting artists and merchants from other parts of France, friends and family visiting from out of town, to enjoy each other's company and celebrate in the festive atmosphere. People filled the Place des Arcades and the town to bursting.

"Will you two stay for the dancing later on?" asked Sabine.

"Dancing?" Niki asked Didier with a questioning glance.

He made a face, like sour lemons and gestured to the end of the square where a section recessed by a few steps. "Later on there will be a dance at the end of the square. It is a larger version of the usual Thursday night markets held through the summer months."

"I take it you don't like to dance," she said.

With a characteristic shrug, Didier said, "I like to dance, but not in public."

She met his gaze with a challenge. A dance floor was a terrific place to put on a public show.

Sabine squeezed Didier's arm and said, "Perhaps this year you will make an exception, for your little Canadian friend."

"*Oui, oui, Girafeau*! You must dance with the monkey!"

Niki had known that Rosaire and his friends occupied a table behind them. Far enough to keep their conversations separate, but close enough to eavesdrop, obviously, and to toss the occasional teasing barb. They were relentless, the little twerps. She shot them a dirty look.

"We mustn't let those idiots–"

But Didier had turned away and resumed his conversation with Rocco about markets in Bordeaux, complacent and apparently inoculated against the poisonous effect of his evil nemesis. He had no intention of drawing attention to himself by dancing, tonight, or any other night.

She sighed. She'd have to find another way. Tonight wasn't going according to plan.

Also, despite trying not to, Niki remained painfully aware all evening of Luc, at the other end of the table. She caught him looking at her from time to time, though he invariably scowled at her. Was it her imagination or was he deliberately ignoring her and her friends? She hadn't seen him since their pyramid stunt earlier. Not that she cared. But she couldn't help wondering if he was mad at her for the way she dismounted into Didier's arms.

On Luc's other side sat a brown-haired man she thought was his friend Charles. Amélie wore an elegant pale blue period gown with a wide low neckline that showed her creamy shoulders. She'd rolled her pale hair into a silken bun inside a mesh net, and topped it with a fabric crown, with two sheer streamers that hung down past her ears and across her chin. She looked like every little girl's fantasy princess. Niki's bright genie costume seemed vulgar now, compared to Amélie's splendour.

Whenever Luc threw back his head and laughed at something Charles said, invisible tension wire tugged at her nerves, and she couldn't stop her gaze from darting over to watch. His throaty tenor rose above the din of thousands of revelers and found its way to her ears. To Niki, he was as handsome in his costume as he was in lycra cycling gear, in a different, more dangerous way. A way that made him impossible to ignore.

"Hey, *Petit Polisson*," Alain teased. "Where's your head tonight?"

"What?" She smiled and leaned in. Each time, she had to concentrate harder on pulling her attention back to the group, and to Didier.

"I asked you a question about your work."

"I'm sorry." She spent the next few minutes describing some helicopter rescue techniques they were interested in.

"It is a good thing you are small, no?" Didier said. "You can go up and down the ropes?"

She nodded. "There are pluses and minuses. It can be a challenge if the guy you are rescuing weighs two hundred and fifty pounds. In rope access, you must rely more on brains than brawn."

Just when she felt she had for the moment forgotten about Luc, and was enjoying Didier's company, the hair on the back of her neck would reach out, and she'd look over in time to catch Luc's attention on her, pensive and intense. Instead of pretending not to watch her, his intelligent eyes narrowed, and his sensual mouth pulled in a flat smile that, to her, seemed more exasperated than flirtatious. When at last she questioned him with her eyes, his flashed and creased like he was passing her a coded message. It was as though they shared a secret, but Niki wasn't in on it. It set her on edge.

Meanwhile, Didier's repeated excuses to get up, so he could move around and check out Amélie, didn't escape Niki's notice. It made it even harder for her to hold his attention and advance the illusion that he was enthralled with her, and vice versa. What a tangled web. It would be laughable, if she didn't care so much to help Didier make some progress in his relationship with Amélie, before Niki left town, and that had to be soon.

If this was the way Didier had been making his interest in Amélie known for the past fifteen or more years, it was no wonder he had got nowhere. He would come up with some pretence, head off to get more food, wine, find a toilet, or to greet someone he knew. But somehow in his attempt to draw nearer to Amélie, like a moth drawn to a candle, if only to come within the circle of her light, his nerves would get the better of him and he would end up veering away so she never even saw him.

Niki saw him though, gaping at her from a thousand miles away, like a sad puppy. If you wanted to know where Amélie was, you had only to follow Didier's gaze. Niki also saw that others noticed. Rosaire and his cronies made it a blatant sport, and the more they drank, the louder and more obnoxious they became. Didier, so intent on his own obsession, was blind. A prickly ball of tension built under her solar plexus.

She stood up. "I'll say hello to Amélie."

Didier looked like she'd punched him in the stomach.

She glanced at him, but then back at Sabine. "Have you met her? She's responsible for my costume." She waved a hand over herself. "I wanted to thank her again. Anyone else want to come?"

"I'll come," Sabine said, standing up. "Maybe she can make some pieces for me. I'm always looking for new performance costumes."

Without singling Didier out, Niki set her hand on his shoulder and squeezed a little. "That's it?" She could feel his tension, but he was being obstinate, refusing to take the bate, his gaze averted. "All right then. See you soon. I'll get another bottle on my way back."

Sabine looped her arm through Niki's as they squeezed their way past the crowd to Amélie's end of the table. "Nice try."

Niki tensed. "What do you mean?"

"I see what you're up to. With Didier."

She ventured, "How well do you know Didier?"

"I'm from Eyrée so I've known him for years."

"But what you said earlier…"

Sabine nodded. "I was trying to advance your cause. But I think if you want to give people the impression you and Didier have a little thing going on, you both have to stop staring at the others."

Niki's heart kicked. "Pardon?"

Sabine laughed. "I have acute powers of observation, especially in matters of the heart."

"Pah!" Niki scoffed. "Didier is the only guy I even know here, except for Alain and Rocco, I mean."

"Sure."

They came up to Amélie.

"Amélie!"

"Niki!" She stood up, and they embraced and kissed, then Niki introduced Sabine, and like two good French women, they too exchanged les bises. Then they analyzed and admired everyone's costume and complemented Amélie's eye for colour and fine details. "How did the pantaloons work for you today? Did they slow you down at all?"

Niki met Sabine's eye with a smirk. Then her gaze glanced off of Luc, who watched their exchange.

"I should say not. Did you not hear about our pyramid?"

Amélie shook her head, no. Given Luc's reaction to her dismount Niki heaved a sigh of relief. If that's why he left so suddenly.

One of Amélie's friends spoke up. "Ah, was that you? Amélie it was quite a spectacle. Your friend was the queen of the show."

"Sit down, join us?" Amélie said. But the chairs were full and jammed into all available space in the crowded hall.

"Thank you, no. I just wanted to say hello, and to thank you. And introduce Sabine."

The two women spoke for a moment longer about Amélie's clothing, and Sabine's wardrobe needs before they took their leave. Niki kept her eyes on their exchange, yet sensed Luc's rapt attention.

"I have to find a toilet. Meet you back at our table?" Sabine said with a squeeze to her hand.

Niki nodded and made her way to the wine vendor at the perimeter of the square to buy more wine for her friends.

As she was paying, she felt him again, his warmth behind her sending a shiver of awareness up her spine and neck like a fever. Her shoulders came up and her head tilted back as she arched back in an unconscious reaction.

Two solid, warm hands gripped her shoulders and squeezed, releasing the tension. He gently brushed her hair to one side, his fingertips grazing her neck, his touch setting off a delicious chain reaction of tingling skin, pooling heat and fluttering in her stomach. She found her body leaning into him as he continued to knead her trapezius muscles. Mmm, that feels so good.

He chuckled, making her wonder if she'd moaned aloud. "Are you having a good time?" It was strange to hear English spoken when she'd been communicating only in French. And he didn't sound mad.

Like an entrancing charm, his warm wine-scented breath skipped across the bare skin of her neck, and wove into her consciousness, capturing her in a blanket of intimacy. Goosebumps danced across the surface of her skin. Why was she reacting to him this way?

"Hey!" she said, pulling out of his grasp. "Yeah, how about you?"

He nodded, his gaze slipping down to her shoes and back up again, lingering on her mouth, before smiling into her eyes.

"Thank you for helping my friends this morning," she ventured. "It wouldn't have been half as interesting with just the four of us."

His dark brows twitched in acknowledgement. "If I was motivated to help anyone, it was only you."

She swallowed to dislodge the lump in her throat. "Right. Well, that's super but, it's not about me, eh? I don't need any help."

"So you've said," He gave his head a little shake. "How's your romance going?"

She lifted her chin and her smile was tight and dismissive.

He sighed, his blue eyes burning into hers, past any defenses she'd constructed. As if to reinforce the non-verbal message, he said, "I'd love to knock down those walls and find out what's on the inside of that fortress of yours. What are you so afraid of?"

Her smile fell. "The only walls around here surround Petit Bergeron."

"Sure," He huffed. "If you say so." He turned to the vendor and asked for three bottles of the local red. "Have a pleasant night, Niki Ballantyne."

CHAPTER 15

Before she got back to the table, she sensed trouble. She still felt rattled by Luc and his presumption. He always got a reaction from her. Why was he flirting with her when he was with another woman? He didn't seem like the philandering type. Niki felt the irresistible draw between them, too, but you couldn't act on all your urges. No matter how potent.

Now she picked up on another kind of tension.

Rosaire and the others were up to their antics, working the crowd, trying to get a laugh. Rosaire's sidekick Izar had somehow found a stuffed monkey, one of those gangly ones with velcro on its feet, and had it tied around his neck, his face in its crotch. With an echo of her earlier arousal, it reminded her of her encounter with Luc this morning, ten feet off the ground, before she could feel outrage on Didier's behalf.

Izar stomped around in a clichéd imitation of a "giant," moaning, while the others jeered and teased. "How's your new pet monkey, *Girafeau?*" they taunted between loud guffaws.

It was bad enough that everyone could see and hear what they were doing. But that wasn't enough for them. They had to turn it into a parade, prancing between the tables, getting louder and louder, working their way closer to where Didier sat.

She looked at him, her heart pounding like a timpani in her chest. He kept his gaze cast down, peering into his wineglass, his large square brow lowered in thought, his jaw working. She slid back into her seat beside him and placed her hand over his. He tensed but didn't acknowledge her in any other way. His complexion had darkened with the shame and rage he kept locked up inside.

Niki's vision blurred, and an image of Sam flooded her mind's eye. Bullies always knew how to identify and zero in on their victims. Like they had a sixth sense about their inability to defend themselves. They found the weakness, the wound, and attached themselves like leeches, bleeding the life from them.

Of the countless times she'd come upon Sam being bullied at school or on the street, there was one time in particular she could never forget, as clear as yesterday. She was seventeen. Sam had just celebrated his fifteenth birthday.

She knew school was hard for him. Despite his brilliance in mathematics and memorization, he struggled to keep up with grade nine English and Socials and the twisted social milieu that was junior-highschool, rife with raw adolescence and raging hormones. Language and people were hard for him. There was something about understanding the world in a broader context and putting those ideas into words that paralyzed him. She knew he'd had to give a presentation in class that day. Even though his teachers knew he had special needs, and tried to support him, they never seemed able to spare him from those experiences that were most painful for him.

That day's presentation had gone badly. He froze up, like he often did. No matter how much she helped him prepare, no matter how well he did practicing at home, when the time came, something about the way his brain worked interfered with his memory. He would panic. Then he'd say strange things. And then the teasing and laughing would start, making it worse.

Expecting to find him upset, she skipped out of her last class early so she could wait for him by his locker, and make sure he got home okay. But he didn't show up. Over fifteen minutes past the bell, she knew something had happened, and tense with anxiety, went in search of him. His usual hiding places, in the dark wings of the theatre, under the bleachers in the gym, in the reading alcove at the library, came up empty. He was nowhere. Her chest and gut tightened, and shivers ran up her spine and neck as she recalled her escalating panic that day.

It was her job to watch over him. To protect him. From the bullies, and from his own volatility. Sam was the sweetest, most loving and playful person she'd ever known, but did strange things when he felt stressed. Behave erratically, push the boundaries of normal, acceptable behaviour. But if she were there, she could help calm him down. That had always been her responsibility—her super power—to maintain the bubble of calm and safety around Sam, who was neither typical nor atypical. From their earliest days as toddlers, she had possessed a special talent for reading him, anticipating his triggers, and soothing him. Their parents saw it, and bless them, exploited it. Whatever worked. They themselves were high-strung and ill-equipped, as evidenced by their father's eventual desertion. Whatever was best for Sam, her mom said. Whatever was easiest, Niki said.

The experts said he was on the autism spectrum, but because he could express himself, get through most subjects in school well enough, and seemed to get through his interviews without freaking out or shutting down, they always sent him back into the lion's den to cope without the support Niki had always felt he needed. They said normalisation was best for him. They didn't know what it was like for him.

That day, she had found him in the boys' showers off the gym, huddled, crying, crouching in the corner of the farthest stall, his pants missing, obscenities scrawled all over his legs and his backside with a Sharpie. Sam could never defend himself. The perpetrators were long gone; she found him alone, unable to comprehend the cruelty of his fellow students.

"Sammy, Sammy," she'd run to him, put her arms around him, held him tight, feeling hollow in her powerlessness. She should have been there earlier. She shouldn't have allowed this to happen. He trembled, catatonic with terror. "Who did this to you?" She tugged the spare pair of sweatpants from her backpack because, yes, this had happened before, and helped him dress, while he trembled and sobbed like a baby.

All he could do was bury his face, and her own tears of frustration would follow. She knew why, too. Whenever they'd retaliated by going to the principal, either with or without her mother's involvement, things always got worse for him. They both felt so powerless. That was the thing about bullies. They were smart, and they were sneaky. They covered their tracks, and blended in when the heat got too hot. Or laughed it off and make it appear to be all fun and games. They'd been through it all before. And yet they feared worse.

Days like this, Niki felt like the worst failure. Not only did she feel suffused with the heat, dizziness and nausea of Sam's pain and humiliation shiver through her like a fever, but she was taut with dread she'd also have to face the justifiable wrath of her mother, who always assumed Niki had the power to stop this kind of thing but was negligent. How could she let this happen? Why wasn't she there?

As though Niki weren't herself a student struggling to survive highschool, with challenges and dreams of her own. But that didn't matter. She didn't matter. She'd go back in time if she could to prevent it all from happening. Do whatever she could to spare him this torture. She knew she deserved the blame her mother poured on her. Where had she been? Didn't she know she couldn't leave him alone after school?

Muscles cramped and ticked in her jaw from clenching her teeth, and she scrubbed at her face with fisted hands, finding her eyes wet. There'd be days of recriminations and silence while they all dealt with the fallout, Sam's withdrawal and seclusion, his mute suffering. All she could think was–next time. Next time she wouldn't leave him. Next time she'd catch those bastards and stop them forever...

That time had been the last time. She never got another chance. They'd killed him.

Or as good as.

It left Niki filled with rage. Unspeakable rage at Sam's helplessness, and her own inability to protect him. Blood heated her veins, pounding in her ears until she was ready to explode. With an overpowering urge to inflict violence on the bullies that hurt her brother, she pounded her fists on the tabletop, the tension that stiffening her body, radiating out from the lump of pain in her gut.

"Niki?" Sabine touched her arm, peering at her with concern.

She blinked her attention back to the present moment. Witnessing Didier's incapacitation when faced with the same cruel and pointless humiliation Sam had endured until he could endure it no more made Niki's blood boil. All she could see were the idiots who continued their charade like those stupid, vicious puppets, flaunting their cruelty in front of complicit audience. With each taunt, twisting the knife in Didier's heart, and in her own.

The clamour of voices, laughter and music built to a crescendo in her head and then seemed to fade away to a throbbing silence. Her eyes locked on Rosaire's ugly, laughing face, the stupid expression on Izar's as he danced around with his monkey, pretending to kiss it, moon over it, fuck it. They got closer and closer.

Niki felt herself rising to her feet, her hands flexing and clenching into fists, her lips holding back a stream of raging invectives. She couldn't help herself as adrenaline flooded her body. A force had built up inside her for years and could not be contained. Her heartbeat pulsed in her head as the heat of her anger flooded through her limbs, crashing like asteroids hell-bent on destruction. Her pounding blood seemed to rise out of her gut, push through her chest to her burning throat and demand release through her grinding teeth.

She didn't remember moving toward them, but suddenly she was up in Izar's blurred face. Turning to Rosaire, her body tense and ready to fight, a torrent of words poured from her throat with no sense of what she was saying. She barely registered the shocked faces in the crowd, mouths gaping, eyes wide.

∾

Luc wrapped his arms around her and frog-marched her backwards out of the market hall with steady pressure until they could duck under the shadows of the arcade at the edge of Place, even as the stream of swearing and threats of physical violence continued to spew from her throat. His heart pounded in his chest as he fought her. Though small, she was strong.

Niki didn't seem aware that she was being physically removed from Izar, from Rosaire, from the crowd that was staring at her in open-mouthed shock. She sobbed and screamed, her words incoherent.

She wrestled against the tight grip that held her. Like a wildcat, she was so strong he could barely contain her flailing limbs, thumping fists.

"Shh. Hush."

"Let me go! Let me go!" she cried and fought, but her hysteria eased under his touch, so at last he loosened his grip. She spun, her fist up, ready to strike. He cradled her cheeks and sought to hold her dark eyes.

"Calm down, Niki. Calm down. It's okay." Luc kept his voice gentle, and he repeated his words over and over until she calmed and her wild gaze came into focus. He knew when she finally saw him, because a puzzled expression emerged in her troubled eyes as they traced over his face in recognition.

Then he wrapped his arms around her and held her tightly. Her arms slid around his waist and held on, as though she needed his solid anchorage. "It's okay. It'll be okay." He soothed her and stroke her hair until her shaking stopped, even though he didn't know if it was true. He didn't have a clue what made her snap, and what she was reacting to aside from the infuriating but commonplace antics of Rosaire and Izar. Nothing they hadn't all seen and heard a thousand times before.

He pulled her away from his shoulder and with his thumbs, stroked the tears that marked her cheeks, wishing he could erase the wounds that caused her such intense pain, as a fresh tide obliterates all trace of footsteps from the sand.

She lifted her fingertips to her cheek, a look of surprise on her face, as though she was unaware she'd been crying.

"W-what happened?" Her voice trembled weakly.

He shook his head. "Something triggered you. It was an impressive freak-out. But it's a good thing you said all of that in English. Hopefully, most of the locals missed it." Though Luc didn't, and what he heard raised questions, many questions. Who was Sam? Why was she calling Izar and Rosaire not only bullies, which was understandable, but murderers?

"What? What did I say?"

"You don't remember?"

She scowled, her eyes flickering. "All I remember is a red rage." She shook her head in defeat. "No."

"Ah, well. It doesn't matter. I think it'll be awhile before those guys poke fun at Didier again. You're really scary for such a small person."

"Really? I stopped them?"

Luc grunted. "In a manner of speaking. But listen." He held her chin gently in his fingertips and lifted her face so he was looking straight into her eyes. It was almost too dark to see the bright dancing green he knew lived there in her better moments, in the sunlight. Instead, he caught the hard gleam of reflected light from the square beyond, sharp and obscure.

She was so close, her warm breath fanned his face, stirring an animal thirst that scattered his thoughts. He cleared his throat and cupped her shoulders with palms.

"You put an end to their mischief for the moment, and I'm not sure I understand why. But I don't think you did Didier any huge favours just now." Luc shook his head at the realization. "When all this is over, and you've taken your personal demons and gone back home, he'll still be the giant of a man who couldn't fight his own battles."

For a long moment, Niki didn't speak. Her frown spoke to confusion, and her lowered gaze to embarrassment.

"I just couldn't stand another moment of the injustice and cruelty and I... I don't know. I was thinking about my..." Her gaze darted to the left, then drifted over his shoulder as he felt her tense under his hands, locking on some ghost in the shadows behind him. He thought she had a better idea than she let on.

"Who?"

"Someone I knew... who was bullied a lot."

He squeezed her arms trying to exorcize the image. "You snapped. I get it. Some things are hard to watch. But you really lost it, and embarrassed everyone, including Didier and Amélie, and that just isn't helpful." He tried to smile to soften his criticism, but his face felt stiff. "It's not your place to be his guard dog, Niki. He's a grown man."

She glared at him. "Who are you to drag me out of there and scold me like a child?"

"Whoa, whoa. I'm only trying to help. I didn't think you'd want to be known as the foreign chick who lost her shit at the festival."

"Too late for that," she huffed through her nose, the momentary flare of resentment ebbing.

"I get you're embarrassed now. You weren't aware of what you were doing. I get that. I was scared too, for you." His voice tapered off into a gust of breath as he felt awareness of her shimmer through his blood and steal his voice.

Her gaze lifted to his and locked, her thoughts swirling in the impervious forest of her uneasy eyes. "I'm sorry," she said at last and swallowed. "Thank you."

Luc took a small step closer, even as he felt her lean towards him. Or had he just pulled her in unconsciously? The invisible magnetic force that had drawn them together and triggered a storm of unrest inside him shivered and wrapped around them both like a bewitching cord that wound and tightened to keep them together and intimate, and the rest of the world outside this bubble.

Her face lifted, and his tilted, their breaths mingling. She smelled of wine and the musky scent of buttered toast that settled into sun-warmed skin after a long summer day. His lips tingled. He wanted this.

He'd felt the urge to touch her, to kiss her, since the beginning. There was something inevitable about it.

Her eyes reflected his need and acknowledged it. Her tongue darted out to moisten her lips, and that was all the invitation he needed. He bent to connect their mouths at last.

CHAPTER 16

"Hey, Niki! Is that you?"

She lurched back, shock on her face and Luc's heart shot to his throat at the sudden interruption. Or was it the fact they'd kissed at all, however briefly? His pulse already thundered from the kiss, and he felt light-headed. Their touch, at last, had transported him to another world. He desperately wanted to dive in and lose himself. He'd been about to deepen the kiss, just about to reach into her amazing mouth with his seeking tongue, when it was over.

"Aziz?" Niki croaked.

Luc tore his hungry gaze from her beautiful, flushed face.

A tall, gangly, dark-skinned young man approached and stopped by them, grinning. "It is you! Why are you still here?" he said, both surprise and delight clear in his rising voice. A huddle of other young men hovered just behind him. "I thought you'd be gone."

Niki barked out a laugh of disbelief, a taut smile stretching her face. "Aziz! I didn't expect to see you again." She stepped away from Luc and embraced the newcomer, and they gave each other les bises. "The festival. How could I not stay?"

"You found a place?"

She nodded, "With a new friend, yes."

Aziz's gaze slid to encompass Luc, who smiled in acknowledgment.

"Er. Aziz, this is Luc. Luc, Aziz," Niki gestured between them. "But I'm not staying with Luc," she said. "Luc's from Canada, too." As though that clarified everything. She didn't bother to explain to Luc where she'd met Aziz, but he assumed on her travels prior to Petit Bergeron. Like she owed him any explanations.

"Aziz, come on!" called one of his friends, their patience with the little reunion wearing thin. "*Allons*-y. The girls are waiting."

Aziz turned. "Coming, yeah!"

"Hey, is Paul here, too?" Niki asked, touching his arm.

"Yeah, I saw him–" said Aziz, flapping a hand vaguely toward the crowded square. "–somewhere. I gotta go. It was great seeing you, Niki. *Adieu*!"

"Bye Aziz!"

They hugged, and he dashed off with his friends, disappearing back into the crowd in the Place des Arcades.

Alone again, they stood awkwardly. The spell broke, the moment lost, like the last grains of sand falling through an hourglass. Tension rolled off of her. She wouldn't meet his eye.

He watched her pull herself back behind her wall, wishing he could hold on to that moment when her defences were down and she was soft and open in his arms.

She pulled back from him and straightened her shoulders, lifting her chin but avoiding eye contact now.

"I'm sorry you got involved in this. It's become too complicated and I'm sorry for my outburst. But my relationship with Didier is private. I understand the impact on Amélie but I'm handling it." She took another step back and paused. "Thanks for…" she averted her gaze towards the bright lights of the crowded square, giving her head a little shake, her voice dropping to a murmur. "…helping when I lost it."

She spun on her heel and marched away, leaving Luc alone in the dark with nothing but unanswered questions and an unanswerable ache.

It aggravated him they were always at odds when they both wanted the same thing–to help Didier and Amélie get together. Why did she have to make him into her enemy?

She was so open and friendly with others she'd just met–this Aziz, the acrobats, Didier, even Amélie. Was that just a facade he'd somehow penetrated because of this crazy chemistry between them?

If it were a mask, what was hiding beneath it? What made her so alive, and yet so defended from real relationships she travelled alone and guarded her privacy? She already had some kind of special connection with Didier. But what was that really about? Why was she so invested in his well-being? Had she fallen in love with the giant? But who was Sam? Confused, Luc felt compelled to find out.

∾

The house was silent the next morning when Niki awoke. She padded out of her room, expecting to find Didier drinking coffee in the kitchen as he usually was, but she didn't see him anywhere.

"Didier?"

"*Meaow!*"

She looked down to see Minou circling her empty food dish.

"Are you hungry, little puss?" Niki scooped a little food into her dish, and petted her tiny grey head as she bent to eat. "Where's your papa, hey?"

Alarmed that her tantrum had disrupted the morning routine them'd established over the past few days, Niki quickly showered and dressed and went outside to look for Didier. At least his truck was in the driveway, so he hadn't abandoned her.

Though, she wouldn't blame him, after her performance last night. Naturally, the bullies would frustrate her, but she should have more self control. She'd handled it badly. Luc was right. She was that crazy foreign chick who lost her shit–in public.

Luc had come to her rescue. Again.

That's what came of exhibitionism. She was normally a private person, and her parkour was her own kind of meditation, and sport, that had nothing to do with crazy circus-style entertainment. It had been wrong of her to get involved in those public displays of athleticism. Instead of improving Didier's image, she'd drawn more unwanted attention to him, making more of a spectacle of him than he'd even managed to on his own.

And Luc had kissed her! But she couldn't dwell on that now.

Her involvement with Didier had somehow unleashed her feelings about Sam. Her gut rolled over at the memory. Didier was not Sam. She had to remember that. She'd hurt Didier. Damaged his confidence more, exactly the opposite of what she'd set out to do.

Guilt swamped her. She'd been stupid and selfish, when what she wanted was to help him. She had to find him and help him to understand her mistake. And then she'd fix this–somehow.

With or without Luc's help.

Walking toward the studio, she heard hammering sounds and tentatively peeked into the doorway. The sight that met her was mesmerizing. Didier stood over his anvil in the centre of his forge, shirtless, his broad back glistening with sweat. Muscles bulged and bunched as he swung a powerful arm down again and again, pounding the shit out of a piece of red hot metal he held with a set of black tongs in his other hand. Her ears vibrated with the repeated thunk and twang of metal ringing, echoing through the dim space.

She crept forward, not wishing to startle him, and arced around until she saw his face. It was frightening. His brow folded like a tectonic plate, his jaw set and jutting forward, quivering with tension. His complexion flushed red under the veil of sweat that dripped down each side of his face, and his golden hair soaked with perspiration.

Her heart broke at his obvious torment. Her own face and chest tingled with heat, and hot tears burned the backs of her eyes. She couldn't compete with the noise of his hammering, so stood and waited until he noticed her.

Eventually he paused to examine his piece of metal and twitched slightly as his field of vision widened enough to register her presence. He turned to shove the iron rod he'd been hammering back into the fire, and slowly turned back. Without lifting his head, his gaze moved up and locked on her face. They were as red-rimmed as the tip of the iron rod. Despite his embodied anger and frustration, he'd spent some time between last night and this morning crying.

She swallowed. "I'm so sorry. You're right to be mad at me, Didier. I–I–I don't know what–"

He stalked past her and stalked outside, grabbing his shirt off a pole. She followed him around the back of the forge to the creek, where he flopped himself down on the cool, shady grass by the creek. He had a tin cup, and he dipped it into the creek and drank.

"Why are you here?"

She squirmed under his steady gaze. "I don't have an agenda. I wanted to… help you." Her voice tapered off until it was barely a squeak.

"You're doing a fine job. How about you leave me alone, *non*?" He wiped the sweat from his glistening torso and pulled on the dirt-smeared shirt.

There was nothing she could say. She slipped down onto the cool grass beside him, and they sat like that for a long time. She lost track of how long. Her eyes followed the swirling water of the creek as it tumbled down the slight incline, eddying against small boulders in its path. Just like her agitated thoughts.

"I only want your happiness," she finally offered.

"Why should you care about me? We are strangers." His gaze fell on the water wheel, only his sad eyes rising and falling as the blades rotated past, scooping up the water and pouring it out on the other side.

"We are friends. And you remind me of my brother," she finally admitted.

His head turned toward her, a question in his glance.

"His name was Sam. He was tall, for his age anyway. But not like you really. He was just an awkward boy."

"And now?"

"He died when he was fifteen. And there isn't a day that goes by I don't miss him." Her chin quivered, and she pressed her lips tightly together to steady it.

Didier lifted a large hand and set it gently against her shoulder, squeezing. *"Je suis desolé."*

"I didn't mean to make things worse for you, Didier. I'm really sorry."

"I know you didn't." He stuck out his lower lip pensively. "Those idiots need no provocation to behave like they did last night. But I have always felt it best to ignore them."

Niki felt the rage surge up again and clenched her hands into fists. "I know bullies, Didier. They won't ever stop. I wish we could do something about them."

"Last night I realized something," he said, plucking out a tall blade of grass. "You were right. They will never change until I change. And I am sick and tired of being their *souffre-douleur*... their punching ball. No one will respect me until I'm ready to have the self-respect."

She sat up, flooded with relief, and the knowledge that Didier was a truly kind man. "Really? You mean that?"

"Oui."

"What does that mean for us? For our plan?"

He shrugged. "I don't know. The festival is ending. Now life returns to normal. It will be easier with fewer tourists and crowds, *non*?"

"Yes. You're right. But we need a better plan."

We should stay here today. Perhaps they will form their own conclusions. Quieter, too." He cocked an eyebrow in her direction and his grim mouth held a hint of teasing amusement.

"Assume we're... holed up here. Good. Good. One of us could go into town for a few groceries for a romantic dinner?"

"Yes. It should be me. I'll arrange for someone to sit at my booth. You are indisposed today, *non*?"

"Okay." She kicked the tall grass with her foot. "Did you, uh, talk to Amélie last night?"

"Not really. She was concerned about you, but we just exchanged a look. Nothing more."

"Could you say hello today, once you've got the supplies? Reassure her you're just keeping me company because I'm embarrassed?"

He wagged his head back and forth. "I'll see what I can do."

Relieved, Niki walked beside him into the house for breakfast. Later as he pulled out of the driveway, she hoped he could alter his demeanour for a change, and give the impression that his thoughts were on her, waiting for him back at the house, rather than endlessly swirling around his hopeful love for Amélie. He seemed filled with a new energy, and it gave her hope.

And his absence gave her time to mull.

CHAPTER 17

Later in the afternoon, Didier returned from town with the groceries, including a bouquet for her of huge pink dahlias that screamed summer. That made her smile. Niki had returned the favour by tidying up his house and doing a little laundry. Too bad the festival was ending, and soon she would have nowhere to wear her fun new clothing. She liked the bright harem pants, so she opted to wear them again tonight, but paired them with a plain white tank top, and an interesting beaded necklace. She knew it looked hot, because even Didier, who's heart belonged to Amélie, couldn't hide his admiration.

Even though they would be alone and their romantic dinner was, in some senses, fake, it would be good practice for Didier. She intended to play her role. Maybe she could figure out where he tripped up. He'd been charming, though self-conscious, when they had dinner in the square. Then shy and awkward in Amélie's shop. Was it only Amélie? Perhaps he was uncomfortable when alone with a woman.

Didier insisted on cooking the dinner he planned, so she sat at the bar with a glass of wine, and they talked. He was very interested in her job in rope access, the kinds of situations that called for her skills, besides search and rescue.

"How does a little girl like you come to work in this dangerous position?" His eyes stroked down and up her bare arms as he spoke.

"I guess, gradually, is the best explanation. When I was a teenager, I was into mountain biking. That was even before I'd discovered parkour. And the mountains of the North Shore are famous for their mountain bike trails. They're everywhere up there, criss-crossing the mountains, where many people also go hiking."

Didier seasoned the meat, and chopped vegetables, nodding. She admired his swift, confident work with the knife, and the strong sinewy muscles of his forearms as he worked. He said with a smirk, "I'm guessing how it goes." He set down a small dish of olives.

"Are you?" She punched his arm. Solid as a steer. The image of his naked torso, glistening with sweat, muscles of his back and chest and shoulders bunching as he threw his hammer at the anvil, flashed in her mind. She shook her head to clear it. This was supposed to be a pretend date, yet she felt herself warming as the space around them heated with familiar touches and lingering eye contact. "How 'bout you just listen and you'll find out soon enough?"

He laughed and turned to the stove for a moment, then back again, his face sober but his eyes twinkling. "Go on, please. I am captivated."

Inexperienced he might be, but he needed no lessons in flirtation. He had all the right stuff, intelligence, humour, kindness, good looks, and a kick ass body. All he lacked was confidence.

"Well, you're probably right. I didn't get into trouble, but a friend of mine did, and I had to wait there until the search and rescue crew came in and carried him out. I was hooked. That was the start. Then when I was working a dumb job, I found out they wanted trainees…" She shrugged.

"And they didn't laugh at you? Such a little heroine?"

"At first. But I proved myself more than capable. And also useful, because so often when we need to pull someone out, one of us has to drop down on a line, either from the mountainside or from the chopper, and strap ourselves onto the victim. Because I'm light, it's easier on the guys and the equipment to haul us back up."

"I suppose you can crawl into the teeny holes also, yes?"

She pulled a face at him. "Not a chance. You mean like caves?"

He pinched her cheek, meeting her gaze. "Mouse holes, maybe."

She slapped his hand away. Resisting the temptation to reach up and pull his face toward hers for a kiss.

His focus returned to his pan on the stove. "And the rope access?"

"Well, as much as I love search and rescue, it's volunteer work, so I needed to make a living. Rope access training increased my value in rescue work, and also gave me a challenging career that's varied and exciting, and not at a desk, which I like."

"Impressive."

"Tell me about Amélie. What do you like about her?"

He stirred a pan. "She is sweet and kind. She has never teased me or treated me like a monster. And she is talented and clever, as you see." He plucked at the fabric of her special pants, and she nodded for him to go on. "She has many younger brothers and sisters, and cousins. We all know these kids. She is fantastic with children. Affectionate. Wise. She would make a superb mother."

"You'd like to have a family, wouldn't you? With Amélie."

Didier's face flushed pink, and he turned too suddenly, and dropped his wooden spoon onto the floor, and swore. He picked it up and tossed it in the sink, taking a clean one.

"Sorry. Didn't mean to fluster you. But, since we're on the subject, can I ask a personal question?"

His eyes slid over to her, cautious and he grunted. "Another one?"

"Are you a virgin?"

"*Merde*! You have no limits."

"It's important that I know!"

"What do you suppose?" His face went berry red, and his eyes slid past her, concentrating again on his food preparation.

"Well, I didn't want to assume. I'm sorry. It's just that…"

"What was I supposed to do about that?"

"Same as any other guy, I suppose."

He rolled his eyes. "Oh, yes. It's just the same."

"If you'd gone to a big city, you'd have seen plenty of action. Women like novelty."

He grunted, blinking slowly, as though that concept physically hurt him.

"It's important. You need experience. Also, in case no one told you, you must copulate to make children."

He fidgeted, avoiding her pointed gaze. His pulse hammered in his neck like a fluttering bird. He was such a true gentleman, he would die old and alone. Except that she liked that he was a gentleman. It was very appealing.

They finishing their dinner when a knock came on the door. Niki jumped. No one had come here since she'd been staying.

"Should I–"

"Stay. *Un moment.*" Didier rose and stepped to the door, swinging it open. "Luc! *Bon soir, mon ami. Ça va?*"

"*Bon soi*r, Didier. Am I intruding on your dinner?"

"*Non, no*n. Come in."

Niki twisted toward the door. What was he doing here? Had he come to chaperone their dinner date? She still couldn't quite fathom that he'd kissed her under the arcade. Why would he do that after she'd been so awful? She still hadn't recovered from it. What would have happened if Aziz hadn't interrupted them? Would he pretend it hadn't even happened?

"Niki. Good evening." Her stomach dropped at his cool tone, until she lifted her gaze to his to see a teasing light in his blue eyes, with a note of apology.

Yeah, I'll bet he's sorry. He'd come to spy. To make sure she did nothing with Didier that he didn't approve of. But why? That was the question. Her voice shook a little. "Hi Luc."

Luc's gaze flicked to the dahlias in a vase on the table. "Don't fret. Nobody knows where I am."

Hm. She studied him with narrowed eyes. Was that a peace offering of sorts? Was he saying he wouldn't interfere? Then why was he here?

Didier poured and handed him a glass of wine, and in a matter of moments they sat together in the living room like old cronies. Luc made himself at home on the sofa, slumping back into the worn cushions.

Without asking, Didier set down a chessboard and set up chess men, sitting opposite Luc, bending over the coffee table. She frowned and tilted her head.

They played with ease and speed, exchanging few words at first. This was not their first game of chess. Then they discussed something she couldn't at first follow that didn't seem to be about the game. Then she realized it was a book, or poetry or something. They seemed to have strong opinions about it, yet enjoy the debate.

Niki took the dinner dishes to the kitchen and cleaned up. From this perspective she could look back at them without appearing to stare. This evening wasn't supposed to go like this. She was planning to pay attention to Didier, and observe how he was with her, flirt a little. Now she didn't know who to look at.

Didier was kind and handsome, but no one wore a pair of faded jeans like Luc. And Luc's tight navy blue t-shirt grabbed her attention.

The way it stretched across his pecs, and showed off the smooth, rounded muscles of his shoulders and biceps when he reached to move a chess piece, left saliva pooling in her mouth and her breasts tightening.

"You're cozy here," Luc sat back, draping one of his sexy arms across the sofa back, as she moved back and forth.

Didier waved at the dishes. "Leave them, Niki. I'll clean up later."

"It's okay. I can't follow your conversation anyhow." She hoped she wasn't sulking, because she felt left out, and very much as though he'd hijacked her date night with Didier. Her attention shifted between the two men, though, wondering whose attention she most craved.

"I'm sorry, Niki. We'll speak in English, okay? Come and sit down."

She shrugged, while the two of them continued their exchange in English. It was no better, as she wasn't familiar with the book they discussed. She took a seat on the opposite end of the sofa from Luc, though.

"You two do this a lot?"

"Every week, while Luc is in Petit Bergeron," Didier replied with a grin. "I love to discuss French poetry with someone who is well read."

Luc flushed pink and cast his eyes down at the chessboard. "I merely try to keep up with him. It challenges me and gives me something to talk about with my colleagues during the year."

Hm. Neither of them had mentioned that they were quite such good friends. "Do you teach poetry?"

"No. Social Studies and Geography. But I enjoy it."

"So this is where the coaching happens then?"

That got their attention. Both men looked up sharply, and then their gaze flew to each other. Niki watched Luc's throat slide as he swallowed.

She didn't mean to say that, especially in such a sarcastic tone.

"So the two of you have been discussing me," Didier's sandy brows lowered into a straight line.

Big mouth Niki. "Uh. Not much."

"We may have had a disagreement about... this..." Luc tapered off, but gestured between herself and Didier.

"I see."

A beat or two of awkward silence followed.

Didier looked hard at Luc. "Is that why you're here? Not to play chess?"

"No!" Luc cleared his throat. "In fact, that reminds me, I came to invite you to Charles' and Francine's end of festival dinner tomorrow night. About twenty people are coming. The usual crowd."

Didier pulled in his chin, considering. "Ah. I see. *Merci*."

It was Niki's turn to feel awkward, and to glance away.

"You too, Niki." She swung her gaze to meet his and found him telegraphing her a meaningful look. But there were layers to it. He was reluctant, and fearful, but also determined.

Her knee bounced. "Are you sure?" Was he offering her an olive branch?

Niki's dinner rolled in her stomach at the thought of going to a party and she drew her lip between her teeth. After her big scene in the square, did she mind people looking at her? Luc always made her feel so naked, as though he could read her every thought, and knew exactly why she did everything.

"That's the point, isn't it?" His tone was light, but he cast his gaze down. "There isn't much time."

And then there was being around him and Patrice, which made her nervous, confused and irritable. How would he behave when everyone was together? It would be an excellent opportunity for she and Didier to practice their couple skills in front of a small, intimate audience. She could throw herself into her plan. She inhaled and lifted her chin, addressing Luc with a steady gaze. "Thank you. It's kind of you to invite us."

He nodded and stood to leave. "We'll finish this game another time."

Once the door closed behind Luc, Niki turned to Didier, pensive. "Should we take something?"

"Yes. I will bring my mother's special cake," said Didier. "Tomorrow morning I will teach you the recipe. We will make it together."

And at last she kissed him.

On the cheek.

∾

On the way to Charles' house in Didier's truck, Niki held the delicate St. Honoré cake on her lap and gazed at the sky as burst into flames while the sun set over the rolling countryside.

It had been a fun and relaxing day in Didier's kitchen, but now her tension built as she expected the evening ahead, her first public appearance since her meltdown in town.

What would Luc do? How would he behave after last night? What about that kiss?

"I'm curious about Patrice."

Didier didn't respond immediately, and she could almost hear the Rube Goldberg machine clanking and whirring in his head.

"Charles's sister. She was a few years behind in school so I don't know her well."

"Sister! What else is she?"

"Do you mean, what is she to Luc?"

Damn. That's not what she meant. Was it? "Noooo." Her gaze jumped from tree to tree silhouetted against the streaked orange sherbet and grape juice sky. "I mean... what does she do? Does she live with Charles?"

"*Non*. She lives in Toulouse. And she works in fashion retail, I believe."

Figures. "Oh. So that's why she's so... well-dressed."

With her peripheral vision, she sensed Didier's big shoulders lifting. Even though his true love was also in clothing and fashion, she imagined he saw Amélie in a different light. That got her thinking about how she made his clothes for him and how difficult he said that intimacy was. Better to think about him than about Luc. Stay on task.

"Hey, Didier. Since it's so... ahem... hard... for you to go to Amélie for fittings, how do you manage it, eh?"

"You're breaking my balls, little monkey, with your nosey questions."

She waited, but he didn't answer. "Well?"

He heaved a big sigh and clicked his tongue in resignation. "I get drunk."

"What?"

"Just a little."

She brought her hand up to her forehead in disbelief. "Oh. My. God. You so desperately need my help."

A few moments passed in silence, her thoughts again drifting to Patrice and her long legs and blond hair, so exquisitely coiffed. "So why is she here? Are they an item?"

Didier chuckled under his breath, but amusement radiated off of him. "Who? Patrice? I mentioned she's Charles's sister? I can't say for sure. I think perhaps she would like it to be so." He shrugged. "Or perhaps it is him. He's always been here, too, so they grew up together, too. And she visits more when he is here."

"He says he spends every summer cycling and visiting friends all over the south."

"May be so."

"They have a thing every summer, then?"

"Niki. I can't say. Why don't you ask Luc? When we get there you can see for yourself, *non*?"

"It's not important. I only wondered."

"Of course."

Niki's jaw dropped a minute later when Didier pulled into the gravel courtyard of the beautiful manor house with black shutters and pink geraniums she had admired on her way to the adjacent village, Villeneuve-sur-Lot, when she'd suffered both a flat tire and the humiliation of Luc's condescension. When he cycled past her so blithely, he'd only a few minutes ride home. The white Renault sat in front, among several others. He said it belonged to his sister-in-law.

And then he'd gloated at her helplessness. A fresh wave of indignation washed over her as they entered the house. Huh. Patrice could keep him.

More people filled the house than she'd expected. Besides Charles and his wife Francine–an angular woman with her black hair pulled up into a messy chignon, Patrice and Luc, sitting on a sofa like Siamese twins with her arm draped around his neck like a yoke. About a dozen other people, including a few she'd seen in the village, sat and stood around, holding drinks and talking. Didier and Charles made haphazard introductions, and soon they too had a drink in hand and had found a seat in the living room. Through the open French doors there was a long, linen-covered table set for dinner, glassware sparkling in candlelight.

Niki wasn't sure whether she or Didier were the more awkward tonight. The crowd had a sophisticated air of insouciance so unlike her boisterous acrobat friends.

While she had plenty of friends back home, they did things together, search and rescue work, parkour, mountain biking, dog walking. Not so much the dinner party thing. Not that she wasn't a sociable person. But she wasn't part of a cozy little group that gathered, the way these people did. She sensed that Didier had little experience with these situations either. She sat near him and kept her eyes on him. And she felt compelled to touch him, but whether to reassure him or herself, she wasn't sure.

She made small talk with a couple, but soon found their smirks and sideways glances irking her.

"Did I say something funny?" Niki imagined they'd all heard about her outburst in town.

The humour dropped from their faces like melted cheese. "*Non.* No, of course not," said a tall redhead with a British accent colouring her flawless French.

Didier placed a large palm on the back of Niki's head and ruffled her hair. "You have a unique way of speaking French, little monkey."

Her mouth curled in acknowledgment. "You mean I'm mangling it again?"

He chuckled, and this gave the others permission to smile again.

"It's charming. I do not wish you to change it." His hand gentled, and he caressed the back of her head, tangling in her hair. Again a shiver of genuine attraction at his powerful but gentle touch snaked down her spine, and she wondered whether he was playing it up for the crowd as they'd intended. He met her eyes with a twinkle and she was grateful for his low key way of taking everything in stride. It warmed her insides. She needn't get her back up because someone laughed at her a little. Her French was mediocre. So what? Language wasn't her thing.

She took his hand between hers and planted a kiss on it.

"Fine. Laugh at my French. At least I'm not one of those North Americans that stomps around expecting everyone to speak English." She hammered in her best worst southern accent, "Hi-ya there can Aah get a haym burgah?"

There was a wave of laughter.

"And we love you for it, darling," said the redhead. "Don't we, Luc?"

Niki's gaze shot across the room like a laser beam to where Luc sat with his attention locked on her, despite having tried not to pay him much attention. He hadn't missed the prompt and responded in his smooth French, adding to her awkwardness. "*Bien sûr*, Gisèla. Niki's French adds another colourful dimension to a fascinating woman of character."

Her brow knit in response to that, as she puzzled out what he meant, and whether he was poking fun at her. But then she gave it up. "Over the top, but I'll take it." She grimaced at him in fake-friendliness and turned away. Her job tonight was to be Didier's companion, and to make sure everyone there knew it.

Shortly they moved to the terrace, and the long table laden with wonderful dishes of food of all kinds under a canopy of twinkling lights in the trees overhead. They served salads, grilled steaks, ratatouille and creamy pasta. Guests passed dishes around family style, and soon Niki enjoyed a delicious meal accompanied by copious amounts of the local wine, trying and failing to keep up with the multiple conversations that criss-crossed the table.

Her French just wasn't up to the task. Although she sat next to Didier, it was easier to look at Luc, across from her, and follow what he was saying than it was to tune into what Didier was doing. At least that's what she told herself. Gisèla and her husband kept Didier engaged, and the guy on her right turned the other way most of the time, probably because of her lacklustre French.

Next to Luc, Patrice pretty thoroughly occupied him with her constant asides and little touches. Not that Niki cared, but it was becoming increasingly clear that Patrice was a poseur. Luc seemed not as interested as she supposed he ought to be, considering how proprietary Patrice seemed. Despite Charles, on his other side, slapping Luc on the shoulder and frequently bending toward him with private jokes, Luc's attention wandered. Charles was trying to discuss immigration policies of the French versus Canadian governments with Luc. Luc's mumbled replies came half-hearted while he continually straightened and rearranged the silverware that flanked his plate, his gaze jumping from one person to the next. Several times she met his furtive glances, as though he was sending some coded message, leaving her baffled yet again.

Patrice leaned toward him to whisper something in his ear, while plucking a piece of lint from his sleeve. A muscle jumped in his jaw and closed his eyes for a too-long moment. Yet he turned to her with an affectionate smile and pecked her cheek. Afterwards, he doubled down on his food, industriously dipping his fork into everything on his plate as though he followed an algorithm, devouring one bite of each food and rotating his plate before digging into another. What was going on in his head?

To avoid another of his searching gazes, Niki tucked her shins under her ass and raised herself up so she could speak into Didier's ear.

"Are you having fun?"

He bent his head to reply. "I am. Are you?"

She pulled her mouth into a saucy moue. "You're not paying enough attention to me. I enjoyed our baking this morning more."

He tilted his head and contemplated her, a wry smile pulling at his lips. "You're restless. You don't care for all this sitting and *caqueter*."

She blinked at him. Yammering. A word she'd just learned last week. How insightful. That was sure true.

"It's the crowds. I never liked them."

"You prefer to be alone with me?" Was that scepticism in his tone?

"I do, actually," she said, meeting his blue eyes with a coy look.

He laughed his big deep laugh and pecked the end of her nose. In response, she threw her arms around his neck and planted a kiss on his lips, then saw his face flush with vivid colour. "Hey."

"Hey."

She released him, understanding his discomfort with public displays of affection, but had to admit to herself that they grew more comfortable with each other. Although implicitly simple expressions of their growing trust and friendship, she knew how it looked to others.

And she could tell people noticed. She caught a darting glance or an indulgent smile directed at them. Each time she caught Luc staring however, his pensive frown set her heart pounding and her nerves fluttering. Was he disapproving of her interference in Didier's life? Or was he upset about something else?

CHAPTER 18

Luc had slept the restless, overheated sleep of a man who'd drunk too much to help himself endure an unendurable evening. He got up early, soggy with regret, but there was nothing for it now but to sweat it out. So he'd skipped croissants, coffee and conversation, and hopped on his bike to pay penance for his folly.

What was wrong with him? Though he'd pretty much indefinitely postponed any notion of proposing to Patrice until he knew his own mind, she'd been more attentive and affectionate last night than ever. Perhaps she sensed his emotional, and, to be frank, physical withdrawal in the past week. He could hardly bring himself to touch her anymore. And it was true, he felt like a hypocrite. He focussed utterly on Niki and Didier. It ate at him to the exclusion of everything else, and he knew he'd behaved like an ass throughout the dinner party.

His parents had raised him to be unfailingly kind, supportive and honest, and he always maintained at least the surface appearance of that, but increasingly he felt less and less in control of his emotions, as though that brittle surface had cracked and lost structural integrity.

He rode northeast today, because the terrain was steeper, and he needed the challenge. For an hour, he pedalled without a thought to where he went, through landscapes he hadn't visited recently, and the change was good. Then, stopping under the shade of a row of poplar trees for a moment to drink water, his pulse kicked up when another cyclist whizzed past. He'd nearly dropped his water bottle when he recognized Niki, also riding as though the devil chased her despite being two hours out of Petit Bergeron.

After that, he couldn't help himself. It was Luc that chased her, pushing hard on the pedals to catch up. Wherever she went, that's where he was going, too.

∼

Didier was right. She didn't much enjoy sitting around making conversation. Nor did she love big groups. Although baking the cake was fun, and the dinner party was interesting, she came away restless with pent up energy and vaguely disgruntled. Her solution was to get up early and hop on her bike for a long hard ride. There had been so much going on she wasn't spending enough time on her own, or pushing her body until she felt renewed and grounded.

She hit the road with a vengeance, and pushed the pedals until her mind released its worries and all she gave herself over to the air in her lungs, the breeze and the sun on her face, the burn of the muscles in her legs. With no real plan or direction, she rode and rode as the morning sun rose in the pale sky and heated the pavement until it bent the air, turning the ripening fields of sunflowers and corn to a sizzling gold.

With the sixth sense of a cyclist, she knew another bike approached her from behind. As it drew closer, she glanced over her shoulder to have a look, only to find her troubles had followed her.

∼

As he came up alongside Niki, he had no doubt that she was the source of his unsettled feelings. Anticipation filled his chest with lightness and stretched his face into a grin before she even turned to look at him.

"Hello, again."

Her shock at seeing him on her heels was clear. "Why are you here? Are you following me?"

He checked for cars behind them and came up alongside. "No. Coincidence."

"Likely story," she scowled and kept her gaze forward, pushing harder on her pedals.

"We had the same idea today," Luc said with a grin.

"I doubt it."

"Don't be like that. You're heading to the ruined chateau, I'll bet. Let's go together."

"No." She pulled ahead.

He pumped to keep up. "Are you… Did I do something to make you angry?"

"Why would my decisions have to do with you?"

"Maybe because everything I do lately has something to do with you?"

Since the day he'd met her, everything inside him felt upside down. Though he habitually enumerated her faults, and tried to focus on those things that irritated him and unsettled his sense of rightness, he couldn't detach his thoughts from her. Worse, his thoughts were heated, irrational even.

She growled in exasperation and pushed harder on her pedals, taking a run at an upcoming steep hill.

He stood on his pedals to keep up, finding a steady working rhythm to climb the slope. She may flip and bounce like a circus performer, but he had a lot of distance under his wheels and his legs were strong. He pulled ahead, noting her heavy breathing as he passed. Conversation was impossible for several minutes.

When he reached the apex, he stopped, breathless, to watch her climb the rest of the way. His own legs were jelly, but his hangover seemed to dissipate, his head filling with a lightness and a sense of well-being that he suspected had something to do with the little woman in front of him.

Luc had never lacked for women friends. Women liked him. He might not be a huge macho man, but he knew women liked his movie-star looks and his lean athletic build. More than that, he suspected his easy charm and good manners attracted women. Thanks to his wise and loving parents, he did not need to posture and pose. He was secure in his manhood. He knew who he was. And he wasn't threatening to women. So they liked him.

Though they liked him well enough, he'd never felt wildly attracted to any of them. He dated many and had a few middling relationships of a few months length. But nothing ever stuck. No one had ever lit his fire. That was how he'd ended up, on the cusp of his thirtieth birthday, concluding that marrying his childhood friend was his best option for an approximation of the happy ever after that he'd always sought.

Until now.

She arrived, stopping her bike, gasping but trying to hide it. "Why'd you stop?"

He smiled. "Had to see how long you took to catch up." He couldn't stop himself from poking at her. His mind flashed back to the kisses and touches she'd shared with Didier at the dinner party, and his own visceral reaction to them. It looked so genuine to him. He told himself it wasn't real, but his gut reacted all the same.

"Did you enjoy the party?"

Her chin jutted. "Yes, I did. Did you?"

He met her stubborn gaze, admiring her bright hazel eyes, brown flecked with green in the sunlight, the dampness that gathered on her brow and smooth tanned neck, with fine strands of hair plastered to her skin. Without intending to, he blurted the truth.

"No." His jealous gaze slid down her lean arms and defined, bare legs. "I didn't enjoy watching you and Didier together like that."

Her surprise showed in her widening eyes, her brows jumping up and down again. Her lips curled inward, between her teeth, as though she suppressed a smile.

Somehow, his parents had failed to teach him what it felt like to lose his head, or was it his heart? With their secure and loving marriage, they had omitted the lessons about what it was like to be attracted to another human being like an uncivilized barbarian. That's what it felt like on the inside. A turbulent inside he was having a harder and harder time reconciling with his civilized exterior.

He resisted the urge to drop his bike and grab her, pull her towards him and kiss the daylights out of her.

That the object of his savage desire was apparently infatuated with his old friend, despite being advised not to mess with the local alchemy, and evidently having her feelings returned by the shy giant, and throwing everything around her into a combustible mess, didn't help his peace of mind.

The dark slash of her fine brows pinched together. "Why are you looking at me that way?"

Was she aware of his attraction and taunting him with her fling with Didier? Sometimes it seemed so. There's no question the ugly fire that roiled in his belly was jealousy. Maybe she pushed him away because she felt nothing for him.

But no, he didn't believe that.

"Because I want to kiss you."

"Again?" She challenged. "Why did you? I thought you were with Patrice?"

He grinned, his brows jumping in question. "Why? Seriously?"

Whenever they were within spitting distance, the air between them crackled with electricity. When he touched her skin, shocks ran through his nervous system like a seizure. When they'd kissed, he thought he might faint with the intensity of his desire. She couldn't miss that. That just didn't happen without reciprocity.

The look in her eyes that night both acknowledged and denied what they'd done. He didn't know what message his own burning gaze had sent, but it could be no mystery.

"You know why."

Yet she dismissed him. He almost felt as though she disliked him, or feared him. No, that was too strong a word. Something was off though. And he wanted to find out.

There was something unhealthy about her interest and attachment to Didier. His concern grew. And even though his own confused and conflicted motives were more clear than ever, he knew he had to stay close to her and make sure she… make sure everyone was okay.

She moved to cycle away, but he shot ahead. "Race you to Baysée," he threw over his shoulder as he shot down the other side of the hill.

An hour later, they pulled into the hilltop village of Baysée, side by side, their war of wills for the time being put aside. For the rest of the ride, they'd alternated between competitive sprinting to outdo one another, laughing and playfully tossing insults, and cruising along in silent camaraderie, enjoying the long open road.

She had to admit it was fun having a cycling companion, especially one who could match her in physical abilities. It was no hardship, either, being able to glance over and see Luc's fine form in motion, his lean muscles tensed and working, glistening with the sweat of his effort. If she'd indulged in more than a moment of visceral sexual fantasies, using his beautiful body for her dirty thoughts, he'd never know.

They paused in the square, propping up their bikes and sitting on an iron bench under the shade of a large plane maple tree, drinking water in silence, cooling down.

He jostled her out of her reverie when he spoke.

"There's an ancient church that's popular with tourists here, if you want to look. And that restaurant serves huge ice cream parfaits in all the colours and flavours of the seasons, called Amour d'Ete and Abondance d'Automne." He looked at her in invitation, waiting to see what tempted her.

She frowned, reconsidering their budding friendship. If he wanted to kiss her, and she was having x-rated daydreams about him, this new closeness could only lead to trouble. "No, thanks."

He paused, scratching his beard, bemused, and she felt guilty for her sharp words. Why was she being such a bitch? He was never less than charming and kind. Unless his gaze heated, and she knew his thoughts had spiralled into the same erotic places hers had gone.

"I'd like to show it to you. It's a beautiful ruin, and they've got this gift shop in a restored section with amazing local arts and crafts stuff." He tilted his head to the side, studying her. "You'd like it."

"You think you know what I'd like?"

Luc sucked his cheek and eyed her, amused. "What's up? I've seen you at the market. The way you linger around the artisans and touch all their things. I think I know what you'd like."

That stopped her. He watched her? Like a stalker? Why hadn't she noticed him watching her? When was that?

"I'm not in the mood today."

"Is it Didier? Because of him? Because he's not…" He bit off his next words, glancing away, seeming to think better of whatever he would have said. "You can't get attached to him, Niki. You just can't."

She shook her head. "I'm not! It isn't because of him. I just wanted to be alone. Is that so hard to understand? I don't need anyone to make me happy or sad or entertained, or keep me company, okay?"

His gaze drifted to the church wall behind her, and he nodded, tonguing his cheek. "I got it. I'm sorry I intruded on your space. I thought we were having fun."

"I'm not like you, Luc. Or like Didier and Amélie. I'm not desperately seeking domestic bliss. I'm perfectly content on my own."

When his steady blue gaze returned to her face, she felt the lie in her words. Instead of being offended, Luc's expression filled with pity. "What happened to you, sweetheart? Why are you like this?"

"I gotta go back." She picked up her bike and hopped on, ready to push off.

"Bye, then," Luc said, avoiding her eyes as he gazed across the plaza. As she rode away, she felt the weight of his eyes on her back, but wouldn't glance back no matter how much she wanted to see his face. She wanted to wipe away that look of pity. She wanted to see his white teeth flash in a smile again. She almost turned around to apologize for being so awful, but pushed on, swallowing the tightness in her throat.

Niki had plenty of time to think on the ride back to Petit Bergeron. The return trip wasn't as exhilarating as the ride out had been, and she blamed Luc for it. She knew he rode a hundred meters behind her, but kept his distance to give her the solitude she sought. But she couldn't empty her mind and immerse herself in the pure physical joy of the ride, and the feel of her body in the elements.

Instead, her mind whirled with thoughts she couldn't resolve and that she didn't like very much.

Her own lies echoed in her head.

I just want to be alone.

I don't need anyone to make me happy…

I'm perfectly content on my own.

But was she happy? She loved her work, no question. It was challenging and fulfilling. She was contributing to the world. She loved the thrill of speed, height, danger. She needed it.

So, okay, her social life was sparse. She had no constant companion, no one to share meals with. She had few close friends, and no real idea where her life was going. So what? The people who knew her, understood her. She liked herself. She was okay.

Then why, when she thought of Didier and Amélie, their life long entanglement, and bottled up passion, did something in her chest zigzag and leave her breathless and woozy with longing.

She admired and even envied their devotion to each other. Most people would have given up and moved on long ago. Anyone with a healthy sex drive would have looked elsewhere for satisfaction.

But not Didier. His love for Amélie was so absolute he stayed locked in his private hell, unable to have what he most wanted, unable to do anything to change his situation for the better. There was no one in her life like that.

Anymore.

Abruptly, the effort of peddling was too much. She should have rested longer and taken Luc up on his offer to sightsee and eat something. She'd ridden long enough today to drain herself of energy, and her legs were throbbing and quivering like wet noodles, her quads too fatigued to push up another hill. She'd head straight back to Didier's. She needed a power smoothie, protein supplements and a nap.

Thinking of Didier lifted her mood. There was something about his sweet manner and gentle ways, his acceptance and self-control, that she found both endearing and inspiring. Instead of thrashing around trumpeting his masculinity like so many men, he just was. Quietly. Maybe it was just the physical proximity of living with a man that was getting to her. Maybe all that testosterone humming under the surface was making her crazy with lust.

Her harsh words to Luc echoed in her mind. They were lies. Lies designed to hurt, and to push him away. The fun they'd shared had opened old wounds, and reminded her, too painfully, of the playful times she'd shared with Sam growing up. Despite their negligent parents, they'd always had each other.

If she was honest with herself, it was more than Didier's physicality that appealed to her. It was the way he looked at Amélie. The kind things he did for her, his devotion and admiration. If Niki didn't know how ridiculous it was, she'd imagine she was feeling jealousy. Not for Didier so much as for what he had with Amélie, or what he would have with her once Niki got out of the way.

A hollow feeling in her stomach twisted and rolled. It would be nice to have someone feel like that about her. To know that no matter what life threw at you, no matter whether you were rocking it or have a shit day, there would always be someone to share it with, someone who cared more about you than anything else. That together you'd get through, and that you'd always belong somewhere.

You could have that!

Her chest squeezed with the painful truth of that. It was their intimacy she envied. Well, their emotional intimacy. If they could ever get past the social barriers and their inhibitions and hook up, wouldn't that be awesome?

An image of Luc flashed in her mind, and she tried to swat it away.

Still she remembered his intense blue eyes locked on her, and the feeling they always left her with of being exposed, as though he saw everything, inside and out, and understood why she did what she did, and didn't judge her for it, even when he didn't like it. That he knew her.

The thought of him watching her in the market, noticing what she did, what she liked, made a shiver course up her spine to the back of her neck. Why was he so interested in her? And how could she have such a strong feeling about someone she didn't even know?

And she would never get to know him either. Not if she kept pushing him away.

She knew why, too. How could she not?

All her life her mother had told her, be strong, Niki. I depend on you, Niki. I can't always be with you. I won't always be here. Watch over Sam. Protect him. Never had she held her close the way a little girl needed to be held, and coddled her when Niki'd had a bad day. Never had she made space for Niki's needs or moods.

And how could she argue with the logic?

No matter how weak or frightened or lonely she might be, nothing she felt could compare to Sam's pain. Everything about life was that much harder for Sam. It was like he had no skin, and everything, everything about the world burned him like acid. It was all too much. Too bright and too loud. Too crowded, confusing and demanding. Too judgmental. Too cruel.

And so she had no choice. She became what they expected her to be. Strong enough for both herself and Sam. But Sam was gone, and Niki didn't know how to be any other way.

Maybe life was richer when you had someone to share it with.

Until it wasn't.

The problem with that kind of trust and intimacy was the responsibility that came with it. You no longer lived just for yourself, but for the other person, too. She could never imagine being a parent, never mind someone's significant other. How could anyone feel worthy of that kind of commitment?

She didn't.

It was dangerous to get that attached to anyone. She would let them down, and when they left, she'd be alone again. Better to be strong and content within oneself and avoid that kind of pain. Maybe that's what Didier and Amélie deserved, but she didn't.

She had to pull over to rest for when the soreness in her throat and the tightness in her lungs made breathing and cycling impossible. *What is wrong with me?*

She'd let herself get out of shape this past week, lallygagging around Petit Bergeron at the festival. It was time to wrap up her business here and move on. Time to get back to her own life and stop messing around in other people's.

CHAPTER 19

She had to go past the village to get to Didier's house anyway, so she made the extra effort to cycle as far as the parking lot, then dragged her tired legs up the hill to the central square to see who was around and what was happening.

A forlorn scene met her. Most decorations and sets for the Medieval festival were already down. Crews of men stood on ladders and carried loads to waiting open-bed trucks parked in the square where no vehicles had been before. They had removed the colourful banners, and disassembled most vendors' booths and tents. People in jeans and t-shirts milled about and strolled back and forth.

She sighed.

A wonderful event while it lasted. But real life intruded now and that meant her little chapter of make believe was ending, too. If she could figure out how to get Didier and Amélie to hook up once and for all, and take their relationship to the next level, she'd feel comfortable moving on. Maybe she'd ride to Bordeaux and look up Sabine, Alain and Rocco like she promised.

Not sure of a game plan, she walked to Amélie's shop.

Amélie greeted her warmly when she walked in the door and offered her a cool drink. "Come and sit on my back patio."

"Don't you have customers?"

"I had a fitting this morning. But I am spending most of today cutting, and it is tiring and boring after a while, so I welcome the break."

Niki wandered out through a pair of tall glass doors that might have been four or five hundred years old. The courtyard was a tiny stone gap between buildings, with a few small windows carved high into the ancient walls that framed the space. A pot of bright geraniums bloomed in a corner, and a green vine sprouting from a crack in the stone climbed up the flaked stone wall to the patch of bright blue sky above. Niki took a seat at an diminutive iron table and chairs she thought likely Didier had made for Amélie and her heart squeezed.

She brought two glasses of cloudy yellow liquid with ice cubes. "Are you okay with *pastis*?"

"I've never tried it." Recalling that day in Villeneuve-sur-Lot when Luc had offered it to her, she bent to take a sip of the refreshing drink. It tasted odd, but she said, "Oh, it's good."

Amélie smiled and took a sip of her own. "So, what brings you by?"

"The site of the festival coming down made me kind of sad. I was looking for company."

"Where's Didier?"

"I don't know. I've been cycling all day."

"Ah. That explains it."

"Explains what?"

"I saw him earlier. He was helping with the disassembly. And he was in a foul mood. I've never seen him like that in my life."

Niki remembered the time in his forge when he was mad as a bear. "I have. Have you ever watched him working?"

"Not really. He's done little demonstrations for the tourists. Not serious blacksmithing." She leaned forward. "Is it very exciting?"

Niki stared. Amélie's peaches and cream complexion was flushed pink, and her eyes were dark. She took another sip of her pastis and ran her tongue around her lips. This girl was seriously turned on at the thought of Didier hammering on iron.

"Uh. It was rather... er." Niki embarrassed herself by giggling at the memory, and she felt her own face flush with heat. "I guess you could say it was pretty awesome. But maybe he takes out a lot of his frustrations on the anvil. That's why he's even-tempered the rest of the time."

"Oh, Didier has always been so gentle and kind. He wouldn't harm a fly."

"Oh yeah. Right. I mean... but he really lets that iron know who's boss, if you know what I mean."

After a pregnant pause, Amélie cleared her throat. "Niki. May I ask you a very personal question?"

"Sure."

"Well... everyone knows you and Didier are very close. Em... I mean that, in the short time you have been here, you've been living with him... at his house, I mean."

"What are you asking, Amélie?"

"I was wondering..." she paused, seeming to choose her words. Niki waited. "Um. I guess all the girls have thought about this, but... perhaps you are the only one who knows the answer."

Niki smiled. She understood the question, but she didn't know the answer either.

Amélie's eyes sparkled. Her voice was a mere whisper. "Is it very large?"

Niki shook her head. "I can't say. I believe it's... appropriately scaled. But seriously, I thought you of all people had a pretty good idea yourself." Niki shot a glance toward the fitting room at the rear of Amélie's shop. If Didier told the truth, Amélie had gotten up close and personal with his junk.

If it were possible for Amélie to blush any brighter, she did so now. "I... I... well. No. Not really. I mean. Well... it's one thing to look at it, and another to actually... to uh..."

"Touch it?"

"Uuumm."

"Oh, you mean accommodate it, don't you?"

Amélie dropped her blushing face into both palms. "I've always wondered." Her voice came out muffled between her fingers.

Would it reassure her if she told Amélie she had tried him on for size? Or upset her? Niki decided to play it safe. "And worried?"

Amélie shot upright. "No! Nooo. What has it to do with me? Didier and I are not–"

"Yuh. Right." Niki reached out and took one of Amélie's hands. "Who are you kidding? And if you think I'm jealous, or I'm going to be sticking around this little armpit of a French village, think again." She grinned. "I've got a lovely life in Vancouver that I'll be returning to shortly. Then you can have Didier to yourself. All of him." She twitched a suggestive brow at Amélie, who's eyes widened.

"It's I that am jealous of you, Niki. I wish I had your courage and confidence to be able to get so close to a man like Didier and just... touch him." Her eyes dipped in apology. "I wish..."

"I don't know, Amélie. I'm a very physical person, just very comfortable in my body." She shrugged. "It doesn't mean anything."

"What do you mean? Is it not the most intimate of acts, to share your body with another?"

Niki thought about it. "Not especially. It's organic. Natural. Nothing to fear. For me the most difficult thing is..." she hesitated. Amélie stared at her, open and waiting. Non-judgmental. Like a true friend. "To be vulnerable I guess. I think I mean that in the emotional sense."

Amélie nodded thoughtfully, staring at her glass. "Has someone broken your heart before, Niki? Is that why?"

Niki breathed slowly before answering. It was time for her to take Luc's advice and let down her drawbridge, invite people in. She nodded. "I had a brother who died."

Amélie reached over and set her hand gently on Niki's forearm, placing it there briefly then removing it. That simple gesture carried power. Niki felt her burden lift a little with that one admission.

"Well, I admire your courage. The way you went after Rosaire and those idiot friends of his. I wanted to stand up and cheer." She shook a delicate fist like a little Rosie the Riveter.

"I don't think that was courage." She laughed. "Ironically, I got in a bit of shit for that."

Amelie frowned. "From whom?"

Niki grunted. "Luc. He thinks I embarrassed Didier that night."

Amélie's head shook rapidly. "No. No, I don't think you could do Didier any more harm than his own neighbours and friends have done. But you've shaken things up around here. It's good for him. For me too."

"Humph. Well, I didn't grow up with these weird dynamics so..."

A small bird flew down into the small patio and pecked at some invisible crumbs on the pavement, catching their eye as it hopped from place to place. It chirped loudly and took off again. A few minutes of easy silence passed then, and they drank their pastis.

"Luc is also from Vancouver, yes?"

"Yeah. Strange coincidence."

"Or perhaps fate."

Niki slid her eyes over to Amélie to see if she was serious. "If you believe in it."

∽

When she got home, she had to hunt for Didier. What had Amélie meant when she'd said he was in a foul mood? It seemed unlike him, unless...

Putting away her bike and helmet, she wandered out to the forge to see if he might be there. Sure enough, before she got there she could hear the clang of metal echoing through the evening air.

There he was, as before, shirtless and sweating in the red glow of his fire, beating the crap out of a metal post, his mighty hammer swings coming down like the wrath of Thor. *Clang.*

He really was awesome.

When she'd first seen him last week, first met him in the village, the only thing she could see was his extraordinary size, his awkward shyness, his painful predicament—and that made her think of Sam. But as she'd got to know him, his charm, his kindness and creativity, his strength, Didier seemed not so pitiful at all.

Another clang of the hammer on the anvil brought her back to the spectacular Didier, and while she still felt she could help him with his frustrated love affair with Amélie, and his general lack of self-confidence, instead she found herself not only admiring him, but drawn in to a powerful attraction. Under other circumstances, she could even fall a little in love with him. *Clang.*

For a fleeting moment, she wondered whether Sam, had he lived past adolescence, would have found a woman to love him, in all his awkward, painful shyness. Her heart wept knowing it would never be.

As if he sensed her outrageous thoughts about him, Didier stopped hammering and turned, a frown frozen on his face, a question in his eyes.

"Hey, I heard you were in town."

"Who said this?" He turned back to his anvil and lifted his hammer again. *Clang.*

"Amélie."

His arm stalled in mid-air. "You spoke to her?" *Clang.*

"We had a *pastis* on the patio behind her shop."

Didier put down his hammer, slowly and carefully, and turned toward her. Two long strides and he was in front of her, his huge hands gripping her thin shoulders. "This must stop, Niki."

"Wha–"

His lips came down on hers, sudden and fierce. Just as suddenly, he pulled away, the look of shock on his face disorienting her more than the actual kiss, over before she registered what was happening.

"*Désolé.*" He dropped his hands, shook his head and stormed out of the forge. Cautiously, she followed him to the grassy bank beside the watermill where he always went to think.

"Didier?"

He spoke without turning toward her, raising and lowering his arms in frustration. "I'm sorry. I don't know what happened. Today is such a mess, I don't know what I'm doing!" He paced back and forth along the bank, his big boots crushing the grass.

"Didier. Sit down, please."

He froze and looked at her, then sank down onto his haunches, his expression matching the churning water of the stream.

She cupped his broad, heaving shoulder. "It's okay. Don't fret. Why are you so upset?"

"I don't know if it's being near you or not being near Amélie, but I'm so…" he bunched his hands into fists and clenched his teeth in frustration, then finished his sentence with an impressive roar.

All at once she understood. He was patient and disciplined, but he was only a man. And he needed sexual release something awful. She stepped toward his back, knelt on the grass and wrapped her arms around his broad shoulders, squeezing as hard as she could. She rested her head against his broad back and rubbed his arms. He squirmed in her arms and grumbled incoherently. "Didier, it's okay. It's really okay. If it's any comfort to you, I'm also very aroused by you, even though I know we're just friends. It's normal. It's all the time we've been spending together."

"The make-believe isn't helping. You're always touching me and looking at me with the big eyes. It's making me crazy excited, Niki. And I don't want to feel that way about you."

"And there's nowhere you can go to–"

"No! You know I'm not comfortable with that."

"And you can't court Amélie in this condition."

He groaned again, raked his hands through his hair and flopped onto his back on the grass, knocking her sideways. She rolled to her side beside him.

"Do you know how much experience Amélie has?"

His eyes slid over to peer at her, skeptical. "Experience?"

"Sexually."

"I know what you meant. I don't know. Not much I think. That's part of the problem. I'm so afraid I'll hurt her, or scare her half to death with my clumsiness."

"That's the impression I got too."

His head came up. "What? You talked about sex with Amélie?"

She nodded. "She's quite fascinated with you. And, FYI, I think she thinks we're already doing it." Niki recalled her conversation with Amélie, and the sense that Amélie had encouraged her to help Didier in any way she could.

His head flopped back onto the grass, and his voice came out feeble and resigned. "That was the idea, wasn't it? Lot of good it does me if everyone thinks I have experience I don't… one moment, did you say… already?"

She rolled until she was on top of him, chest to naked chest.

"Oh, no, no, no, no."

"Relax." He was definitely larger than any other man she'd lain with this way, but now she was so familiar with him, the difference didn't seem so great. She wiggled, feeling his long limbs and firm muscles under her.

"Hey, stop that!" He grabbed her around the middle, about to toss her off.

She stopped him by returning the kiss he'd begun earlier. But instead of hard and sudden, she lowered herself slowly, pausing a hair's breadth away to wait for him to stop her, then gently continuing until their lips were melding softly. She waited. He did nothing, but it put an end to his complaints. He seemed immobilized. She stared into his blue eyes until she could see that he understood she was smiling. She pushed herself up a little on his barrel of a chest, stroking the impressive mounds of his blacksmith's pecs and shoulders, and then lowered herself to plant feather light kisses on his nose, chin, cheeks, brows and lips again. With her fingertips, she gently stroked the sides of his face, his ears and his neck.

"Niki, what are you doing?"

Murmuring, continuing along her pathway of gentle kisses, she explained. "I'm trying to help you get over the adolescent notion that sex has to be some kind of life altering big deal. Once you get past your fear and worry, you can relax and just enjoy it for the pleasant, relaxing, playful and sensual experience it should between two consenting adults."

"Pleasant does not begin to describe what I'm feeling."

She lifted her head, really grinning this time. Under her legs, the hardness of his erection made itself known. "I feel it too!"

He closed his eyes, groaning, heat radiating from him.

"Don't hide from me, Didier. Look at me. Feel me. You have nothing to be afraid of. We're friends. You said so yourself. We've become good friends, and we trust each other. Don't we?"

He conceded by making a low noise in his throat, reluctantly.

"Look at me."

He opened his eyes, and she gripped his chin between her fingers and locked her gaze on his.

"Let's just do this. Friends with benefits, eh? Let's do it right now."

CHAPTER 20

"We can't! That would be wrong!"

"Why? Are you getting all moralistic on me? Are you trying to save yourself for your bride?"

He sulked, and she watched him chew on and digest that notion. "No. I'm not like that. But–"

"We wouldn't be the first pair of friends with benefits, and definitely not the first casual hook up. Why not? We'll let off some steam, you'll get a little experience, and I'll get…" she made a funny, lascivious face, "I'll get to satisfy my curiosity about how big and wonderful you really are."

Instead of laughing with her, his face pinched with worry. "You are small. Aren't you afraid?"

She scoffed and made a silly face. "Humans are stretchy. We're made to fit together. I'm not worried."

"You have experience."

"Duh."

He grabbed her middle again and lifted them both as he rose to his feet, setting her down like a child. "I don't know. It sounds dangerous."

"I already explained, I'm not worried about your size. And I won't do anything either of us is uncomfortable with."

"No, it's not that." He turned to her, biting his lip. "You have become a special friend to me, little monkey. I don't want to risk spoiling that. What if–?"

She placed a hand flat against the warm skin of his chest. His heart hammered into her palm like his hammer on the anvil, bam, bam, bam. His sweetness warmed her. She hammed it up, linking her hands and fluttering her eyelashes up at him. "What if we get attached? What if someone gets a broken heart?" She squinted her eyes at him.

A sound like gravel rolling in a riverbed emitted from his chest.

"We both know your heart already belongs to Amélie. And I'm just in it for the good times. And to help you. But mostly because I haven't had sex in a long time and the more I think about doing it with you the more I want it. You know I'll be leaving soon. So there's no time to get into a habit. So why not?"

"Everything is so easy for you. Why are you not in a relationship, Niki?"

"Pish. Not for me."

"What about Luc? I've seen the way he looks at you."

She flicked a skeptical glance over her shoulder. "He's not available, is he? And anyway, I'm just not interested in… that."

"Huh."

She walked away from him back toward the house, putting a little more sway into her hips than usual, knowing he was watching her.

"But I feel it would be disrespectful… to… to use you in such a way."

"You're not using me, dumbass. In case you haven't noticed, I'm very comfortable in my body, and in the world." She flung out her arms and spun as she walked. "Bodies are beautiful. I'm a sensual, physical person, and not particularly hung up about romantic nonsense. There's nothing wrong with two consenting adults agreeing to come together to exchange a little physical pleasure. No strings attached."

He grunted.

"You and Luc play chess, do you not? You discuss poetry? Are you exploiting his brain?" She stopped, hands on her hips and smirked at him. "We're friends now, Didier, and we'll be friends afterwards, I promise."

She continued walking, knowing that despite any lingering doubts he might have, he was only a few steps behind.

∽

"Have you ever seen a naked woman?"

His golden brows twisted. "I do own a computer."

"Has anyone ever stripped for you?"

"You know the answer to that." He kept walking toward her as she sauntered across his great room toward the stairs. She'd never been upstairs in the loft where he slept. She paused with one foot on the bottom step and half turned toward him, making sultry but playful eye contact. Despite his reservations, he was so into this, jaw slack, and she could see his chest rising with each breath. He stood motionless, unable to take his glazed eyes off of her. She was only wearing a tank top over a sports bra, and a pair of bike shorts, but as strip teases went, it would have to do. Slowly she peeled off the tank top, an inch at a time, and finally pulled it off over her head and tossed it in his general direction. He caught it and took another step toward her.

She climbed another couple of steps and sat down on a stair. Then she removed her cycling shoes and sports socks as though they were patent leather stilettos and silk stockings, kicking out her bare legs one pointed toe at a time.

Didier was smiling and rolling his eyes now, even though the bulge in his shorts was painfully obvious. He understood that this was just for fun, for sport, and for pleasure, and he was relaxing. That was her intent. The last thing she wanted was for him to get so nervous he couldn't perform his first time.

Another couple of steps up she paused, peeling off her sports bra. Not an easy feat considering the tight elastic. She distracted him by rotating her hips while she wiggled and struggled to get the thing over her shoulders. Probably that wasn't the sexiest manoeuvre. And since she had no underwear on under her bike shorts, that was it. She ran up the last few steps ahead of him, quickly peeling off her shorts and tossing them off the mezzanine.

While he stomped up the stairs behind her, *fee-fi-fo-fum*, she felt like Jack climbing the beanstalk. At the top, she had a full minute to take in his giant-sized bedroom loft. It almost broke her heart. Naturally an extra long king sized bed filled it, covered by a beautiful snow white *matelassé* coverlet and stacks of throw cushions. The pine plank ceiling sloped overhead, with skylights for nighttime star-gazing. A huge giltframed print of classical nudes hung over the bed, maybe four feet wide by six high. A guy with a sword and armour, and a plump blond sitting on a cloud looking down at him. There were a few cherubs too, and two swans above her, against a shadowy blue sky.

"Wow! Who is that?"

She felt him step up beside her, and at the feel of his warm breath, the hairs on her neck stood up and stretched toward him.

"That's Vulcan, the Roman god of fire, metalworking and the forge. The woman is Venus, his wife, the goddess of love and beauty." Didier stepped up behind her, his voice low and soft.

"It's amazing!"

"The original painting is in the Louvre museum. Francois Boucher painted it in the eighteen century."

"What's he going to do with that sword?"

She felt the tips of his warm fingers against her ribs.

"Niki." She heard a hard swallow. "I don't know if I…"

She spun in his arms. "I know you can." She kissed him again to silence his fears. Her hands found his fly, and quickly before he changed his mind, unbuttoned and unzipped him, sliding her cool fingers between the waistband and his trim hips, pushing down.

He drew in a breath as she freed him, and she looked down, curious what all the fuss was about. Then it was her turn to gasp. He was magnificent. But… normal. Just about right for a man seven feet tall.

"Humph."

A look of panic stole over his features, and he looked down as though he would find something he'd never seen before. "What?"

"Didier. You're beautiful. But there's nothing out of the ordinary about you at all."

"Really?"

She took his silky hot shaft in her hands and tightened her grip gently, knowing this was his first intimate touch.

His response was to suck a breath through clenched teeth as though she'd burnt him.

"You okay? You want to keep going?"

"Mm-hmm." His gaze caught on her hands on him.

She guided him to turn around and sit on the edge of the bed so she could get rid of his shorts. Then she nudged him until he was lying on his back and straddled him, climbing higher until her knees flanked his hips, and she felt his very impressive erection pressing against her between her legs. His hands lay lightly on either side of her torso.

"Touch me."

He slid his large calloused fingers over her skin, from her knees to her hips, up her ribs, igniting a fire in her blood.

"You're making me so hot," Niki said, squirming.

The corner of his mouth twitched, curling up. "That's what I do. I play with fire."

"Now we're talking." She adjusted herself snugly over his hardness and lay down, chest to chest. "I am molten metal in your hands."

Laughter rumbled in his chest. He became bolder, caressing her small breasts, smoothing his hands over her back and her ass, gripping her hips. She felt like a tiny doll in his huge hands, and his callused fingertips excited her skin.

She shifted her weight from side to side, feeling the weight and hardness of him pressed against her centre, and he moaned. "You'd better not…"

"I know. Hey. Do you have condoms?"

His eyes shot open. "Sacre bleu. Yes. I forgot." He rolled to the side, taking her for the ride as he shimmied backwards and pulled open a bedside drawer. He pulled out a package and held it up.

"Did you have this custom made?" she teased, taking it from him. "Please, allow me."

"Apparently there are other extra large men out there."

Laughing, she rolled the condom over him smoothly, caressing the length of his shaft as she did. "Apparently. Ready?"

She rose and settled herself gently over the head of his penis, revelling in his thickness spreading and filling her. All their play had made her more than ready. "Mm. You feel sooo nice." She wanted him to know it all was good.

His face slackened, his eyes losing focus as though he'd seen a heavenly vision. His breath accelerated.

"How ya doing there, mon grand ami?"

His words tripped out one at a time, his breath catching his throat. "I. Am. Doing. Very. Very. Well. Merci."

She slid a little further down his shaft, taking him in her, feeling him fill her. His hips jerked in a reflexive urge to rut. "Hold on. Slowly."

He raised his head and looked down. "I'm sorry. I have not been thinking about you at all. Are you okay?" He seemed transfixed at the sight of their joined bodies.

She smiled. "So far, so good." And slid further down, moaning at the sensations spiralling up and outward from her centre, being filled by his long hard cock. The member in question twitched, and she felt a corresponding throb inside her, the merging of their heartbeats. Holding herself up with her hands on his hard muscled chest, she moved up and down. He was touching her everywhere inside, which was a grand thing. She took all of him in, until she felt the head of his cock bump against her cervix. "That's it for me."

"You're finished?" Didier gasped, confused.

"No darling. You've filled me up, that's all."

"I think this is a fucking miracle," he groaned, looking at the place where their bodies touched, without a gap. "I think women are miracles, gifts from God for mere mortals like me."

"Hey, don't get carried away. I know you're enjoying this, but remember why we're doing it."

She laughed out loud at his bewildered expression.

"Amélie. You need to know a few things."

She gave him a few hints about where a woman was sensitive before, and during lovemaking, and guided his movements so he could give her pleasure. Since she was on top, her own pleasure was significant, and the vibrations inside her built and built almost to the point of pain. Instead of watching him, she moved in rhythmic ways that would soon take her over the edge, while she narrated what she was feeling and why, explaining her anatomy.

"Ni-ki!" he groaned.

She looked down. "Hm?"

"Please stop to talk," he croaked.

A grin stretched her face as she focussed her senses on the intimate connection between them, lifting herself up, holding his head just pressing into her opening, and then sliding quickly down as far as she could. She repeated this again, and again, taking them both over the edge. She felt him twitch and throb and drive his hips upward just as her own climax tore her into a million sparkling pieces.

She collapsed onto his chest, and listened to their heavy breathing, her heartbeat between her ears, and his pressed against her cheek, like a primal drum. Long minutes later, when her breathing returned to normal, she said, "Next time, you're on top. I want to make sure you know how to drive this bus."

CHAPTER 21

By the time Niki and Didier went into the village, he was a much more experienced lover. Once initiated, Didier's enthusiasm and curiosity were boundless, having waited too long in frustrated celibacy. It amazed Niki how quickly he gained skill and finesse. That's what came of being a mature and sensitive man to begin with. And he didn't lack for vigour. She would be sorry to give him up, because she was getting the royal treatment and loving every minute. But not sad, as Amélie would get quite a gift, in her opinion. A grin stretched her cheeks at the thought.

They strolled through the lanes in the village, her legs as relaxed and loose as rubber. She had no desire to run, jump or do anything athletic.

Saturday morning market day was something like the Medieval festival, without all the pomp and ceremony. She recognized many of the vendors, though there was more food and fewer artisans, and no entertainers. Sabine, Alain and Rocco had returned to Bordeaux. Everyone wore ordinary modern clothing. Not a headdress in sight, other than the flat caps still favoured by rural French men.

Didier took a break from selling his wares, so they bumped along side-by-side, meandering through the market booths picking up things to eat. Dry salty sausage from André, soft ripe cheese from Thomas, a couple bottles of red wine from Victor, the guy who had driven down from his winery in Monbazillac. They filled their bags with fresh produce at the local farmers' stalls and were wandering and browsing when they came upon Rosaire, Izar, and Sylvan, the portly, awkward one.

"How is it that those three are never apart?" she asked Didier. "Do they work together?"

Didier scoffed. "No. They work little. Rosaire inherited a farm that other people manage. Izar waits tables some nights. And Sylvan is a spoiled rich kid who dropped out of university. If they had more to do, they would probably not make such a sport of tormenting me."

As they drew closer, the three dropped their eyes and murmured to each other. It was impossible to tell whether they were scheming their next move, or whispering among themselves about the crazy Canadian bitch and whether she'd attack again. Niki stood a little taller, lifted her chin and stepped out in front of Didier, ready to engage in whatever conflict was due.

She felt Didier's large hand close around the back of her neck and steer her to the left. Suddenly they were walking uphill through a narrow passageway, not even a street, more of a back lane, in Petit Bergeron proportions. The old stone buildings nearly touched above them.

"What's going–?"

"I saw you gathering yourself up to scrap like a junkyard dog, little monkey. It's not your job to defend and protect me. Let it go."

"I wasn't."

"Mm-hmm," Didier grunted skeptically.

She sighed. "It just makes me so mad to see them strutting around town like they own the place, looking for ways to make you miserable."

Didier stopped and turned her to face him. "Petit. I'm a long way from miserable this week," he grinned. "Don't spoil the mood."

She pouted for a nano-second. "I'm sorry. Pick me up."

"Eh?" he asked but did as she asked, lifting her with a big hand on either side of her waist. "Are we doing circus tricks?" He grinned.

She took his face between her hands and kissed him, cheerily at first, but the physical echo of their recent lovemaking soon overcame them, and they were fencing with tongues in less than a minute. She coiled her arms around his strong neck. Niki felt the burn between her legs, and wrapped them around Didier's ribcage, squeezing.

He moaned low in his throat and backed her against the stone wall of the alley, pressing his chest against her to hold her there, his hands slipping down to span her butt cheeks, reaching under her to graze her hot core with his fingertips. "Jesus, Didier!" she gasped at the jolt of desire that shot through her. "You'll make me scream right here in town, *mon ami*."

He grunted. "You're right. I forget myself." He let her slide down to the ground, body rubbing against hard body, their eyes locked on each other's, grin matching grin.

The sound of a throat clearing broke their trance. Didier stepped back.

"If this is an illusion, it's quite convincing."

Bright colour rushed up Didier's neck and cheeks and he gawped over her shoulder, a choked sound in his throat. She turned to see that Luc had followed them up the alley, and was now standing with his arms crossed, a wry expression on his face.

"Sorry to interrupt you lovebirds, but I thought you'd like to know that Amélie is coming this way any moment." His voice dripped with sarcasm. "You're a fool, Didier. I didn't think you capable of this," he sneered.

Luc might have released a swarm of bees at Didier, that's how suddenly he fidgeted and twitched, his eyes darting back and forth. Niki realized they were only a few yards from the entry to the lane, and people walking by below could easily look up and see them. As Luc had done.

"We were... I mean, it was only..." Didier coughed. "There's something I need to do. Excuse me." He turned uphill, away from the market and strode purposefully away from Niki and Luc. "I'll catch up with you later, little monkey," he called over his shoulder, without looking back.

She turned her eyes on Luc and shrugged. Then she noticed the dark scowl on his smooth features and the tick in his handsome jaw. His dark hair was now three-quarters of an inch long. It looked hot slicked back at the sides and spiked up on top. Especially with his beard and the hot glare of his intense blue eyes.

"I like your hair," she blurted.

He blinked at her and shook his head. "Are you flirting with me? After what I just saw?"

She lifted her chin and said, "You don't know what you just saw."

"I have a clear picture of what I just saw burned into my retinas." His mouth pulled into a taut line, as she felt chastened.

She tossed him a dirty look and turned away, crossing her arms over her chest.

He spoke to her back. "You think you're helping him."

"I know I am."

He stepped closer and dropped his voice to a growl. "What if Amélie had seen you?"

"It's okay. She already thinks we're fucking," she hissed back, turning to face him.

"You are fucking! Obviously." His nostrils flared, and his dark brows bent into a V under a lowered brow.

"Why are you so angry?"

He stepped closer. His face was inches from hers, and he leaned toward her, his eyes raking her face, locking on her mouth. He seemed to be in some kind of pain, his chest rising and falling. He was gritting his teeth, his lips pulled back. She thought he would kiss her, or bite her.

"Are you falling for him?"

"No!" she barked, but then hesitated and pulled her eyes away, thinking, under other circumstances, that might be true. More softly, she repeated. "No. But I admire him very much. He's a great guy. You shouldn't have made him feel bad."

"He is a great guy." He dropped his gaze, lowered his head and combed a hand through his short dark hair, setting it at odd angles like a cornfield after a storm. "So you are falling for him. That's what it looks like."

Niki shook her head, needing to convince him. "We're just good friends. And we know what we're doing. It'll be okay."

He shook his head, his gaze wavering, unable to stay on her face. "What about Didier? He might get attached. He lacks experience—"

"Not anymore." She grinned at him. Was she egging him on?

He groaned. "Do you have to flaunt it? You're a freak." He leaned close to her, so agitated. His pupils dilated like a madman's, and his lips glistened. It was strange seeing such seething emotion on his usually so calm, cheerful, picture-perfect face.

Regular chiseled planes gave way to creases and shadows and revealed a dark side of Luc that Niki hadn't seen before. Maybe it was her recent physical intimacy with Didier that had her all jacked up, but she had to hold herself back from closing the distance and roughly kissing his furious face.

"Jeez, who's the freak? You're acting like you're jealous or something." She pulled back. "We're having fun. Why are you so bent out of shape? Don't be such a prude!" She shoved him roughly away, her palms tingling at the contact with his hard chest. Softening her tone, she added, "What business is it of yours what either Didier or I do, anyway?"

Luc blinked, as though she'd slapped him. He raised his palms, facing out, and stepped back. "You're right. It's none of my business."

Niki scowled at him. Was he hurt? Why did she want to take his face in her hands and sooth his anxiety with kisses? Why were images of her tongue on his skin flashing, unwelcome, in her mind? Why were her hands shaking? Why did her eyes burn? She nodded curtly to shake herself out of her heated daydream.

Then Luc stepped back, shoving his hands back into his pockets, angling away from her. "I don't want anyone to get hurt. That's all." He stalked away, head down and shaking.

I'm not a prude. Infuriating woman.

Luc stalked down into the busy *Place des Arcades*, uncertain where to put himself. How dare she make him feel like he'd done something wrong? She was the one messing around with someone else's boyfriend. Sort of. Though everyone knew Didier had never even asked Amélie on a date, never mind claimed his rights, so to speak.

Luc wasn't wrong about Didier. He loved Amélie, as everyone knew, and Niki would ruin their epic romance by confusing the poor bugger with casual sex.

Luc huffed.

"Luc?"

He wasn't Victorian in his attitudes. And he wasn't born yesterday. He didn't have a problem with casual sexual relationships, as long as both parties consented and were happy about it. Which they appeared to be.

He and Patrice had been hooking up casually for the past two summers, with no expectations.

Luc moaned.

"Luc? Ça va?"

Well, none until he'd got it into his foolish head to complicate matters by thinking they must spend their lives together as a family. He felt terrible now he'd given Patrice any hint of his intentions and raised her expectations. How wrong that felt today.

Luc raked his hands through his hair.

"Hey, man, what's the matter with you?"

Luc glanced up, scowling, at Victor, one of several men moving sets around, and clearing the square of festival decorations. "What?"

Blinking, he looked around the square. People were everywhere, and he'd stormed through without seeing them.

Victor made a wry face and slapped him on the back.

His feelings for Patrice were lukewarm compared to the raging passion Niki ignited in him. He was more upset about finding Niki and Didier locked in a passionate kiss than he was afraid of Amélie's feelings being hurt. It was he himself who was hurting.

"Luc? *Ce qui se passe?*" What happened? Someone grabbed onto his arm and stopped him.

He spun and growled and slammed his fist into a stack of empty wooden crates. Pain exploded in his hand as they toppled and slid and crashed to the ground.

"Luc!" "Luc?" "What's going on?" Several voices shouted at once.

Someone shook his arm. "Luc!"

"Amélie!"

"Are you hurt? Did something happen?"

Amélie peered at him with concern, her blue eyes warm with compassion, while people scrambled to right the collapsing pile of crates, grumbling. She grabbed his hand, looking at it in shock.

He glanced down. Blood seeped from scrapes and skinned knuckles. "How can you stand it, Amélie? If you love him, why don't you do something about it?"

"Luc? Shh. Calm down. What happened?"

He pulled back. "Nothing. Nothing." She was unperturbed, yet surely understood exactly what had been happening between the man she loved and the usurper. His usurper. "Do you feel no resentment? No frustration?"

Amélie's mouth curled. "Aha. You mean am I not jealous?" She laughed softly. "*Non.* I am not jealous. Didier will come to me when he is ready."

Jealous? Was he ripped apart with jealousy? What an ugly sensation. His jaw ached from clenching it so tightly, and acid still swirled in his stomach, making him nauseated. He would never utter them, but angry insulting words had risen unbidden to his throat to cut down his rival. Words he'd never even thought about his friend Didier. But some primal instinct had made him wish to annihilate the competition.

But could he blame Niki? Didier was a great guy. If she had a special talent for breaking down his paralyzing shyness, why wouldn't she find him attractive, and want to get to know him better? He had a good build, was good-looking, intelligent and talented, and perhaps most of all, he was kind and gentle.

Unlike Luc, who'd been behaving horribly out of character since he'd set eyes on her. What had Luc ever done to Niki but criticize and insult and tease? And his own flirtations must have come across as sleazy, as it was clear he was with Patrice. Niki must think him some kind of two-timing Lothario.

"*Pauvre* Luc," Amélie commiserated, stroking his damaged hand. "Be patient. It will all work out."

He gave her a pained expression, aware how outrageous his reaction was. Behind her, he caught of a glimpse of *Grand-Mère* Bougie standing with her hand in the deep pockets of her apron, her leathery wrinkled face folded in a toothless grin. Her kerchiefed head bobbed up and down as though she thoroughly approved of the chaos that reigned in the village.

He groaned once more, shook his head, huffed, turned away and continued stalking through the square, aware of a trail of sympathetic laughter in his wake.

What right did he have to criticize their affair? As Niki so plainly pointed out, what business was it of his what she and Didier did?

He firmed his jaw, suddenly crystal clear and determined in his intentions. Unlike Amélie, he wasn't content to wait patiently while fate took its course. He'd make it his business from now on. It was time to set things straight.

CHAPTER 22

"You're sure you don't mind? You'll be all right getting supplies with only your little bicycle?" Didier asked, his arms full.

Niki stood in the flattened tall grass outside Didier's forge while he finished packing the bed of his truck with an amazing assortment of metal objects, some in crates, some too large to package. He covered it all with a huge tarp and fastened the edges down with bungee cords.

"I'll be fine. Don't worry. Have a great time and kick some ass in Carcassonne."

"You won't forget to feed Minou?"

She tilted her head and smiled. "How could I? You've reminded me eight times."

He tossed his duffel bag into the passenger seat and slammed the door. "D'accord. Well, I'd better begin. I have a three-hour drive before my first meeting."

He wrapped his long arms around her and squeezed, lifting her off the ground, and she hugged him back. They stayed like that for a long minute, rocking, saying nothing.

The run-in with Luc in the village had shaken Didier and he couldn't rest until they'd had a "talk". He determined that their affair must end. Immediately. He felt that each pleasurable encounter now he'd conquered his fears and phobias was a further betrayal of his love for Amélie. It would be wrong to continue. And dangerous to his hopeful future. "You are positive you're all right. I am not hurting your feelings."

She reassured him with another smile. "Truly. I told you so."

He nodded. "It is best this way. Before we are too accustomed to each other."

They'd agreed to make a clean break. Now was the perfect time for Didier to undertake the business scouting trip he'd always longed to do, before his thirtieth birthday. He was still shy about his conspicuous size, but also filled with a new determination. He was a new man, master of his own life.

She was glad he'd decided to go and pursue his dream, but also a little sad. Their fun and romantic tryst was over.

When he got back, they would return to being platonic friends. They would host a celebratory dinner and invite all their friends. And after that, she would pack her bags and leave. Her heart squeezed. She'd miss her new friend a lot.

The moment he rumbled down the drive and out the gate, she got herself ready. Double water and no food. Energy gel. And no GPS today. She had no plan other than hitting the road and peddling as hard and fast as she could until she could ride no more. No matter how long it took. She'd ride all day if she had to, and half the night to get back home, as long as she could feel the adrenaline in her veins and her mind was blissfully empty.

Empty of Didier, their friendship, their incredible lovemaking that had sidelined her despite her best intentions, all the entanglements of this little French village. Including the inconvenient attraction that drew her to the schoolteacher, and him to her. It was time to move on, and she needed to purge herself of the emotions that kept her here. She needed to cut ties and prepare to return to her own life, as hollow as that seemed from where she now stood.

She filled Minou's dishes and her own water bottles, locked up the house and tucked the key under a flowerpot beside the driveway. Lifting her bike, she hopped on and pushed off with a heavy heart.

The next four hours disappeared in a blur of pavement and ripened fields. She didn't stop for anything, taking whichever road took her fancy at the moment, grinding up hills and coasting at breakneck speeds down the inclines, whizzing through villages or bypassing them altogether in favour of the long uninhabited stretches between.

At some point, she knew she was returning in the general direction of Petit Bergeron, the muscles in her legs going limp, and cramping. She'd ridden hard and nearly erased the swirl of emotion that left her so confused. She'd felt more joy, anger, sadness, love and regret in the past two weeks than she remembered feeling in a long time.

The final thought she wrestled with on the long stretch south was her last encounter with Luc, still puzzling over what had made him so angry. His face flushed and jaw jutting like a boxer, she didn't understand why he was so out of sorts. And though he had made her feel as though he knew exactly what she was thinking, she couldn't for the life of her figure out what he was thinking.

She never even heard the truck coming.

CHAPTER 23

Lying sprawled in the field, Niki analyzed what went wrong. Consciousness ebbed and flowed, so she had no idea how much time passed after she'd swerved, spun out, flipped over and flown off the road. The truck had barely nicked her, but it was enough, at her speed, and catching her unawares, to lose control, hit gravel on the verge of the road, and start a hopeless wobble in the front tire. She'd flipped ass over teakettle into the air. That's the last detail she could recall before waking up.

It was all over in a flash. The impact must have knocked her out, because the next thing she knew she was alone in a farmer's fallow field, the birds chirping, the sun slipping lower in the sky. The truck was long gone, the driver either oblivious or scared. Profound stillness was enveloped her. She could hear beetles scurrying in the grass beside her. Perhaps she could hear the earthworms burrowing beneath the soil. There was also a steady, rhythmic drumming in her ears.

It was very peaceful, her vision veering in and out of focus. Sometimes she stared at the stalks of grass and wildflowers that bobbed above her, just on the edge of her field of vision. Sometimes she gazed for long periods at the unrelenting blueness of the sky overhead, forgetting where she was. The sun was hot on her face and bare arms and legs.

She tried to lick her dry lips and found she had no moisture in her mouth. She smelled only dry dust in the summer field, the vegetation already too dry to give off any scent of life. Attempting to swallow ended in a feeble coughing fit that caused pain to ricochet through her whole body.

Some time later, she tried to get up. She found she couldn't. Something was wrong, terribly wrong. Sharp pain arrowed through her legs and groin, and her arm wouldn't move at all. No amount of willfulness could get her body to respond to her commands to push itself up off the ground.

Then the quiet and the emptiness of the field, and the unrelenting brightness of the sky, took on sinister qualities, because she realized it could be a very, very long time before someone happened upon her. She squinted again at the sun hanging in the blue dome of sky. Perhaps too long.

∾

"Nik-Nak?"
"What?"
"Whatcha doing?"
"Having a nap, Sam."
"Are you tired?"
"Mm-hmm. I like to sleep in the sun. It's warm." She lifted her head, squinting into the glare of the sun, and saw him standing over her, looking down. His hands hung at his sides, limp. He tilted his head.
"Can I sleep with you?"
"Sure Sam. Come over here and lie down with me."

He did, and she felt his large, soft, awkward body shift and snuggle up beside her in the grass and drape a heavy arm over her stomach. She was even less comfortable, but then, she liked to cuddle with Sam. She closed her eyes again. They lay for a while, just being. Being together.

Kissing his broad forehead, she asked, "How was school today?"
She felt his shrug against her.
"You had art today, didn't you? Was that fun?"
She felt his body stiffen. Heat radiated from his face, tucked against her neck, like a furnace. Then she felt the wetness of his tears as they leaked onto her skin, hot then cool, her skin tightening.
She whispered. "Tell me, Sammie. What happened?"

He sobbed, garbling his words in wetness. "I made something for you."

"A drawing? A painting?"

He nodded.

Another couple of minutes ticked by in silence. She knew not to rush him, especially when he'd had an upset. He'd tell her when he was ready. More time passed, and she thought maybe he wouldn't. She fought to stay awake.

"I painted a garden for you. And they took it."

"What was in the garden?"

"You and me. Just us. In a garden."

"That's sweet, Sammie."

"Say the thing?"

"The garden thing? From Hitchhikers's?"

"Yes."

"'Isn't it enough to see that a garden is beautiful without having to believe that there are fairies at the bottom of it too?'"

"Yes. It's gone now."

"I'm sorry, Sammie."

"They broke it, Nik-Nak. They poked it with a stick and ripped it in half, then stomped on it."

She waited, letting the rage that flooded through her ebb away before she could control her voice and speak. "I'm so sorry, Sam. That was wrong. But I'm still glad you painted a picture for me. I'm sure it was beautiful, and it means a lot to me. Thank you."

"But I wanted you to have it. To remember us together. For when I'm gone."

"I won't forget Sam. And you're not going anywhere. We'll always be together."

"Uh-huh." He nodded again, sighed, whispered, "So long and thanks for all the fish," and then she heard his breathing slow and flatten out into a steady rhythm. He'd fallen asleep in her arms.

Then it was her turn to shed tears, which slid from the corners of her eyes, down her cheeks, falling into the grass where she lay. She never would leave Sam, no matter what. That was a promise she'd made first to her parents, then to Sam, and finally, to herself. He was her responsibility. Even though she was crap at keeping the bullies away, and couldn't protect him every moment of every day, at least she was here to comfort him afterwards.

Their bond gave her life meaning. It was who she was. There was no room in her life for anyone else, even though that sometimes made her heart ache with loneliness. Sam needed her, and she loved him with all her heart. As long as she focussed on Sam, she'd be all right.

Exhaustion overcame her.

Those were her thoughts as the field melted away, the buzz of insects grew faint, and the wide blue dome of the sky faded to blinding white light.

CHAPTER 24

"Niki? Niki!"

"Sam?" Why was he calling to her? She was right here.

She felt him kneel beside her, his hands touching her all over. There was panic in his voice.

"What, Sam? Did you have a bad dream?"

"Niki! Where does it hurt?"

She sighed, letting her breath out slowly. She croaked, "Kind of everywhere." Funny. He didn't sound like Sam.

"Jesus. Jesus." He stood up. "Hang on, sweetheart. I'm calling Charles."

∼

"She's over here. Careful. I don't know if anything's broken."

"*Merde.* She looks like hell."

"Do you have a blanket or something we can use?"

"*Oui. Oui.* I'll get it."

∼

"Niki? We'll lift you, okay?"

For some reason she was listening to English voices, then French, then English again. It was confusing. Where was she? She vaguely noticed being prodded and jostled and lifted, of sinking into a soft hammock, swinging and more jostling, and then the rumble and vibration of a vehicle.

∼

Her next awareness was of bright whiteness again, but this time harsh. Lights, curtains, coats. Someone poked and prodded her. Beeps and murmured voices.

"Niki?"

"Mmm."

"Can you wake up? The doctor says you can go home."

She tried to shake her head, but it hurt. "I don't know. I don't think so."

"It's okay, sweetheart. I'll take you. Where's Didier? Do you know where he is?"

Fragments of thought fit together and started to make sense. She opened her eyes, squinting at the light. "Where am I?"

"Hospital in Villeneuve-sur-Lot. But we can take you home now. Nothing's broken. Where's Didier?"

She thought for a moment. Didier. Didier was... where? "Mmph. Carcassonne."

"What? Shit."

"It's okay. It's good. Ts'a good thing." Now she could focus her eyes, and realized that Luc stood beside her, looking down, his expression concerned. "Why are you here?"

"I found you. I'll explain later. We'll go to Charles's house if Didier's away."

"I have to feed Minou!"

"What?"

"I have to go to Didier's. I have to feed the cat."

∼

Luc had almost missed her. He'd just been starting his ride, perhaps half an hour north of the house. It was only the slightest flash of colour in the field that had caught his eye. Then the skid marks in the gravel verge. What might have happened to her if he'd not seen her bike by the side of the road? He couldn't bear the thought.

"Luc."

He stood at the side of her hospital bed, his jaw tight, stroking her hand as she drifted back to sleep yet again. He couldn't lose her, not now.

"*Mon Frère*." Charles chuckled softly, gripping his arms in a way that somehow managed to both reassure and taunt. "*Tu porte ta coeur en écharpe*. You are as obvious as Didier with his unrequited love."

Luc screwed up his face. "Really?" He wore his heart on his scarf?

"*Oui*. You watch her constantly, you follow her, your sad eyes searching and searching for her. You can hardly think of anything else lately. You're worse than your friend Didier."

Luc tucked his chin in, breaking eye contact. Mentally he reviewed his own thoughts and actions over the last week or two. It was true. What started as intrigue and irritation had morphed into infatuation. There was no point in denying it. His face heated, his collar suddenly too tight. He stretched his shoulders to loosen his shirt and cleared his throat.

"Does Patrice say anything?" Yesterday, catching Niki wrapped around Didier, their tongues down each other's throats, had rattled him to his depths, and he'd decided, only then, to make her love life his business. He wanted her. He needed her. She belonged with him. Somehow, he had to convince her to give him a chance. It wasn't about Didier and Amélie at all, though he wished them well and genuinely worried about this forged affair between Didier and Niki. If that's all it really was…

He tensed, his hands drawing into clenched fists. No. There were words circling his consciousness to match the swirling emotions that burned in his chest when he thought of Niki. Words he wasn't ready to reel in and pin down. But the need was real and strong. This obsession was something new for him, and yet it was as familiar as the painful longing that had ridden his back like a monkey since he was a child. Since he'd looked with love and envy at his parents and felt both safe and somehow, excluded.

And now this. His gaze drifted back from the floor back to Niki's battered face, the bandages, the beeping monitors. His monkey, in the flesh.

"Everyone knows, *mon ami*."

Luc met his sympathetic gaze with chagrin. "I'll talk to her. As soon as possible. Once I get Niki settled and comfortable at Didier's."

Charles gave a classic Gallic shrug. Did that mean Patrice wouldn't care? Or did it mean Luc deserved whatever wrath was coming his way? Well, either way, he'd find out soon enough. He couldn't put it off any longer.

The doctor entering interrupted them, at last, with her assessment.

"*Bonjour, messieurs.*"

"*Docteur,*" said Luc stepping toward her and shaking his outstretched hand.

"You are family?"

Luc darted a glance at Charles, seeking support.

"We are close friends. She is in France on vacation, so there is no one else."

"I see." The doctor withdrew a pen from the breast pocket of her coat, lifted a chart and scanned it with the point of her pen. "*D'accord,* she can go home. The injuries are superficial. However, there are some badly pulled muscles that will take time to heal, especially around the dislocated shoulder, and the groin and right leg. I doubt she'll walk for a few days. She'll need bed rest."

She bent over Niki, lifting her eyelids. Then she looked up, casting her gaze from Luc to Charles and back to Luc. Whatever she saw in Luc's expression, she addressed him directly.

"Also, there is a possibility of concussion. Keep her awake for the next few hours and observe her. The symptoms may progress." The doctor counted them on her fingers. "Watch for confusion, lethargy and the desire to sleep, headache, irritability, sudden tears or memory loss, especially around the event. Nausea or vomiting. Anything unusual."

Luc swallowed. Did Luc know her well enough? Would he remember and notice? But he nodded. He would take care of her. He would keep her safe. Whatever happened next for them, if there were or could ever be a them, he wouldn't let this tragedy rob him of his one chance at true love.

∽

Once Niki had explained where to find the hidden key, he opened the door and turned on some lights. He came back to get her. Lifting her gently into his arms, he carried her to the door. Behind them, the car pulled away, fading into the night.

"Did Charles leave?"

"Yes. He went home."

"What about you?"

"I'm staying with you. You can't be alone."

"It's okay. I'll manage."

"No. No, you can't. You can't walk. And you might have a concussion. The doctor said I have to watch you."

She was too weak and groggy to argue with that. It seemed to be true for the moment, however uncomfortable it made her feel to be an invalid.

Luc brought her into the house and stopped. "Where do you sleep?"

"There." She pointed. Her room, for another week.

Luc elbowed his way in and set her on the bed, plumping the pillow under her head. "Comfy?"

"Fine. Fine." As comfortable as possible under the circumstances. Everything hurt, and it was impossible to shift her weight even a bit without shooting pain in her groin, leg and shoulder. Whatever drugs they'd given her at the hospital were clearly wearing off.

He went away, and she heard noises from the kitchen, cupboard doors opening and closing, dishes clattering.

Then he was back with a tray. "It's not much, but it's all I could find." He set the tray down and helped prop her up a bit more. "It's just some soup. I know it's weird on a hot evening, but it's probably good for you."

"Not hungry."

He ignored her, balancing the soup and bringing a spoonful to her lips. She turned her face away. "Niki, eat something. You haven't eaten all day, I'll bet. Where did you go?"

"Riding. I don't know."

"What happened? Why did Didier leave? You were crying when I found you."

So many questions. She was silent, remembering her dream, or hallucination, or whatever it was. Sam had come back, and they'd talked. She couldn't remember that incident ever happening exactly that way. Perhaps her mind had mangled several memories. She wondered what he meant, for when you go away.

"Niki?"

She turned to Luc, and studied him while he looked at her, his brow furrowed and his blue eyes intense and assessing. The blue of his eyes seemed to draw her in, like the bright surface of a pond, cool and welcoming, accommodating and forgiving.

"I thought I was dying," she croaked. Her voice was still hoarse from dehydration.

Then she accepted the spoonful of cooling soup he held for her, and the rest of the bowl he fed her, one spoon at a time, without a word.

It was weird and disorienting.

Her waking memories of Sam were always the best memories. Their time growing up. Their time alone together, doing all of his favourite things. His sweetness and trust. And also... also the times she needed to comfort him. The bad times.

It was her dreams, or rather her nightmares, that were the worst. When she remembered Sam in a dream, he was already dead, surrounded in a litter of orange peelings, like fallen autumn leaves, Mom's empty medication bottles beside him.

This time, maybe because she was delirious, it was different. Sam never spoke to her. He never said things she didn't understand. What did that mean, To remember us together? For when I'm gone? As if... what? Did Sam think because she'd gone travelling she'd forget him? Abandon him?

What was she even saying? Did it come out of her subconscious? Or was it really Sam, trying to tell her something?

An image of the old gypsy woman at the market flashed in her mind. What had she said? *"Vous devet vous preparer au changement... C'est l'heure."*

Prepare for change. It's time.

None of it made sense. Why had so many strange things happened since she'd arrived in Petit Bergeron? Her life was all in turmoil. Meeting Didier, who reminded her so much of Sam. Meeting Luc, who got inside of her and turned her upside down. Losing her cool with Rosaire and his cronies, when she never lost her cool. And now this accident and strange words from her brother from beyond the grave. Coincidence? It was all too much. Probably the effects of the drugs, she thought, as her eyes drifted closed.

She was vaguely aware of Luc sitting beside her, stroking her brow. Each time she dozed off, he'd touch her gently, murmuring words of comfort.

CHAPTER 25

"I said I don't need your help anymore! Why won't you listen?"
He was ignoring her. Again.
"Luc! Go home. I want to be alone." She moaned in frustration.
Nothing but the sounds of him puttering in the other room. Water running briefly. His soft footfalls on the wooden planks of Didier's house. And there wasn't a damn thing she could do about it.

It was infuriating and humiliating, having him here. It was almost as if he mocked her in her helplessness. He'd apparently slept on the sofa last night after he'd deemed it safe for her to sleep. First, he'd tortured her by waking her up repeatedly. Then she'd slept a long time, awakening when the sun was already high in the sky and the heat of the day had built. She'd had to suffer the indignity of having him carry her to the toilet and back, and feed her yet again, soft eggs and toast.

Her right arm had a bandage from shoulder to fingertips and hung in a sling. It was dislocated at the shoulder, badly cut and scraped, he said. Her left hand was also bandaged and burning.

And though she hadn't had the luxury of attempting it, she suspected she would have a difficult time getting around on her own. She wasn't sure if it was her legs or her torso, but every muscle screamed with pain at the slightest attempt to shift her weight, never mind stand up. Not that she didn't want to try, but Luc hovered and made sure he brought everything she could need, insisting she not move without his help. They'd also bandaged her legs in spots, and she was bruised badly in others. Her difficulty shifting her weight spoke to sprains as well. She must have bounced like a cloth puppet, tearing everything as she flipped over and over.

He appeared in the doorway, holding a glass of water. "How can I leave when you can't walk to the toilet or feed yourself?"

"I can feed myself," she sulked, glaring out the window.

"Barely."

"I'm not used to having people do things for me. I don't like it."

"That's too bad. Here." He held the glass of water close and pressed two pills to her closed lips.

She resisted, then remembered the last time she'd refused the acetaminophen. She didn't welcome the full brunt of the pain of her multiple injuries. Damn it! How could she have been so careless she didn't hear the vehicle? She was usually very safety conscious.

She'd spent her entire life working to avoid ever needing help from anyone. It had always been her job to be strong, supportive and solve problems. If she felt pain, sadness or loneliness, well, those were things you just dealt with on your own. You got over them. There was never anyone you could rely on to prop you up when you felt weak, so you couldn't ever let yourself feel weakness.

Now look at her. Helpless as a baby. It made her want to scream in frustration.

She took the pills on her tongue, tasting salt on his fingers as she did, then accepted a few sips of water to wash them down. Warmth gathered in her belly at his touch. She didn't want to find him attractive, but how could she avoid it? Now she was trapped in the net of his intolerably gentle care.

"You're an asshole, doctor."

"Yeah. Apparently. But you're the sweetest patient I've ever had." He chuckled and left the room.

"Fuck off," she mumbled, and closed her eyes, feeling safer and better cared for than she ever had before.

It's a damned good thing she was so helpless, and so damned easy on the eyes, or he'd have thrown in the towel long ago. Or thrown the towel right at her snarling face! How could one small woman be so prickly?

He scowled into the dishwater.

Luc was a patient man. As a teacher of kids, he'd had to learn to maintain equanimity and humour even when the most obnoxious of teenagers did their best to provoke him. But he never reacted, he never lost his temper. He never gave up on them. He understood, implicitly at first, and in time through real concrete experience, the most antagonistic and disagreeable kids cried out for help, for understanding, and for love. Now he understood all those years of training had prepared him for this moment.

Her. Niki. The worst patient in the freaking universe.

He smiled as he cleaned up the dishes and fed the little grey cat. For all Niki's belligerent behaviour, she was more alluring than ever, maybe because her vulnerability showed through the cracks. Which made her all the more defensive. And, at least to him, obvious.

Walking quietly to the door of her room, he peeked in. She dozed again, all the rough edges melted away. Dark lashes lay lightly against her smooth, sun-bronzed cheek, strands of her dark hair strewn across her pillow and the elegant column of her neck, bared now as she lay with her face to the wall. She was just a girl. A young girl despite the impenetrable armour. A beautiful girl who drew him powerfully against his better judgement.

She wasn't what he wanted. She would never give him the life of which he dreamt. Why would he be fascinated by a woman who could never give him what he wanted, and would be too much work, and bring chaos into his life? It made no sense.

Luc was a man in command of himself and his life. He was organized and orderly, calm and conscientious. He was self-aware. He'd thought.

She was tough, resilient, and stubbornly independent, but he'd met no one so reluctant, so downright unwilling, to show vulnerability, or accept help from another person. What the hell had happened to her to make her push people away?

Except Didier, of course. He was the only person she'd allowed close. To everyone else she was friendly but cool. Why? Was it his vulnerability? Was she drawn to help him because of his helplessness?

Luc couldn't be glad she was so badly injured, but the opportunity it gave him to spend time with her, and get to know her better, made him happy. After all his watching her from a distance, she remained as much an enigma to him as she had at first. And his compulsion to be closer to her only increased with time and proximity.

His thoughts circled and circled. It was pointless to revisit the arguments. Patrice was so elegant, competent and mature. A woman who fit into his dreams of family, home and security. He'd always strove to replicate the image his parents created with their loving bond.

Now, he was coming to understand he'd picked up on something else. Something under the surface which wasn't so tidy. Beneath the idyllic family atmosphere they'd painted was a passion for each other superseding anything else, perhaps even love for their children.

Was that why he'd always sensed he was missing out on something? Had he picked up on the simmering undercurrent of devotion they had for each other?

Although Patrice looked like the perfect mate to fulfill his illusion of happiness, it was Niki who awoke his sleeping heart.

It was Niki, in all her inelegant wild irrationality who compelled him and fired his blood. Yes, she was hard work. He could tell, even beyond the challenges of her current discomfort, she would be hard work. She wasn't someone he could control, and he didn't believe she was in control of herself either. She was as unmanageable as a storm. Was that what he wanted, anyway?

No woman had ever awoken in him such a powerful desire to connect, and to protect and... and to possess in the most primal sense. It contradicted everything he was–rational, calm, controlled... civilized!

She was what he wanted. She was what he'd fantasized about and searched for his entire life, under the surface. Even though he was losing control of himself, and he was certain he would lose his perfect dream if he pursued her. Like Odysseus compelled by the Sirens, she would tear him to shreds, or he'd crash on the rocks just coming near.

Yet he couldn't stop himself from trying. He had no Penelope, no home to return to, not without his heart.

But how did one woo a porcupine?

∽

Over the next few days, Luc patiently nursed her back to health, despite her complaints. He cooked for her, and he was a decent cook too. Once she heard mumbled male voices in conversation in the yard. She assumed Charles had come by, probably to bring groceries, and perhaps his personal things, as Luc's shirt changed shortly afterwards. She shouldn't notice or care, but he smelled so good, fresh and masculine.

Luc insisted on spoon-feeding her, since her one half-decent arm was hopelessly clumsy, and she dropped a lot of food when she tried herself. He teased her and told her amusing stories about people and events in the village that made her laugh despite trying not to.

Whenever she asked, he carried her to the bathroom, averted his gaze while he pulled down her pyjama bottoms and eased her onto the toilet, left the room until he heard the flush, then came back and reversed the process, laying her gently back in bed.

Once a day he brought a basin of scented warm soapy water and gave her a tender sponge bath, leaving her for a few minutes to tend to her private parts. He sympathized when her body gave her trouble, though she tried to hide it, tutting and soothing her with sweet words of endearment like a child. He attended every subtle shift in her expression, every indrawn breath, and seemed to know which parts hurt even more than she did.

And through every moment, he was damned fine to look at. She was never in so much discomfort it escaped her notice. He could be a model, he was that breathtakingly handsome, with balanced features. Her eyes revisited his chiseled jaw and brow bone, so exquisite. The shadow of his beard and the straight line of his nose. That mouth. Except, perhaps, that he wasn't all that tall. But more than tall enough for her. She pushed that thought away.

To make matters worse, he was so thoughtful, gentle and patient, she hated him for it. The longer she lay there, helpless, the more her frustration grew, and the more Luc became her punching bag. Even that, he took with equanimity, giving her space when she lashed out with harsh words.

One afternoon after she'd eaten, he cleared the dishes away then brought two cups of coffee to her room, and sat down in the chair beside her bed, handing her one.

"Coffee?" She made a face at him. "So I'm not required to sleep all the time anymore?"

He smiled and took a tentative sip of his hot coffee. "You'll sleep again, I'm sure, if you need it." He set it down and picked up a book.

"What are you doing?"

"Entertaining you."

She groaned and threw her head back onto her pillow. "So your idea of entertaining me is to give me coffee to force me awake and then torture me with some boring French poem?"

His smile was smug, and she didn't want to admit that the fact he was both funny and intelligent made him way too interesting to her. "That's about it. Now be a good girl. Lie back and listen."

She did as he bid, and he surprised her when he began to read some kind of poetry in French. She only knew it was poetry because of the rhythm and cadence of his speech, his soothing, lilting voice, which she loved the sound of no matter what he was saying. He could read an instruction manual and it would be sexy and compelling. And though she knew his French was superb, this took it to a new level. She could understand some the words, but her French was not good enough to understand the poetics, or the hidden meaning. She closed her eyes to absorb the music of his voice.

And yet, as he went on, images formed in her mind, and sensations took shape. His voice was just deep enough to be resonant, with a slight huskiness to the texture, so that the sound of it made her think of sensual things–melting chocolate and sugar crystals, flaky croissants from the patisserie; the feel of ancient limestone arches and pillars cool against her calloused palms and the way parkour energized and empowered her; conjuring images of kisses, caresses and languorous Sunday-morning sex. It also brought up emotions–like joy, sadness and longing. His voice carried emotion in its notes, reminding her of a speaker on the verge of tears.

For no reason she could understand, her face began to heat, and her throat to thicken. Her eyes burned as tears filled them and forced themselves out from under her lids. She lay still, hoping they would reabsorb, or that Luc wouldn't notice, but felt the hot tears sear a path down her temples, cool, and disappear into her pillow.

Luc's voice continued for a time, then faded and finally stopped. Instead of opening her eyes and looking at him, she lay still, like an ostrich, pretending that what she couldn't see didn't exist.

CHAPTER 26

"Niki?"

The poem moved Luc, too. It was one of his favourites, and it was, romantic, in aid of his cause, though she would likely not realize that. But he didn't understand why it would make Niki cry. His acknowledgement seemed to make it worse, and her tears flowed in earnest. She pressed her lips together, but they twisted anyway, her chin quivering. She turned her face to the window wall to hide it, but a sob tore from her chest.

He shifted to sit at the edge of the mattress, feeling the heat of her body against his, and placed his palm gently on her good shoulder. "What is it?"

She could only shake her head and gurgle. It meant–go away. She wasn't comfortable showing emotion, let alone weakness, he knew.

He stroked her brow gently. "It's been a shock, I know. But you'll be okay. It's just your body recognizing that it's been through a trauma. Now it's releasing the adrenalin that the accident caused."

She shook her head again.

Despite his assurances, he knew that was only partly true. There was something else, a wound that went deeper than her dislocated shoulder and torn hip flexor, deeper than the superficial scrapes on her skin. Something about her situation had opened that wound and made it bleed afresh.

Another sob convulsed her, ripping out of her throat, shaking her. Still she fought it. Luc continued to caress her brow and her hair.

She reached her good left hand up and shoved his arm away. "Leave me alone!" Her voice was a wet, soppy mess, and she sounded like a spoiled child.

"Hey. Hey. Calm down."

"This wasn't the idea at all. I'm supposed to be on vacation. I was having fun. This shouldn't be happening. Everything's gone to shit." She turned her head to face him, her drowned eyes filled with recriminations. "Why are you being nice to me? Why do you care? I don't want your attention. I don't want your kindness. Just bugger off!"

Luc stood up. He'd stiffened under her sudden rebuff, but he understood she was hurting, and hating being weak and in pain. Turning his back to her, he picked up a quilt to refold it and set it at the foot of her bed. "So, let me see if I've got this right. It's okay for you to get involved in other people's lives, it's okay for you to help them with their problems, but it's not okay for anyone to help you when you're in need."

"I don't need you! I don't need anyone!" Despite her anger, her tears continued to flow, strangling her voice.

Luc continued to putter around the room, not looking at her, straightening clothing, blankets. He noticed one of Grand-Mère Bougie's bound herb bundles on the dresser. Picked it up, he inhaled the mix of sage and lavender, and set it down gently. "Right. I understand."

"Shut up!"

"Tell me about Didier. What was that about?"

"Nothing. It was about nothing. Why are you always looking for reasons? Didier and I are friends. Friends with benefits. Big deal."

There was nothing left to tidy, so he stood gazing out the window at the tall grasses in Didier's yard, laying flat from neglect and trampling. "I don't believe you. "

"Well, I don't care if you do. Mind your own business."

Luc paused in thought, but also to give her some room to breath. He'd learned, from dealing with his students, that a relentless interrogation resulted in a tantrum, or shutting down. It was better to leave them stewing about the ideas you'd planted, and just be there. After a few minutes, during which he could sense her squirming in discomfort, he continued, keeping his voice calm. No pressure.

"I understand Didier's challenges. Anyone with a caring heart would have wanted to help him." In the silent interlude, she had opened her eyes again and looked up at him. Luc sat in the chair, peering at her, locking gazes with her large, wet eyes, so she couldn't look away. Holding onto the connection.

"Helping people is what I do. It's no big deal."

At last, a crack. He sighed. "I understand what you've done for him, and trust me, I admire you for it. But why you, Niki? What was so compelling about Didier and his problems that made you go against your solitary nature and get involved? Not just involved, but… you reworked your whole trip to make things change for him. Most people wouldn't have done for their closest friends what you did for him. That takes a lot of commitment and conviction. You put yourself at great inconvenience and risk to help him. But why?"

"Why do you care? What's it to you?" Her rigid muscles began to tremble under his relentless focus.

His shoulders lifted in a tiny shrug, and he blinked and looked away again. The question surprised him. "Who can say? In the same way you needed to get involved with Didier, I needed to get involved with you. The moment I met you, you stopped me in my tracks and shook me up. I can't say why. Maybe it's just timing. I'm at a crossroads in my own life, and suddenly there you are, making me see things differently. Making me want different things."

"What do you want?" She eyed him suspiciously.

"I'm trying to figure that out."

"I can't help you."

"No. Maybe not. I'm trying to understand why you made such an effort to help Didier. Usually you keep people away. You're so tough. So independent and stubborn. Then this…" He flipped a hand, palm up. "This fake affair."

She frowned. "It's not fake. Just, no strings."

It was his turn to frown. "It seems extreme to me."

She lifted her left shoulder a titch. "He was uncomfortable with his body. I'm comfortable with mine. I could help him. That's all."

He continued to gaze into her eyes. "There's more."

The tears were back, welling in her shadowed eyes. She didn't want to answer him.

He whispered, an invitation, not a command. She wanted to, he could feel it in his gut. She was so bottled up, so alone in her suffering. "Tell me."

"Damn you! He..." her throat collapsed, and she tried again. "He reminded me of... my brother, okay?"

WTF? Blood rushed to Luc's ears, and his eyes shot open wide. "Your brother? So you slept with someone who reminded you of–"

"Not like that! Jesus!"

"Like what?" His hammering heart slowed as he strove to understand. There was something about Didier.

"Sam was special. He was on the spectrum. And... he was bullied. He..."

Luc drew in a breath, held it, noting she spoke of him in past tense. She would share her story with him. He didn't expect it so soon. A fluttering started in his belly and shimmered outward in waves until his skin tingled. He struggled to keep his voice calm, almost disinterested. The opposite of his true feelings. "Where's Sam now?"

Between her tears and her sobs, she murmured, "He died. He died long ago."

"Hm." But something about Didier raised him from the dead. She had some unfinished business with this brother of hers. "How did he die?"

She squeezed her eyes shut, as though seeing and trying to erase the images she saw. "He... he kil... he comm... committed...," she choked out.

His heart thumped. Suicide! No wonder she grieved. Luc was back by her side, stroking her gently. "Shh. I get it."

While she cried, he stayed beside her, stroking her brow and hair, her shoulder and hip. When the tears at last subsided, he spoke again.

"Tell me more about Sam."

The story poured out of her. How her whole life focussed on little Sam, making everything okay for him. Until one day he wasn't okay. One day when he wasn't so little anymore, life became just too much for him, and she wasn't there to pick up the pieces and put everything into perspective for him, sooth him and distract him, protecting him from the bullies like she always did.

"Poor Niki," Luc murmured. "Who was taking care of you? Where were your parents?"

She stiffened and glanced away. "They weren't..." She pressed her hands to her chest, and a tight, high-pitched moan leaked out of her, as if her poor heart was speaking of its own disappointment and need. "… available," she whispered. "Dad left long before, when I was eight. It was just Mom. Poor overwhelmed Mom. So I had to help. We had to think of Sam and help him. My job was Sam's protector. I learned to take care of myself."

Her entire childhood? Through all her own growing pains and challenges, her own hopes and dreams? Even if her mother had struggled with a special needs child, what kind of parent did that? His heart contracted under a sudden heaviness as Luc tried to envision what that had been like for her, so very different from his own loving, supportive childhood. "I'll bet you did. And what about now, Niki? What do you need now?"

She turned away and closed her eyes again. "Nothing."

"What about Didier? Why get involved with Didier?" He knew the answer, but he had to ask.

"Someone had to stand up for him."

"Why you?"

"Who else?"

He sat in silence, stroking her shoulder, touching her soft mussed hair with the tips of his fingers, pondering the mystery of Niki until his own tears were too close to the surface to tolerate. He thought about her toughness, her independence and spunk. Brittle but resilient. And the wall around her heart that kept everyone away. He picked up the hairbrush on her side table and dragged it gently through her hair, smoothing the tangled strands.

CHAPTER 27

On the fourth day, he stood in the doorway and asked, "Would you like me to wash your hair?"

Niki closed her eyes and gritted her teeth, willing herself to be kind. He didn't deserve her irritability, but she wanted to be free and private. Every kind and caring act grated on her nerves. "Why? Does it look greasy?"

"Niki..." She was trying his patience, she knew from the tone of his voice.

"What do you want from me, Luc?"

Leaning in the doorway to her room, he slipped his hands into the pockets of his faded jeans, and she couldn't stop herself from admiring how they hugged his lean, muscled thighs, and bulged over his package. Cripes, she had to get out of here. She had to get away from him. She was missing Didier and the way he'd awakened her carnal thirsts.

"I don't want anything from you," he said. "Just anticipating your needs. I want to make you more comfortable."

"Well, who asked you to do that?"

He sighed. "Has no one ever taken care of you before?"

A moment passed while she quickly replayed her childhood, her life. "No. And I like it that way. I prefer to do things for myself, so you're really getting on my nerves with all this nursemaid shit."

"So you don't want your hair washed."

"I'd fucking love my hair washed, Luc! My scalp is itching like hell. But I'd rather do it myself, thank you very much."

"How do you intend to do that?"

"Piss off."

He went away and left her to scowl and grumble for a half hour. He returned with a stack of towels and a basin of steaming scented water. Without a word, she submitted again to his tender ministrations. He tucked towels under her, and supported her neck and aching shoulder while her head tipped back over the basin, cupped in his strong palm. He poured cup-fulls of the lovely lavender scented sudsy water over her head. His strong hands were firm and delicious as he gently stroked her brow and massaged her scalp, worked up a lather, and rinsed her hair again until it squeaked.

While he quietly worked, she knew his calm face hovered inches over hers. She kept her eyes averted, staring out the window at a lone apple tree in Didier's yard, the ripening fruit hanging on the drooping branches. Still she was painfully aware of the shape of his strong jaw beneath his trimmed dark beard, the intensity of his steady blue gaze focussed on her face and hair, the sweet scent of tea on his breath fanning her cheek.

He didn't say a word, or force her to meet his eye.

His touch soothed and comforted her, and yet his closeness left her agitated. Not only frustrated at her own helplessness physically, which maddened her, but increasingly defenceless against the rising tide of desire his constant nearness fuelled. The more he touched her, the more he filled her with a shimmering liquid heat that pooled in her core, and throbbed between her legs.

Once he'd towelled her hair dry, he picked up her hairbrush and ran it gently through her locks until it was smooth and straight. He fanned it gently with the hair dryer he'd found in the bathroom, likely Didier's since she didn't travel with one, combing his fingers through it.

"Your hair is beautiful. I love its silkiness," he said, his voice thick. His warm hand slipped over her crown, and let her hair slide through his loose grasp, pulling gently before releasing it. Her scalp felt wonderful.

"It's as ordinary as can be."

"Nuh-uh. It's like dark chocolate. Chocolate silk, thick and straight. And now it smells like lavender."

"Right. You can go."

He swallowed, shook his head a little. He set her back on her pillow, gathered up his supplies and left. A little while later, she heard him walk outside, and the door close.

Well.

She'd got what she wanted. He'd left. Now she could be alone, and wallow in her feelings of guilt for being such a hag, missing his steady presence with an ache in her chest, and longing for his return.

Some time later, she wasn't sure how long had passed because she'd dozed, utterly relaxed after the scalp massage and shampoo, the sound of the door signalled his return. So. He hadn't left her alone for good. Chagrinned, she realized she needed to use the bathroom.

"Luc?"

He moved around in the other room.

"Luc!"

He entered her room and stood beside her bed, his expression inscrutable. "Yes?" He'd changed into a loose fitting tank top and bike shorts, his golden tanned skin and hair wet with perspiration.

So he'd gone for a ride. Her face and neck tingled with shame. Her voice came out a tiny squeak. "I have to pee."

"Just a sec. Let me towel off first." He left and came back rubbing himself with a small towel. He tossed it down and lifted her, and she suppressed a sigh at how much she loved his strong arms. His bare skin was hot and damp, his dark arm hairs plastered down. Her nostrils flared as she took in his fresh musky scent, with grassy notes, and the sweetness of apple as though he'd stopped in a field for rest. "It's killing me you got to ride while I lie here like a dead fish."

"You'll be back in the saddle soon. Give yourself a chance to heal."

Emerging from the bathroom, he took her to the living room sofa instead of to her room. "Would you like a change of view?"

"There you go again, anticipating my needs."

"Excuse me for living. I thought we could chat while I make lunch."

"Fine. Yes, thanks. I'm losing my mind in there."

He set her down, turned on some music, and returned to plop Minou into her lap. "Here's some company for you. I dare you to yell at her. I'm going to shower."

His reprimand silenced her, and she was glad to hold and stroke the little grey cat. She tried to ignore the sound of water running, tried and failed to turn her mind away from the image of Luc's naked lean muscled cyclist's body streaming with hot water, his strong gentle hands lathering himself with soap. An arrow of hot desire shot from her breasts to her womb and she clenched her inner muscles, leaving her aching.

Minou nudged her.

"What would your Papa say if he saw me acting like such a bitch, hey? He'd regret ever taking me in off the street. I wonder how he's doing in Carcassonne."

The little cat's response was to stare at her with wide, round yellow eyes and knead her stomach.

"Yeow. You need your nails trimmed, little girl."

She shifted her weight to remove Minou's claws from her tender flesh. Minou folded her paws and nestled down onto Niki's chest. She blinked and her eyes closed to half mast.

"What I want to know, Minou, is why he stays. I've been horrible and no matter what I do or say, he carries on being thoughtful and gentle and caring and patient. I mean, what the fuck? What's wrong with him? Any sane person would have kicked me in the teeth and ridden out of here days ago."

Minou's steady purring soothed her as she settled in for a nap. Niki closed her eyes, too, and exhaled, listening to the music flow over her.

"What's the matter with me, Minou?" she whispered.

Noises from the kitchen woke her with a start, causing Minou to leap off and dash out the open door. Luc was in the kitchen in a clean t-shirt and shorts, his legs and feet bare. His back was to her, and she watched him chop and assemble salads, shifting his weight from one leg to another. She loved the bunching of his glutes and calf muscles as he moved. She shook her head and looked away.

"You're awake," he said, walking toward her with a tray.

"Yup."

"You looked really sweet snoozing there with Minou on top of you." He grinned, his tanned face creasing at each side of his mouth, and she couldn't stop herself from smiling back at him. "I was kind of envious. She looked cozy."

"Ah…"

Luc set the tray on the coffee table and sat down beside her, shoving her over gently with his butt to make room. He turned to peer at her.

She felt the weight of his gaze, steady, penetrating, questioning.

"Why is it I always feel you know what I'm thinking, but I can never figure out what you're thinking? It's not fair."

"If it's any consolation, at the moment, I have no idea what you're thinking. And I'd happily tell you what I'm thinking."

Is that what she wanted? "Uh. Yes. Sure."

"Well. I was thinking you're looking much better. Not just because your hair is clean." He grinned again, and she felt her breasts tingle and reach out to him. "Are you feeling a bit stronger?"

"Yes. I'm not so preoccupied with my aches and pains."

"Can you stand?"

She nodded. Maybe. "I'd sure like to try."

He helped her to sit up, removed a salad from the tray, and set it on her lap. He'd created a beautiful salade composé, with slices of cold chicken and apple.

She picked up her fork. "This looks delicious. Thank you."

One side of his mouth quirked up. "What? No threats of harm because I made you lunch?"

She stuffed her mouth full of lettuce and chicken so she wouldn't have to reply, and he laughed. She rolled her eyes, loving his laugh, the way he tossed his head back, his teeth white against his beard.

After lunch, he helped her to her feet instead of lifting her. Leaning on him, with his arm supporting her around her ribs, they hobbled together outside. Her hip and groin were tender. By the time she'd gone fifteen feet, she was ready to sit down. He helped her into a patio chair and sat down beside her.

Pulling out a newspaper, he shook it out and began to read aloud. He chose headline news first, tossing in little editorial comments in between, then he told her about the new films were out this summer, then moved on to the social page. Even though he was reading in French, his tone implied he lampooned the rich and famous people he read about. He made faces and used different voices to mimic the characters he was ridiculing. She didn't read in French, except for menus and train schedules, so was surprised that she not only understood him but was thoroughly entertained. They both laughed so hard she moaned and cried, because her ribs and shoulder pained her.

"I'm sorry. I didn't mean to cause you pain."

She shook her head. "It's good to laugh. I enjoy listening to you read in French. You're so good at it. You have a great voice, and…"

"And?"

"And I... I'm... glad for your company. I was bored and... I really enjoy hanging out with you. I'm sorry I've been such a bitch."

"That's putting it harshly. But you have been a rather difficult patient, I'll give you that."

She made a wry expression, glancing away and then back, and their eyes locked. "Why did you stay?"

He twisted his lips to the side. "I couldn't leave you alone in your condition. But... Niki, if you can't tell by now." He swallowed. "I'm fond of you. I mean, even when we first met I... I'm very attracted to you."

Niki felt a giddy fluttering in her chest at his confession and struggled to breathe. Her eyes met his, and she knew he could see that the attraction was mutual. She tore her gaze away. There wasn't anything she could say in response, so she carried on, forcing her next words through a dry throat. "What did you mean when you said you were at a crossroads?"

His eyes wandered past her, across the yard. "I've decided I'm ready to settle down. But... but my life is complicated. I live and work in Vancouver, and there's a woman there that I've been seeing quite a while who's ready to take it to the next level. But I spend every summer here, in France visiting good friends. And..."

"Oh, I see. And you spend the summers with Patrice."

A rosy blush coloured his cheeks. "Recently, yes."

"So you had to choose."

His mouth pulled into a line, and he shook his head. "I'd made no commitment to either of them. First, I had to decide what I wanted. About where to live and work but also... what else I'm looking for."

"In a partner."

He sniffed and nodded. "I like Patrice, and the other woman, too. But I'm not in love with either of them. And I've been wondering if that kind of love is just for fairy tales. Maybe my expectations were too high, and I would never feel that way."

"And?"

"Then I met you."

Their eyes met and held. Niki's heart thumped a strong steady beat in her ribcage, as though it were fighting to escape. Her skin tingled all over. Again she fell into the dark blue pools of his eyes, as though she'd find all the answers she sought there.

"But once you and Didier..." he broke off, shaking his head and breaking eye contact. He looked at his hands, resting on his thighs.

Did he expect her to say something? How could she respond to that? She couldn't tell him she'd been attracted to him since she'd first seen him on the ramp, since that night in the square, by the puppet show. She couldn't tell him that when he was near, she followed him with her eyes, hungry for touch, or that the sound of his mellow voice melted something inside her. Could she?

"You want to know about Didier and me." It wasn't a question.

His Adam's apple slid up and down his neck. "I don't know if I do."

"You know why I did it."

He turned to face her again, his face flushed and his eyes sparking with... something akin to anger. "I understand. But was it really necessary to... to the extent of..." He shook his head.

"He was so stuck, and his self-esteem was low. And it worried him. He was afraid of himself, his lack of experience. He told me I was a catalyst for change. I'm not sure if I knew that's what I was doing. I just followed my gut. He needed help, and I wanted to help him."

"And what now? Are you just going to walk away? You're involved. You could hurt him. Have you thought of that?"

"No. I mean yes. It's all okay. We knew going into it what we were doing, and it's over. People take sex too seriously. We're good friends. Everything's fine between us."

"Why did he go to Carcassonne then? Did you have a fight?"

"No! It's something he's wanted to do. And we needed some space, so the timing was right."

"So when he returns?"

She grinned. "We'll see. He's supposed to ask Amélie out on a date."

Instead of inspiring a corresponding grin, Luc's face was suddenly sombre. His blue eyes burned with intense heat, and again she felt as if he could see right into her soul. He stood up, and without breaking eye contact, bent over her until he brought his face down level with hers. He kept coming, brushing her lips softly with his, and waited a beat. Two. Three.

She kept her face upturned, feeling her nostrils flare with desire. A tiny sound of yearning emerged from somewhere deep inside her. When she didn't pull back or protest, he kissed her again, more firmly this time, holding her jaw lightly between his fingertips, sliding his fingers to caress her neck. His tongue stroked her lower lip, and she opened her mouth to let him enter. As their tongues met and danced, a powerful force seemed to compel her forward, as though in this very kiss, in his embrace, lay her salvation.

CHAPTER 28

He leaned in, his kiss becoming more ardent, until her chair rocked back on its rear legs and he stumbled forward, touching her shoulder as he braced himself.

"Eeyahhhh!" She shouted, half into his mouth, as pain blasted through her.

He lurched upright, grabbing the chair and steadying it. "Oh fuck! I'm so sorry."

She sat for a moment with her eyes closed, waiting for the sudden flood of pain to subside. It didn't take long. The waves of heat that rose from her liquid core soon subsumed any thought of the pain. She opened her eyes to find him bent over her, one hand supported on each arm of her chair, his eyes filled with concern and remorse.

"Are you all right?"

She felt her face stretch into a sultry smile and reached her left hand up to cup his cheek. Looking deep into his blue eyes, she saw his expression morph as he realized she was thinking about anything but pain. The sharp bright compassionate sky blue darkened to a heated indigo. "Niki?"

"Take me inside, Luc."

His eyes widened in disbelief, but he didn't hesitate. He scooped her up in his arms and swept her into the house, marching straight back to her little room with its narrow bed. Setting her down gently, he ripped off his t-shirt and came to her, covering her mouth with his in a hungry kiss before she had half a chance to admire his lean, ripped torso.

He broke the kiss to say, "Are you sure you want this? What about–?"

She opened her mouth and pressed it against his to stop his words, reaching with her tongue, eager to show him how much she wanted for him. He responded in kind, and in moments they were both panting, moaning and grunting with curbed desire.

He sat back, his hungry eyes raking over her body. Lifting one hand, he set it gently on her stomach, caressing gently, grazing the underside of both breasts, one after the other. Her nipples tightened and her breasts throbbed with the need to feel his touched. She felt her ribs arch up to meet his caress, begging for more.

"I've been hot for you for days, lying here suffering while you walk around strutting your stuff in front of my helpless eyes."

He laughed, breaking the spell. "Strut? It wasn't exactly easy on me washing you and touching you every day." He planted kisses on her face and chin and neck as he spoke. "But Nik, this won't work." He sat back. "As much as I'm dying to bury myself in you and rut like a bull, you're not ready."

"Keep talking like that. I am so ready."

He laughed softly and pecked her mouth, then again, and again, as though he couldn't tear himself away.

His words and hers triggered a corresponding flush through her body, and she felt a gush of wetness between her legs in anticipation. She felt her nostrils flare. "I need you, Luc. I can't wait."

"I'm here for you, but we're going to have to get creative. With your pulled tendons, I can't bear to hurt you." She'd been wearing her usual soft baggy sweatpants without underwear, to make dressing easier. Luc inserted his thumbs under the waistband and started to slide them downward over her hips, dragging his fingertips over her hot sensitive flesh as he inched them down, exposing her to his eyes for the first time. Or was it?

"Hey! Who undressed me the first time, when I was unconscious?"

His mouth slowly curled up at the corners, while his shadowed blue eyes peered at her from beneath hooded lids. There was nobody else here.

Her hips lifted, reaching for him, his touch, his caressing eyes. "It was you, wasn't it? All this time you've been such a gentleman, averting your eyes, but you saw me naked already."

His smile stretched into a grin, and his answer was to lower his face to her belly and plant a gentle kiss there. "If it's any solace, I was too concerned about you to be aroused."

"Liar. You're a man, aren't you?"

"Okay, but I gave myself shit for it." He tossed her sweatpants aside, laying his hot palm over her mound and pressing, holding it there until she thought she'd die of need. His eyes drank her in, and his breathing sped up. He applied just enough pressure to tease her and cause her hips to press back, searching for more. More targeted pressure. More satisfaction. The aching emptiness inside her throbbed.

"Touch me, Luc."

"I plan to." Instead of doing what she thought he'd do, what she wanted him to do, he slid his sensitive fingertips across her quivering stomach, across her ribs, and slowly pushed up the hem of her tank top, exposing her small breasts an inch at a time. His hands shook. "I've wanted you for so long, it's been killing me watching you with him. I can't believe this is me, touching you at last."

She shushed him. "Don't talk about that."

"I love this spot." He bent to kiss the soft curve of flesh at the bottom of one breast, sliding his lips up to circle her nipple with his tongue. She sucked in a breath and pushed her ribs forward, wanting more. The movement caused a jolt of pain to shoot from her shoulder up her neck. "Ow!"

He sat up, pressing his lips together, sucking in his cheeks. Dipping his chin, he peered up at her with pinched eyes. "I don't know, Niki."

Her voice came out whispered and urgent. "Please… please don't stop. I promise I'll be still."

"You'd better, or else…"

He kissed her again, slowly, luxuriously exploring her mouth with his hot tongue, nipping and nibbling on her lips, travelling along her jaw to lick and suck at her sensitive neck, while his palms lightly covered her breasts, circling and rubbing with just the right teasing pressure. His touch was electric, his skill out of this world. Under his expert hands, she forgot Didier and every other lover she'd ever had. Luc brought a whole new level of amazing.

She tried to hold herself still, despite every cell straining up toward him, wanting to touch him all over. A vibration deep within built and built until her entire body quivered. He anchored her with one hand, cupping her between her legs, exploring her wet folds with the tips of his fingers, maintaining the steady, maddening pressure on her clit. She moaned into his mouth.

He paused for breath, gazing into her eyes. "I want you so fucking much."

He turned his body, shifting his hands to hold both her hips in his grip, his thumbs lying on either side of her vee, caressing gently, reminding her of where he wanted to be, where she wanted him. He scowled at the foot of her bed, where there a wooden slatted footboard stuck up above the mattress by eight inches. "There's not much room here." She could see him trying to puzzle out the logistics of loving her without hurting her. "Sideways it is, I guess." He shifted her hips a little toward the edge of the bed, and knelt to kiss her between the legs.

"Take off your shorts," she hissed.

He shook his head. "There's no way, Niki, with your pulled hip flexor. No way I'm gonna–"

She smiled. "There's nothing wrong with my mouth."

He looked stricken, his eyes unfocussed as he realized what she meant. "Ah–"

"Don't argue with me. I can be a real shrew if I don't get my way."

He didn't take much persuading. He stood up and dropped his shorts to the floor his magnificent erection bounding free.

"Stop."

He stopped. "What?"

"I just want to look at you. You've had the advantage over me. Give me a sec to take it all in." His eyes jumped to hers at her suggestive language, and she smiled again. Then she let her gaze drop from his face downward, caressing his taut, lean muscled body with her eyes, lingering on his beautiful cock. For all he was maybe fifteen inches shorter than Didier, the difference between their dick size was negligible. She adored his body. While Didier was buff, he was also beefy. Luc had no spare flesh. He resembled the idealized statue of a Greek god, every muscle defined but long and lean, from hours and hours of cycling. It excited the hell out of her, just looking at him, he was so perfect.

"Okay. Come here."

He stepped to the edge of her bed, bent and kissed her again until they were both straining and moaning and he had to hold her still. Her teeth vibrated with the intensity of her need. Then she pushed him away, and he turned and straddled her, a knee on either side of her hips, exposing his tight little biker's ass and full, taut scrotum to her eyes. In an instant, his mouth lowered to her core, darting his tongue out to lick, then zero in on her hard, swollen nub. He sucked gently at her heated flesh, and she would have screamed, but chose that moment to reach for him with her good hand. He jerked when she grazed his balls with her calloused palm, and brought him long and hard, to her mouth. He stiffened and released a guttural moan as she gripped him firmly but gently, and circled the head of his cock with her tongue, round and round, slowly slipping more and more of him into her mouth, teasing and tracing the ridge on the underside with her curled tongue.

He grew even harder, and she felt his pulse throbbing in his swollen member, even as she lost all sense of time and space as he flicked at her tender flesh with his tongue, then dove into her, sucking, flicking, exploring her depths in turns. Her trembling had become violent with the effort to hold her injured limbs still. It was as though restraining her natural animal movements channelled all of her passion into the tiny muscles, and to the surface of her burning skin.

Letting him set the pace, they found a common tempo, his body rocking in time with the movements of his talented tongue. In synchronicity, she squeezed him and slid her wet lips and tongue up and down quickly again and again to his rhythm. Their shared passion built to a frenzied crescendo that blocked out all other sensation, even her latent aches and pains, until they crested together like the finale of a huge symphonic movement, moaning, rigid, like a frozen serpent eating its own tail for eternity.

Afterward, he slid from her mouth, trembling in his effort not to collapse on top of her frail body. Turning around, he slid into the gap between her and the wall, kissing her, so their flavours mingled on their tongues, hovering in that place of bliss for several long timeless moments while their thundering hearts calmed. "... most amazing... thing... ever..." he croaked, burying his face in her hair and going still. She agreed. For a long time, she couldn't tell where he ended, and she began.

∽

The last thing Luc wanted was to leave Niki's side, but he had to speak to Patrice before spending another day in Niki's arms, in her bed, without taking care of his affairs. So later in the evening, while she slept soundly, he slipped out and rode back to Charles's house.

This whole thing had caught him utterly by surprise. He'd expected to have to wait longer, fight harder, to get to this point, if it was destined to happen at all. He hadn't even known what the status was of her fling with Didier, when this all started.

He knew their chemistry was off the charts, but he hadn't realized that their forced intimacy was having the same effect on her as it had on him. My god, if he had to strip the clothing off of her incredible body one more time he thought he'd explode. Apparently all the touching, steamy eye contact and growing closeness had had the same impact on her.

He thought he'd have more time to speak with Patrice. He was going to anyway, there was no going back now, and he knew it, but he'd been cowardly and put it off. He was painfully conscious that he'd given Patrice the wrong impression. As they'd been lifelong friends, and were as close as a family, the last thing he wanted was to hurt her. It didn't seem like something he wanted to tackle when he couldn't commit the proper time to see it through. To spend as much time as Patrice needed explaining. Now he was forced to rush the matter so he could get back to Niki quickly.

This was something he had to do. Even if Niki didn't want to be with him. He would never settle for something less than real just to satisfy some arbitrary life list, some imaginary deadline, or some idealized dream. What he felt now was real, so real and so powerful, he would never settle again.

When he pulled into the driveway, both Patrice and Charles' cars were in the drive. He paused. He would rather deal with them separately. Those were two completely different conversations, in his mind.

He found them sitting together at the dinner table, finishing their wine and talking.

"Hey you two," he said, strolling in. "Where's Francine tonight?"

"Visiting her sister," Charles replied. "Have you eaten?"

So, he was stuck with Charles. Luc shook his head. He couldn't eat anything at the moment, though he suspected he was hungry. He and Niki had stayed in bed all afternoon, talking about their travels, their lives, their likes, and their families, playing, gently, with each other's bodies, finding pleasure again and again in subtle and creative ways, without actually consummating, so to speak, their new relationship. That was an event he could hardly wait for, despite being thoroughly spent.

"What's up with you? You look thrashed?" Charles asked.

"Uh." Luc swallowed, suddenly nervous, and accepted a glass of Bordeaux from Patrice, who sidled up and gave him *les bise* as she passed with dirty plates in her other hand. He kissed back absently, his mind whirling. "I've just, um, not been sleeping well. Strange place, you know." Why was he prevaricating?

Charles raised his brows and gave him a condescending smirk. He never could pull one over on Charles. They'd known each other too long. In fact he'd be shocked if Charles couldn't tell he'd had sex. Charles could always tell. It was, in fact, how Charles first found out he'd been sleeping with Patrice, though they'd been sneaky about it. Charles had always teased him for being so transparent.

"I was hoping to speak with Patrice," Luc mumbled. "Alone."

"I see," said Charles, rising.

Patrice stood behind him. "Don't be silly, *cher*. What could you possibly say to me that Charles can't hear?" She patted her hands in the air in her brother's direction. "Stay. Don't get up," she commanded her brother, almost sharply.

Luc detected a strange tension in the air between them. Messages were passing back and forth with eye contact and subtle facial tics that Luc couldn't help but notice, but also couldn't decipher.

"Fine," Charles sat back, resigned, and topped up his wine glass. "I will stay and witness. I admit I'm intrigued." He peered at Luc, eyes narrowed. "*Commencer, mon frère.*"

On the spot, Luc stalled by drinking more wine. Then he took a chair and indicated that Patrice sit as well. Perhaps with a table of glassware between them, she wouldn't slap him. Although she could throw something breakable at him.

This was the hardest thing for Luc. He never could stand to disappoint others. Especially those he loved, his family and closest friends. He would go to great lengths to ensure their happiness. He'd do anything for them. Well, almost anything. He couldn't marry Patrice. That was just wrong.

Realizing he was holding his breath, he exhaled, puffing his cheeks, searching for the right opening.

"Okay. I'll just say it, since we've known each other so long. And take whatever consequences you decide I deserve."

"*Mon Dieu, crache le morceau.* Spit it out already," Charles grumbled.

Luc glared at Charles, then met Patrice's gaze steadily. "I have something important to tell you."

Patrice stared back a long moment, then pulled something from her lap and set it on the tabletop, her hands resting lightly over it. He glanced down and was utterly horrified to see the small velvet jeweller's box that had been, to the best of his knowledge, at the back of his sock drawer in the guest room. He froze, his heart hammering and his head buzzing. Fuck!

"Luc?"

He forced himself to look up, meeting her gaze again. She waited, patient and expectant, but for what? Were they both sitting here expecting to hear his proposal? Did they think he would propose with Charles sitting there staring at him? The irony was overwhelming. He glanced at Charles, horrified to see him struggling to hold in laughter. Without thinking, he kicked him under the table, hard on the shin.

"*Merde!*" Charles barked, his face screwing up in pain.

Why was Charles behaving like a child? Why was Luc? This was serious adult business. That was the problem with knowing these two all his life. And they knowing him.

He sighed. "Fine. Look. Patrice." He met her gaze steadily, bravely. "I know we've been hooking up these last two summers. And it's been lovely. And I know I've likely been acting like… I mean perhaps giving you the impression that… that I think we have a future. A permanent future. But I've been thinking, and… and… it just isn't right. I love you, cherie. But I love you like a sister. Well, not quite a sister, since we've… you know. But as a friend. A dear, dear friend. But I can't follow through on…" He gestured at the box under her hands. "I thought maybe, but no."

The room fell silent. Luc continued to stare at Patrice's face, awaiting her reaction. It came slowly. As he spoke, her expression remained placid. Then her delicate brow crinkled slightly, her eyes widening, as she realized he wasn't saying what she had expected him to say. He scrambled to explain.

"I've... fallen for someone else. I didn't expect it to happen. I didn't see it coming, I–"

Then he watched her face tighten with emotion as she held in her feelings, her eyes going glassy and her lovely lips pressing together firmly. Finally, she dropped her head onto her folded hands, and he sat in stunned silence and watched the top of her blond head, and her white shoulders shake.

He grimaced as guilt swamped him. "Patrice. I'm so, so sorry. *Ma chere.*" Dragging a hand through his hair, he choked on the sudden tightness in his throat. I'm such an ass! He'd only been thinking about himself, and Niki, and been so absorbed with her accident and their new relationship. He'd completely neglected Patrice, and now he was dropping her like a hot rock. He'd completely taken her for granted.

He leapt from his chair and rounded the table, taking her shoulders between his hands and dropping his mouth to the top of her head. He kissed her there, murmuring words of comfort. "*Je suis desolé. Je ne voulais pas te blesser.*"

Lifting his eyes to Charles, he was confounded to find his best friend in the throws of silent laughter. What the fuck? He stood upright. Patrice too was in hysterics, of the comical kind.

"What am I missing?"

Patrice turned to him, trying to bring her laughing face under control, and speaking in a soft and soothing tone. "Luc, Luc. Stop worrying. I'm not hurt." She took his puzzled face between her hands and met his gaze earnestly. "First of all, you reek of sex. Yuk." She pinched his cheek and Charles' laughter burst out loud. "Charles and I were talking over dinner about how to let you down. I found the ring while looking for something a friend left here." She lifted the ring box as evidence and it sat there on the palm of her elegant hand like a beacon shining a light on his idiocy. "I'm sorry we invaded your privacy. I assumed this was for me, and I was trying to think of how to let you down easy, to not hurt you, cher."

He closed his mouth and frowned, taking the box. "It was for you. I'm sorry. I'm a fool."

"It's all right, darling. Remember, we know you well, and we love you always."

A light went on in his head. "You would have said no. That's what you were talking about before I came in? How you would reject me?"

She nodded, and glancing at Charles, this was confirmed. "I tried to convince her she had nothing to worry about. I knew, since the hospital, that you were lost."

"What we've been doing, it's..." She shrugged. "You know, *cher*. It was fun for a while. But it wasn't... I love you, too, Luc, but the earth, you know, it didn't move." She gave him a sly side-eye, for of course he knew what she meant. Their shared intimacies had been... pleasant. He never knew that she expected more. But she was a French woman. Perhaps he should have known.

He pressed the heel of his hand to his chest as the pressure lifted, and an all over sensation of giddiness filled him. "So. We're good?"

She smiled. "We're good."

He felt his face stretch in a wide smile as the feeling of relief swamped him. "Uh... I have to go back. Niki's sleeping, but, she needs me."

Charles stood up, still laughing, and slapped him on the back. "Go, go."

CHAPTER 29

The next twenty-four hours passed in a blur of laughter and passion as Niki and Luc indulged in their newfound intimacy. All Niki wanted was to be well again so she could get as close to him as possible and engage in some athletic lovemaking. Sadly, the pulled muscles in her hip, legs, abdomen and shoulder made a large movement of any kind painful and difficult. Spreading her legs was one of the most difficult things of all, and she shuddered at the thought. Her new goal, therefore, in between heated eye contact, long, delicious kisses, and teasing bedroom talk, was to work on physiotherapy and get her body working again.

"What do you think you're doing?"

"Walking," she replied, although it could barely be called walking. Her steps were tiny and stiff, and she couldn't cover much distance, but she wouldn't give up.

In two strides he caught up with her. His arms came around her, his mouth to her neck, sucking and biting. "You're very easy to catch."

They both laughed, and she shoved his arms away with her good hand. "Leave me be. I need to rehabilitate. And soon."

"What's your hurry?" There was laughter in his voice.

She turned, and that was another ten minutes of hot and heavy necking.

"You aren't ready for physio, Nik, let alone full-on sex. You need to heal. Give yourself time. We can wait."

"I can do it. I'm fit. If I send my body the signals it needs to get back to work, it'll heal quicker." She began another tedious lap around the sofa.

"What kind of work did you have in mind?" he teased.

"Would you leave off, already!"

And later, when she had exhausted herself, Luc lay down with her, wrapped his arms around her, and they dozed together. When one of them stirred, the other awoke, and they began again with gentle and curious caresses that slowly built in intensity, until the lust overtook them, and frustrated them with their inability to take their passion to fruition, at least in the conventional way. They were like two hungry and creative teenagers, forbidden the ultimate act, and restricted to small, stolen gestures. The advantage they had was that no one was there to catch them at it, and they were not obliged to keep their clothes on. Niki thought they'd pleasured each other in all possible ways by the end of the long day.

Luc was a tireless and creative lover. She encouraged him to slip in from the back, even though it would be more awkward, and she was still stiff, but he said no. He wanted to wait, and look into her eyes, kiss her mouth, when they joined. It sated her, and yet she was still hungry for Luc's body. How could she not be? Until she had his cock buried in her, and, as he liked to say, rutting like a bull, she would still want more.

Wanting her consumed Luc. He kept himself busy, continuing to take care of her every need, although she stubbornly hobbled around trying to get mobile again.

While she resolutely pushed herself through an endless series of exercises and stretches, he cooked, cleaned and, when there was nothing else to do, sat and read his books. His concentration, though, was fragmented because he couldn't stop himself from looking up and just taking her in. Every line and curve, every mannerism and determined expression that flitted across her brow, fascinated him.

Yes, he wanted her. But he was secretly, perversely, glad she still couldn't move around much. Something told him he should relish every moment she was stuck here with him at Didier's farm, alone together. She was a force of nature, and couldn't be contained for long.

Some instinct, some feeling in his gut, told him if she could, she'd slip out of his grasp as easily as a wisp of smoke.

She hadn't asked him to take her into the village, yet, and he hadn't suggested it. They'd only just discovered each other, letting their barriers down. It was too soon to spoil their bliss with outside influences. They would come soon enough. Didier would come home eventually.

If he could, he'd preserve this idyllic state forever. Strangely, for all the dating and casual relationships he'd experimented with, he'd never lived with a woman and he'd never experienced this cocoon of intimacy, domestic comfort, post-coital torpor and affection with another woman. But he liked it. He liked it a lot.

Maybe this was some part of his makeup he instinctually knew. Maybe this was why he'd always known he wanted marriage and a family with some special woman, if he could only find her.

He loved that he could glance across the room and take his fill of her while they were each engaged in different activities. As though they connected wirelessly, she seemed to sense he was thinking about her, feel his eyes caressing her skin, and she would look up, meet his hungry gaze and smile. In those moments his heart felt full, and he was dizzy with happiness.

And just as he wallowed in those feelings, he would realize he was playing with fire. She filled him up, made him feel alive, but he knew part of it was that he was out on a ledge. This was risky. Crazy. Dangerous. He might risk everything for her, just to feel this passionate and complete again. Maybe, even, every day. But did he expect too much?

A terrible weight pushed down on his chest, crushing the breath out of him, pushing upward to fill his throat with an ache as though his heart knew the danger and wished to flee.

Every time forever thoughts meandered through his head, he recognized how foolish he was being, letting his heart run wild with a woman he'd just met, a woman he, truthfully, hardly knew, except to know this one thing. That she was a woman who was terminally afraid of commitment. Probably she would take his open beating heart, stomp on it with her restless shoes, and leave it in the ditch, bleeding pulp.

∽

While their everything-but lovemaking sated her body, and still left her frustrated from desire, there was another part deep inside Niki that was shaking with fear. Being with Luc wasn't like being with Didier, where she knew at the outset why she was there, what would happen, and that she would go back to being Niki Ballantyne, footloose and fancy free. Back to her fast-paced and independent life. It wasn't just about physical pleasure. Being with Luc was nothing like that.

He was different.

If there's one thing Niki understood, it was her body and its environment. But her inner world was a dark, scary place she hadn't explored. She wasn't sure she wanted to. Nobody had made her feel anything like this. Nobody made her feel anything at all except pain. Until now.

It scared the bejeezus out of her.

She couldn't help but wonder if it was Luc himself, or Luc's self-professed desire to settle down with the right woman in the immediate future that frightened her. He was the perfect picture of the man she'd never known–protective, devoted, caring. Growing up without a father, she hadn't known it. Was he even real?

Perhaps Chief and the other guys she worked with in search and rescue had that quality. It took a selfless, brave and big-hearted man to do that kind of work. The ones who were merely thrill-seekers never made it in the field. You had to have it together and care, really care, to be a successful search and rescue worker. There was too much on the line. Everyone had to trust their fellows, and to trust, you had to connect to life. You had to want to get in, make the rescue and get out alive. You had to want to go home again at the end of a shift. And that took a team. Maybe it was that powerful connection with life that drew her to the work. Maybe those incredible men were part of the reason she loved going out on a mission.

But that's not what she was looking for in a relationship. Was is? She was in the prime of her life, only twenty-six years old. She enjoyed her freedom, in more ways than one. And she wasn't about to give up her hard-earned position on the search and rescue crew, or on her exciting rope access contracts, to stay home and raise somebody's babies.

The very thought of such cloying domesticity made her break out in a cold sweat, even though he was a man she wouldn't mind spending more time with. A heaviness settled in her chest as she realized she'd have to tell him he'd set his sights on the wrong girl.

But then she thought about Patrice, with her silky blond hair and fashionable, elegant clothing, snatching up Luc and forcing him to be her whipping boy in Toulouse. She didn't think Luc would like that at all. He was better than that, but he really wanted to settle down.

What about this other woman back in Vancouver? He said he wasn't in love with her either, but they'd been seeing each other for quite a while. He knew her better than he knew Niki. He would probably end up marrying her if Niki cut him loose. Then they'd bump into each other at the Save-On-Foods back home. Wouldn't that be...

Her stomach rolled, and tension grabbed the back of her neck. A burning sensation pressed at her eyelids. That would be horrible.

The thought of Luc settling with another woman, belonging to another woman, even one she'd never met, made her skin creep with tension. It felt wrong.

She'd have to avoid him. In her own hometown. Even though they didn't know each other before, now they'd run into each other all the time. She pictured herself darting into the frozen food aisle to hide from him.

She chuckled. This was becoming absurd.

First, they had nothing except a brief, very awkward fling going on. It wouldn't amount to anything in the time they had left. Second, she couldn't even imagine conflict with someone as easygoing and steady as Luc. That was one thing she liked about him. No angst. He was like a safe harbour, soothing her stormy seas.

Luc strolled into the living room, wearing only a pair of boxer shorts, jarring her from her circular thoughts, forcing her eyes to follow his movements, as he always did. He flashed his gorgeous smile her way and her heart cat-leapt and back-flipped like a *traceur* in her chest. All her doubts and fears fled out the window like a startled bird. One thought remained. She wanted him.

She cleared her throat, pursuing another direction her thoughts had taken her. "Doesn't Patrice wonder where you've been all week?"

He stopped, staring at the floor. "We talked last night. I popped over while you slept."

Her stomach hardened. He'd snuck out to see Patrice last night? After they'd spent the afternoon in bed together? "Hedging your bets?"

"Not funny. I'm not... we're not..." He sighed. "We're like family. I felt I had to make my... our new situation clear."

Luc would do the right thing. Naturally. "Don't do anything rash on my account."

His brows shot low over darkening eyes. "What does that mean?"

She couldn't meet his penetrating eyes. Why was she being such a bitch about it? "Nothing. Just that... you're so clear about what you want. I'm not."

"My reasons for talking to Patrice have nothing to do with what you and I do. I just feel differently now."

She shrugged.

He strode over. "Don't get weird on me Niki. I never meant to freak you out with my confessions. It's just changed things for *me*. My feelings I mean." He reached across the back of the sofa and caressed her cheek with his knuckles, frowning down at her.

She caught his hand in hers and smiled up at him, his nearness, his scent making her stomach flutter with desire. She tried to ignore the twitches of adrenaline that surged through her limbs. The urge to run, and jump and flip jolted through her like a bolt of electricity. But her injuries kept her here, immobile, gritting her teeth. Then he bent to kiss her on the lips and carried on his way to the other room.

Aaaaahhh! Now she was panicking. Not wanting to say or do anything to alienate him or drive him away, all the pushing and pulling was happening inside her head, inside her heart. But the result was that she felt herself withdrawing from him. Already.

A space was opening up. It made her feel a little safer. But it also made her world feel like it was spinning slowly, coming to a stop.

CHAPTER 30

Late the next morning, the front door banging open startled them awake. Luc bolted upright and leapt from the bed, lending credence to the feeling they were teenagers involved in illicit petting.

Niki's heart pounded against her ribs. Didier was home! She whispered, "It's Didier."

She wasn't sure why she felt the need to hide the fact they were together but Luc seemed to agree. He scanned the room, grabbing his clothes and pulling them on, straightening and folding hers. "Stay there. Lie down."

She did as he instructed while he pulled the quilt over her naked body and smoothed it. Blinking at her, he reached for her hair, combing it with his fingers, tucking it behind her ears. He gestured for her to lie down and pretend to sleep. With one last glance around, he kicked a few stray things under her bed and picked up the tray with the remnants of last night's meal on it, and moved to the door.

"Luc," she hissed.

He turned.

"Your shirt's inside-out."

"Fuck." He set the tray down, ripped off his shirt, giving her one last peek at his gorgeous, rippled chest, flipped the shirt right side out and pulled it back on. Then he picked up the tray and opened the door, while she flopped back down and closed her eyes.

"Hey there, Didier," she heard Luc whisper.

"What?" Didier's shocked voice. "What are you doing in my house?"

"Shhhhh," Luc hushed him and led him away from her door, perpetuating the ruse she was still sleeping and he'd popped in her room to tidy up. Then she heard their low, murmuring voices without making out the words. Didier's voice rose once, in shock. Luc would be filling Didier in about her accident, and how he came to be staying in Didier's house.

Would now be the time to 'awaken?' She was eager to see Didier after his trip, a mix of excitement and dread swirling in her gut. After the past few days, she wasn't sure how she felt about either of the two men. That they stood together in the kitchen talking about her sent a shiver of unease up her neck. What was Luc thinking? What about Didier? Could he tell that she and Luc had become lovers? If so, what would he think of her? Would he be hurt?

Suddenly all the intimacy and complexity of being in any relationships at all overwhelmed her and she had a strong urge to return to her solitary ways. Mentally she shook herself. So many unusual events had happened in the past couple of weeks. Was there something magical in the water of this old Medieval village? Or maybe it was the French country air.

How would she feel when she saw both men together? It wasn't as if she was in a real relationship with either of them, but anyone would agree this was a weird situation. She would never have allowed it to happen if not for her accident, her resultant helplessness, and that she was vacationing in a village in France. None of this was normal.

Jumping from one lover to another was not her habit, let alone in the same house, in the same week. In fact she hadn't really had a regular lover for several years, and few sexual encounters in the meantime. Now she had more on her plate than she could handle. The weight of it hit her in the gut like the thrust from a helicopter blade, churning.

She heard footsteps nearing, and forced herself to lie still, feigning sleep. For now, it seemed the easiest solution. The door opened a crack.

"She's still sleeping," Luc whispered.

"Okay. I'll check on her later. Thank you for everything, Luc. I'm so relieved you found her when you did and could stay and care for her." Worry coloured Didier voice.

"Not a problem, man. My pleasure. Although I'll warn you, she's not the easiest patient. Kinda cranky. She really doesn't care much for being helpless and depending on others."

Oh, thanks Luc, for the dig. She smiled at his teasing comment, clearly meant more for her than for Didier. She'd earned it.

Both men shared a quiet chuckle, leaving her scowling at her eyelids.

"I'll keep that in mind."

She must have fallen asleep again, because she woke up sometime later when Didier brought a tray with tea and pastries into her room.

"Didier! You're home," she pushed herself up to look at him. He seemed different than she remembered. Huge, for sure, and still handsome in his fresh-faced blond farm-boy way, but something else had changed. He stood straighter and met her eye more directly. His smile was ready and confident. "You look great. How was your trip?"

He frowned. "I'll tell you all about it later. Tell me how you are. I can't believe this happened to you the moment I left. I feel terrible."

"Don't. It's not your fault. It just happened."

Didier came in and set the tray down on the bedside table. He'd made her a toasted croissant with cheese and a mug of tea. Where did all these lovely, caring men come from? If she'd met one before, she might have hung on to him, and she'd be an old married woman by now instead of having adventures in the south of France. She felt heat flood her face. Where had that thought come from?

"You're so lucky Luc found you."

The truth of that hit her in the chest like one of Didier's hammers. "I am, really lucky." If he hadn't come by, recognized her twisted bike and taken her to hospital, nursed her this past several days… well it didn't bear thinking about. She owed him a lot.

"He saved my life. Is he still here?" She lifted her mug and took a sip of tea, keeping her eyes down.

"No. He went back to Charles' place. He said he hadn't been back since he brought you here."

"Ah." Except that one time. Naturally, he'd be eager to return to his own life once Didier was here to take care of her. Maybe he'd had second thoughts about Patrice. She should have expected as much. She wondered if he'd told her the truth about Niki, or had left that door open.

Maybe their time together was just an anomaly, a brief interlude caused by opportunity and proximity. Maybe she misread all his affection and enthusiasm, and over-reacted. Maybe it meant no more to him than her brief fling with Didier, and he thought it was over. That should come as a relief.

So why did Luc's sudden abandonment leave her feeling so desolate? After all their intimacy, he hadn't even said goodbye.

∼

Luc didn't want to leave her, but being in Didier's house was awkward. Seeing Didier, knowing what he'd done with Niki, what Luc himself hadn't yet done, drove him mad. And he could hardly explain to Didier what had been happening between Niki and himself in the past few days, could he? That wasn't his news to share, with Niki pretending to sleep on the other side of the bedroom door. Except for his confession to Patrice and Charles, that was still a private matter.

Luc had to acknowledge that, though he didn't like Niki's radical intervention, it seemed to have shaken Didier out of his complacency. He really had more confidence now. Was that his new worldliness, or the trip to Carcassonne? Or was it just Niki's no-nonsense acceptance and friendship?

Still, he'd rather be with her than anywhere else. She consumed him. But he could tell she felt… something, some kind of reticence about their being together. She had pulled away from him, like a dagger dragged from a wound. Awareness of his own vulnerability, the threat of his life blood spilling out of the gaping hole she would leave in his heart if she left, chilled him to the bone.

He was being melodramatic. And intense. *No wonder I scare her.*

He filled his lungs and let out a huge sigh. Maybe he'd built this up too much with all his dreaming and planning for his perfect future. Still, this was real. Niki was real and what they had together, well… it wasn't his dream, but it was his heart's desire. Now he didn't know what to do about it, except he couldn't let her go.

CHAPTER 31

Niki knew one thing. She had to get mobile again. Lying around doing nothing, and being waited on like an invalid was making her squirrelly, and she also needed to get back on her bike or she'd never be ready to complete the last leg of her trip and fly home on schedule. She was due back at work. She needed to ramp up her intensive recovery plan.

And it was also long past time to get out of Didier's house. Although they were both doing their best to be lighthearted about it, there was a definite undercurrent of tension. She wasn't sure, though, if it was the residue of their previous intimacy, or whether it had something to do with what Didier had deduced about her and Luc. Either way, he needed his privacy, and she needed hers. With the festival over she ought to find a room in town for her last few days.

"Let me help you with that," Didier said, rushing to her side as she attempted to dress herself.

"No, please, Didier. I have to do it myself. A little effort and stretching is good for my recovery."

"But I can see you struggling. Your shoulder still bothers you."

"It will for some time I imagine. But it doesn't matter. I'm an athlete. I'm used to pain. I need to get on my bike to finish the trip."

"That is not a good plan, little monkey. You can change your ticket and fly out of Toulouse, or I can drive you to Bordeaux to catch your flight. It's only about an hour."

"I can't ask that of you, Didier. I want to do it this way. It's what I set out to do."

He shook his head, frowning. "When must you leave?"

"Less than a week. But I want time to explore Bordeaux, too, once I get there. And I won't if I'm lying around here. The plan was not to spend three weeks in one village, and a week of it lying in bed."

"I can't see it. You can barely walk."

Finally dressed, she hobbled out to the living room. "I'll be fine. But I need physio. I need to move around before my muscles atrophy. Hey can you get me some things in town?"

"Of course."

She described the supplements she needed for her recovery. It was a long list of minerals, bioflavonoids, anti-inflammatories, and collagen and enzyme supplements. She wrote them all down and handed him the list.

"Merde. You eat all this?"

"If I want to heal I do. Do you think you can find it?"

He shrugged. "I know who to ask."

He followed her to the yard. She hobbled over to his shop, and around the end to the watermill and creek. It was cooler here in the hot August afternoon. But she didn't let herself sit by the creek and relax. Instead, she walked back and forth, and did some small, gentle exercises, testing the range of motion of her pulled hip and shoulder. The right side of her body would be tender for months, but she was in excellent physical shape, so she could handle it.

Glancing up, she found him standing, watching her. "Don't you have work to do?"

"Plenty of time."

"Tell me about Carcassonne. Was it a success? Did you get new business?"

He broke into a grin. "I did. I met with a few shop-owners and got orders for several small items they want to stock. Some of my blades and household things. But the best part was getting to know Georges Lousiers."

His face lit up, and she paused her exercises to listen to him, enjoying his enthusiasm.

"He's the director of historical artifacts for the town and reports to the local agent for UNESCO responsible for the heritage site. He set me up for an interview to add me to the list of pre-approved contractors for site restoration work overseen by the Centre des Monuments Nationaux. It's their responsibility to plan and schedule this conservation and development work."

"That sounds important, Didier. Wow. Good for you."

"It is. It's what I always wanted and worked towards. In the study of my craft, I've always been interested in conservation and restoration, and now it has paid off. They admired my work, and my knowledge."

"So you'll get contracts?"

"I'll be able to bid on them, yes. It's all I can ask for."

"I'm so happy for you. Come here and give me a hug, Girafeau."

He strode toward her and wrapped his arms around her. Only a second's hesitation let her know he was still thinking about the last time they had embraced. She had to admit, being close to him again, smelling his scent, triggered a few firings of her own nervous system in places she didn't want.

"Hey there, you two. What's this? The tryst by the mill?"

Niki and Didier leapt apart. Her heart raced, and she felt heat flood to her face. "Hey! Hi, Luc." Meeting his questioning gaze, she lifted her chin. They hadn't been doing anything wrong. Why was he so possessive?

Didier cleared his throat. "You're back." She heard the silent 'already.' Was it her imagination or was he as uncomfortable with Luc as Luc was with him? Unfortunately, that only lent credence to Luc's suspicions.

Luc strolled up to them and stopped, his hands in his pockets. Niki shied away from the sharp expression in his piercing blue eyes. Was that garden variety jealousy with a dash of anger? Was he questioning her behaviour with Didier? Or was it just that she felt a little guilty that her own body had betrayed her by jumping to attention at a little physical contact with him?

"I wanted to see how my girl was doing." Luc grinned, but she sensed tension behind his wide smile. That 'my girl' was no casual choice of words. "I'm glad to see you up and around, Nik. How are your injuries?"

"I'm... great." She hated the unnatural reserve between them. "I dressed myself today," she boasted with a smile, trying to add a little humour to diffuse the friction.

"Excellent!" His eyes roamed over her body.

And somehow with that one word, Luc made her feel as though he was undressing her with his eyes, and then her nerves were rattling for the second time, proving the tingle she'd got from hugging Didier was a mere ripple compared to the storm of desire just looking at Luc whipped up. She swallowed the lump in her throat, suddenly feeling as though her skin were ten times as sensitive as it had been a moment ago.

"What are your plans, Luc?" Didier broke in.

Luc shrugged. "Just popped over for a visit. It felt cramped at Charles' place this morning so I needed some air. Guests have arrived for the weekend."

Her eyes shot to his, blinking, his words raising questions in her mind. Was Patrice being a shrew about the breakup?

"Do you have time to hang around? I want to stop into the village to speak with someone, but I didn't feel comfortable leaving Niki alone."

Amelie! "You should have said something Didier!" she scolded. "I'm perfectly all right by myself. There was no need–"

"Ah, well. It doesn't matter now." His eyebrows lifted. "Luc is here."

The eye contact between Didier and Luc lasted just a little longer than she would have liked. It made her feel more like a pawn in a game than the master of her own destiny, and she bristled at the thought.

"No problem, man. I'll stay 'til you get back."

"I can stay by myself!" She sounded petulant even to her own ears.

"Merci." Didier smiled at her, a little awkwardly, she thought, and turned to leave. He turned back. "I'll get that medicine you wanted."

"Thank you!"

"I could have got that for you," Luc said.

She raised a brow. "When?"

As Didier's truck bumped out of the driveway, Luc turned to face her. "Are you mad at me?"

She huffed. "Of course not. Why would you ask?"

"I don't know. You seem distant."

Luc and she faced each other by the side of the creek, neither speaking. His beautiful blue eyes mesmerized her as his gaze slowly combed her face and body.

"Because I left. You okay?"

All the tension drained out of her body at his gentle tone. "I missed you." As his arms came around her, she melted against his hard chest, drugged by his scent and the feel of his hands against her skin.

"I missed you, too." He lifted her chin to gaze into her eyes, tilted his head, quirking his lips just before he set them against her mouth, setting her on fire.

~

They turned back to the house, arms around each other, their bodies molded together. "You did leave in a hurry yesterday."

One side of his mouth twitched up. "I wasn't sure what you wanted. How you were going to handle it... us. Didier." He shrugged.

"I thought you took care of that."

His brows inched closer together. "I didn't say a thing."

She dipped her chin and smirked up at him. "You didn't have to. You're channeling caveman."

He chuckled and pressed a kiss to her forehead, but pink tinged his cheeks. "Sorry."

She started her slow way back to the house. "Do you want something to drink?" She thought her discomfort was because of Didier, but it was worse now she and Luc were alone.

"Sure."

Inside, he insisted she relax on the sofa while he got them cold drinks. Pastis again.

"Do you like this stuff?"

"It's an acquired taste. Where did you have it before?"

"I don't dislike it, but... it's strange. Amélie gave me some."

His gaze darted to her face. "I didn't know you hung out with Amélie."

She studied her glass. "There are many things I haven't told you."

"Things you don't want to tell me?"

"No, Luc. Things I haven't had time to tell you!"

"Why are you angry with me?"

She threw herself back onto the cushions with an exasperated groan. "I'm not angry!"

Instead of getting defensive, he laughed and said, "Oh, good. 'Cause that'd be really confusing." He shook his head and lifted his glass to his mouth, keeping his eyes averted. She felt like an idiot. She loved that about him. That way he always kept his cool and called her on her shitty behaviour.

"I'm sorry. I'm just frustrated."

His eyes swung over, and the corners of his mouth lifted. He blinked slowly, acknowledging her apology.

She sighed. "I suppose Patrice has come for the weekend and you're avoiding her."

His lips curled in a small smile. "Jealous?" He set his glass down, came over to her and crawled onto the sofa, bridging her body, bending down to kiss her. Against her will her face lifted to his in response, straining. He nibbled at her lips, licked her, and kissed her more deeply, triggering a surge of lustful stirrings between her legs, before sitting back. "Does that sound like me?"

"Not really, no."

"I spoke to Patrice the first time I went back. It's all cool. In fact I was… quite deluded in that direction so there are no hard feelings. I wanted to be here with you. I had to get out of the crowded, noisy house."

"So you didn't really want to see me. You were just looking for escape."

"Oh, yes I did. I ached for you the moment I left." He leaned forward and kissed her again. He kissed her so thoroughly she was squirming and moaning beneath him in a matter of minutes. "You do that rather well. How mobile are you now?"

"It hasn't been that long since I saw you."

"Too bad." His kisses travelled from her mouth, across her jaw, and down the side of her neck, while his talented fingertips traced a delicate line up her arm and down the neckline of her tank top, grazing the tops of her breasts, calling them to attention. His voice was thick. "It feels like an eternity since I touched you." With a finger, he pulled down the shoulder of her tank, his lips following the margin of exposed skin, until his mouth covered her hardening nipple. He grunted and took it between his teeth, teasing lightly, before sucking and flicking it with his tongue.

A moan rose up from her swirling belly. Suddenly all the distance that had opened up between them disappeared like a flash of lightning. Instead, once again, he had blurred the line between him and her. She felt his erection grow between them, pressed against her thigh. Her legs moved apart to make space for him in between.

He lay a hand gently against her hip. "Careful sweetheart."

His murmured endearment fired her desire. She moaned again and shook her head in protest while attaching herself to his mouth hungrily, luring him with her tongue.

It was his turn to groan. "Jesus." He plunged his own tongue into her mouth, exploring and sparring with her, conveying his need.

My God, he was a champion kisser. All thoughts disappeared when he touched her, except the need to be closer. The need to join. "Luc. We have unfinished business."

He froze for a split second, and to make her point clear, she spread her legs a little further, testing her limits, and pressed herself up into him, putting pressure exactly where she wanted it. It set them both afire with lust, and she felt his corresponding push and the slow, languorous rocking of his hips as he groaned and rubbed himself against her heat. His arms trembled and her response was to quiver from head to toe, as though he were the stone, and she the ripples.

He gasped. "Do you think we can?"

"If it weren't for our clothing, we would be already."

His smile was slow and hot. "Then we'd better get rid of this clothing real quick, before I explode with need for you." His mouth closed over hers in another achingly sensual kiss, with deep slow thrusts of his hot tongue, and teasing nips of his teeth on her lips, filling Niki with the most luxurious warmth, like a furnace deep within that built and emanated its heat until her limbs were languid and trembling with desire.

He sat up to slide her sweat pants down her hips in that way she loved, trailing his fingertips, his eyes never leaving the line where a new inch of skin was being revealed, second by second, as though he thought it the most fascinating sight.

"Do you have a condom?"

"Oh, hell, yeah. I wouldn't come near you without one, just in case."

"Looks like today's your lucky day."

Once he'd dispensed with her pants, his mouth landed on her belly, his tongue teasing her navel, darting across her skin, lifting gooseflesh wherever he went. He did that thing with his palm again, applying heated pressure over her mound, making her body dance with need. How did he know to do that? He seemed to know a lot of things about her body. She wanted to hand it to him on a platter.

"Now you. Quick."

He laughed. "You can't want this more than I do. But I'm going to do it right, even if it kills me."

"You're killing me. I know that. Come on. Condom, condom. I need you inside my box, pronto."

"My, my, you're a demanding little wench." He stood up to drop his shorts and made her watch while he slowly opened the packet and rolled the condom over his gorgeous hard cock. It jumped under his touch.

"I told you. I'm a girl who knows what she wants and demands to get it. Hurry!"

He defied her by moving slowly, carefully. He lowered himself over her, moved her leg gently to the side, positioning himself at her opening. "I thought you said you didn't know what you wanted." He kissed her again, stalling to torture her, diving into her mouth with his tongue, in and out, in and out, mocking her.

"That was then," she gasped. "This is now. I want you. Inside. Now."

He stopped moving, sobering. "Look at me, Niki. Say my name."

Their gazes locked. She fell into his indigo eyes, utterly absorbed. Safe. Home. "Luc, pleeeease!"

She got what she wanted. Never once taking his eyes from hers, he slid into her in one thrust, slow and steady, stretching her, holding her hips steady with his hands, to prevent her lifting while a torrent of incomprehensible, seductive French streamed from between his clenched teeth. A cry tore from her throat. The trembling began as she strained against his grip, pressing up into him, her need for him desperate and intense, feral. She growled.

His lips brushed her cheek, and he whispered into her ear, "Easy, baby, easy. Make it last. Oh, fuck! You are so beautiful." He slid slowly out, drawing in a long breath, luxuriating in the feel of their most intimate parts touching, so sensitive. "You fit me like you were made for me, Niki. I knew you would. I knew the moment I saw you. You're meant for me."

They were both shaking now, and his slow movements brought them to the brink of ecstasy within another few strokes. All their times together, devouring every inch of each other, had primed them for this moment. It didn't disappoint. His deep kisses filled her, his pulsing cock filled her, and she throbbed with a glorious ache that climbed and climbed, higher and higher, until on the cusp of agony, she clenched, broke, coasted over the brink, floating, taking flight. Time stopped as they locked in the moment together, rigid, vibrating, panting. Then an aftershock ripped through them with a violent shudder, and they collapsed, Luc's weight coming down onto her for a moment.

But only a moment. He would never forget, never be careless with her. He was always attentive of her needs and her comfort. "Mmm. Sorry, baby." He slid to one side, squeezing in next to her on the narrow sofa, even as she continued to tremble and gasp, wrapping himself gently around her. "Someday we'll do this in a nice big bed. Won't that be fun?" With one hand pressed gently into the hollow of her lower back, his free hand caressed her cheek, and wiped tears from under her eyes with his thumb.

She shooed away the dark part of her mind that demanded to know if they had a someday to look forward to. If she would ever let that happen.

CHAPTER 32

Before slipping into oblivious sleep, she had murmured, "Luc?"
"Hmm?"
"You're amazing," she whispered.
When she awoke from her doze, he stared at her, his heart in his eyes.
"Hello."
"Hello."
He kissed her lightly, his eyes never leaving hers, as though he could see right into her, shining a light on every dark crevice and corner. A small part of her shrunk away from his intensity, his searching intimacy.
"What's wrong?"
She swallowed. "Nothing."
One corner of his mouth twitched up in an almost smile. "I know you. You can't hide."
She whispered, "What if I want to. What if I need to, sometimes?"
A frown lowered his brow. His hand gently touched her chin, lifting her gaze to his. "Don't be afraid of me, Niki. I would never hurt you."
She looked back into his penetrating eyes for a long moment, then pulled her gaze away. "You're very intense, Luc. I'm not used to it."
Luc shifted his weight to give her more space, bringing one hand up to caress her cheek. He gently turning her face until she was looking at him again and waited a beat. "Niki. I love you. I think I fell in love with

you at first sight. I feel like some magic charm has enchanted me, compelled to give you my heart. I'm utterly bewitched by you. It hit me so hard. I've never felt like this before, about anyone."

Panic thrummed in her chest like a chopper blade, fast and hard. She squirmed. The weight of his words pressed in on her like the walls of a cell, and the urge to flee rose up in her. His body over and around hers suddenly felt too tight, too close, too oppressive.

"I… you know, I think I need some air." Guilt swamped her as his face fell. He opened his arms, hands up, releasing her. She could see the hurt in those naked blue eyes of his, that saw everything, but also hid nothing. She'd disappointed him. "I'm sorry, Luc. You're moving too fast for me. You're going places I've never even thought about." She pushed at his chest, and he took the hint and got up, freeing her. She hauled her half naked body from the sofa and scrambled for her sweats, struggling to get them on with her stiff hip and awkward arm, feeling the after effects of their brief but intense connection.

He reached to help her, but she swatted him away. "I've got it. I can do it myself."

He sighed. "Of course you can." He picked up their glasses and carried them to the kitchen, not bothering about his own shorts, unself-conscious. His lithe naked masculine body drew her gaze, but she forced herself to look away, and heard him walk to the bathroom and close the door.

She limped outside. Standing in the tall grass with her hands on her hips, she breathed in the fresh scent of the French countryside, which carried on it cut hay, peaches, from somewhere far away, grilling meat as families prepared for the evening meal. Such a beautiful place, it made her heart ache.

The sun hung low in the sky like ripe fruit, bringing with it a vivid spectrum of violet and persimmon and pink, jumbled with shadowed mackerel clouds along the horizon. The colours blurred as she blinked away tears. She fervently wished she were on the road, pushing hard, careening along one of these endless small country roads, the breeze in her face, her mind empty and free from burdens.

Her pulse raced at the thought. She turned and walked back to the side of the house where her bicycle leaned, unused this past week since the accident. Damaged from her crash. She hadn't been thinking about that. Maybe Didier could look at it. Or maybe she'd have to buy or rent another one, if it would take too long to fix, though that was a big waste of money. She gingerly squatted down to examine the dented frame, scraped gears and mangled handlebars.

"Planning your escape?" Luc stood behind her. He'd donned his shorts and t-shirt.

"Can't I look at my bike without it meaning something?"

In the long silence that followed, she'd thought he'd gone away, but when she glanced over her shoulder, he still stood there.

Their eyes met. She knew she was being waspish but couldn't help herself. How could you long for something so much that you knew you shouldn't want? She was so confused. No lover had ever pursued her like this. No one had ever cared about her this way. Had they? Had she ever stuck around long enough to find out? Or had she already been a mile down the road before the chance occurred?

"You're right. I'm sorry I'm pressuring you. It's not fair. I–"

"Stop being so fucking nice, would you? You don't always have to apologize!"

"Why do you have to make it so damned difficult to love you?"

It was her turn to stop and stare.

Because I don't deserve to be loved.

A flush had risen to his face, his blue eyes were dark and his raked hair spiked with frustration. He was angry. Finally.

She'd pushed him too far. Her muscles went rigid, and her hands shook. A tight band cinched around her ribs, crushing the air from her lungs, ramming into her fluttering heart.

"You know what you are? You're a liar and a thief."

"Huh?" She wanted to stand up, to face him, but she couldn't. Her muscles were stiff, and she wasn't strong enough to lift herself up without crawling on her hands and knees and pulling herself up on something. Either that, or asking for his help. And she wouldn't do that.

"You're lying to yourself about us, Niki. What we have begun here is not a casual thing. This is life changing, what's happening between us. You can't run from this."

"I'm not running. You're being melodramatic."

He ignored her protest, continuing. "And you're a thief because… Niki, you've stolen my heart." His voice wavered, and with it, her resolve.

"I never promised you anything." Her throat thickened with a sudden rush of tears. She was such an ass.

He reached for her and hauled her upright. His next words were shredded, rasping, anguished. "Not in words, maybe. But you made promises with your lips, with your eyes." He tapped them lightly as he spoke. "With your hips and your sighs. This body you trust so much, Niki. It told me the truth."

She trembled from holding back the feelings that overwhelmed her at his words. "Please stop. I'm just sensible. I'm taking care of my needs. Is that so hard to understand?"

He dropped his hands and stepped back. "What do you think you need? To keep people away forever? Do you really want to be alone forever?"

Her entire body was quaking now, and breath came with difficulty. Her voice was shrill. This whole encounter made her want to hit something, to take her bike and toss it at him and his smug judgements. "I'm fine on my own. It's always worked for me."

Luc's eyes were glassy and red-rimmed. "You don't have to do this. You don't have to be the tough one, dealing with everything all alone. I can take care of you. You can trust me. I won't hurt you."

"Leave me alone."

His eyes shot blue fire, and his nostrils flared. "Let me add one more name to the list. Coward. I didn't think that was true when I first met you. I admired your adventurous spirit, your risk-taking, your joie de vivre. But now I can see it's true. You run because you're afraid of everything. You run and you jump but you're afraid of living."

Uncontrollable trembling started in her cramped legs, gathered strength in her bowels and radiated up and out through her whole body. She leaned back against the wall of the house. He was right. She couldn't breathe. Or speak. Or even blink. Her stomach was a rock, cementing her in place, when what she really wanted was to be away from here, flying, running, jumping away. Free.

"Nik, Nik. I'm sorry. I wish you'd give me a chance to show you. Loving brings endless rewards. But you've got to let yourself be loved. You've got to risk vulnerability, let yourself fall into another's arms. Before you can be fully alive, you've got to learn to trust."

Niki couldn't think of anything to say to that. How could she explain? She did trust him. He was everything she could want in a lover, in a partner, in a friend. She didn't trust herself. If he relied on her, she would let him down.

At her continued silence, he huffed out a frustrated sigh. "I can't stay here. I'm going back to Charles' place." He shook his head. "I'm leaving for Bordeaux soon anyway and going home. I have to pack up my things."

There were no words to bid him goodbye. She wished it weren't goodbye. But neither was it au revoir. The best she could do was to wish him Adieu. Go with God. But she said nothing, and at last he turned and walked away. He got on his own bike, strapped on his helmet, and pedalled out of Didier's yard. She watched him until he disappeared into the shadows of the leafy trees beyond Didier's fence. Only then did she allow the tears to fall.

CHAPTER 33

What a complete idiot! Luc pounded the pedals, not because he was eager to get back to Charles', but to get away from Niki as fast as he could. Before he lost his shit.

He might be an idiot, but he was no fool. He knew he was reeling from her rejection. He was raw, open and vulnerable after their incredible lovemaking. For him, they'd just crossed over into a new land of wonder, intimacy, connection and trust. For her, obviously a different reaction.

He felt sick with it. He couldn't stick around and wait for the full impact of his pain to surface. And he wouldn't stick around and be the object of her guilt and pity. He'd bared his feelings, laid out his heart for her, and she ripped it from him and stomped it till it bled.

He squeezed his eyes tightly closed, and pushed harder on the pedals, tearing up the pavement. Within seconds he hit a pebble and his front wheel wobbled. Slamming the brakes, his bike skidded to a stop in the dirt at the side of the narrow road and he planted his feet on the ground before he killed himself.

A cry ripped from his throat.

Luc wasn't a man to lose his temper. He couldn't remember a situation that warranted it. Irritations and disappointments were part of life, and he could process them, handle them, find a solution. He was also compassionate and understanding, and good at putting himself in other people's shoes.

This. This was different. This was raw, primal pain. And he didn't know how to process it. He didn't know what to do about it. He only knew it hurt, and he was mad as hell.

At Niki?

Hell, yes. At Niki. There was no way she didn't feel what he felt. It was visceral and ran deep. The feelings—not just the powerful physical attraction that drew them together—but the wordless sense they belonged together. The innate knowledge they belonged together. The inevitability.

She could imply that he was a naïve romantic, was impractical or had let his dreams colour reality, but she was wrong.

She was a liar and a thief and a coward. And he was furious with a universe that would damage a beautiful, vibrant, lovable girl so badly that she'd run from the huge, all-encompassing love he offered her. All that they could be for each other. The life they could make together. It might be messier than he planned, but oh, it would be wonderful.

As Charles' house drew nearer, he knew he couldn't go back there. Not yet, anyway. Not like this. He felt too tender and bloody.

Maybe I am a fool.

Was this crazed feeling what drove spurned men to commit atrocious acts? He released a long breath, trying to purge the tension that consumed him. Pushing off, he continued cycling past the driveway toward Petit Bergeron. He'd find something to do. Some distraction to diffuse this madness that consumed him.

After another twenty minutes of cycling, he was calmer, but no happier. One of the first person he saw when he mounted to the Place des Arcade was Didier. Even if the giant weren't as conspicuous as a billboard, anything that reminded Luc of Niki was sure to draw his attention, the way one's tongue tormented a broken tooth.

Didier stood talking with two older men Luc knew to be artisans. He laughed and gestured animatedly, out of character with his more reserved demeanour. More relaxed and confident in his bearing. The trip he took to Carcassonne had been fantastic for him. Why hadn't he done it years ago, if he wanted to?

Luc shied away from the obvious answer. He really didn't want to admit that Niki's friendship, Niki's… benefits… had been the catalyst that drew the shy man out of his shell of defeat, and out of the limiting inhibitions of a lifetime. But it was true. It all fit together.

A thought flitted past, teasing him. Why had someone else not taken the trouble, seen what it would take to help Didier before? Why had not Luc found a way?

Luc might as well let him know he'd left Niki alone. At least that way Didier wouldn't stay away longer than necessary, and Luc wouldn't need to worry. As if.

Just as he moved towards him, Didier bid his friends farewell and strode purposefully toward the lane that led to Amélie's shop and home. How did he know that's where Didier went? He just knew. There was a look in his eye, of determination and boldness, that seemed almost foreign. No trace of Luc's concern that Didier had gotten emotionally attached to Niki lingered in his mind. Didier was as committed to Amélie as he ever was.

Luc hesitated. He wanted to make sure Niki was all right out there on the farm alone. But he couldn't, he wouldn't, return himself. So he wanted to make sure Didier went home. But how could he interfere with a man on a mission? A man so obviously in love, and determined to win the heart of his girl, that no one should stand in his way.

No. Niki wasn't Didier's problem.

Niki was Luc's problem. For better or worse.

He didn't need this kind of trouble. Before Niki, he may have been unhappy. Not unhappy exactly, but unfulfilled. But life was simple. Orderly. Predictable. Until he met her.

He wanted her to be happy. He cared about her. He wouldn't force himself on her. Reluctantly, he admitted, she had a point. They hardly knew each other. They'd only met two weeks ago. How could he be sure he wanted to be with her long term? He focused too much on his end goal, not allowing the relationship to grow naturally.

But she wouldn't let it grow. She'd thrown him out. His own fault, he supposed. But that's okay. She needed time to think. Maybe he wasn't what she wanted. He had to allow for that possibility. He couldn't force his naïve and idealistic view of life and relationships on other people. He couldn't control her any more than he could hold a hurricane in the palm of his hand.

Unconsciously, Luc had trailed Didier to Amélie's open door. He hung back, watching as he ducked to enter the tiny shop. Luc stood near the door, flattened against the sun-warmed limestone wall, hidden, curious, undecided.

"Bonjour, Didier! Tu es revenu," came Amélie's sweet voice. She was pleased to see him. No hesitation or resentment, that Luc could detect. She must have found his jealous rage laughable.

"Amélie," said Didier, his resonant voice a gentle caress. She could hardly mistake his intentions. At least Luc thought so. "Comment ça va?"

"Bien. I'm glad to see you. I missed you."

"And I you, Amélie. Very, very much."

As they exchanged niceties, their voices weaving around each other like classical flute and bass, like vine and pole, Luc pondered how different his exchanges were with Niki. Sly, snarky, imbued with innuendo, sometimes sharp, sometimes spiced with teasing humour, and utterly thrilling. More like a jazzy saxophone and clarinet duet, somehow more viscerally connected to each other, tapping into something earthier, primal. Each voice asserting itself and drawing out the other, making his blood run hot.

His interactions with Patrice, in contrast, were civil and interesting, but made no music at all. He saw that now. All this time as he'd been longing for a connection with someone, with a woman he could call his own, he realized he'd needed that. That intangible he couldn't quite find the word to describe. Even if... no, he could never go back to Patrice. Not now. For his thirtieth birthday, instead of his youthful dream, he'd got a broken heart, and, he supposed, the wisdom and sorrow of manhood.

His body buzzed with the need for Niki, as if, in leaving her, he'd left a piece of himself behind at Didier's farm. But what could he do? She'd rejected him and all he was offering. Groaning he tipped his head back, bumping it repeatedly against the stone like a lunatic.

Pulling his attention back to the romance unfolding around the corner, he could no longer make out words. Didier's voice dropped to the murmur of water over stones, Amélie's rose to a whisper on the wind. Both evoking emotions deeply felt.

Humph.

A couple walked by, greeting him, eyebrows raised. "Bonjour, Luc."

He nodded, smiling and strolled further from the door, as though it were his intention, and waited until they'd passed down the lane. Doubling back, he jerked as Didier bent and emerged from the doorway.

"Ah! Didier! There you are," he said, his face stretching into a fake smile.

Didier stretched to his full height, pulled his shoulders back and grinned at Luc.

Luc crossed his arms and shook his head, laughing. "I see."

"What do you see?"

"Progress, of some sort," Luc replied. "What's new?"

Didier flushed. "Amélie has agreed to go to market with me tonight and have uh… dinner and wine."

"Ah. A date. Marvellous. Congratulations, man."

"Are you looking for me? Why are you here?"

"Um." Luc considered confiding in Didier, but reconsidered. "No, no," he said lightly. "Are you going home before…" He gestured at Amélie's doorway.

"Non. I need to talk more with Serge. Then drive to Villeneuve for a few things and be back in time for dinner." His eyes held a question that Luc ignored. Why was he not at the house with Niki? Well, he'd find out, eventually.

Luc nodded. He'd hold his tongue then and leave Didier to his errands and his big date. What was the point of either of them worrying about Niki? She wanted to be independent. She chose solitude. Let her be.

It was beyond his control now. He had only to deal with the fallout. His life was different now.

CHAPTER 34

It relieved Niki that Didier didn't return home until late the night before. She couldn't have faced his questions, and she knew her puffy red eyes would have given her away. Instead, she'd spent the evening organizing her few things and packing and repacking her saddlebags, thinking about being on the road again. Heading home. Back to life as she knew it.

Just to be safe, she'd called the airline to find out what her options were, in case she wasn't able to get to Bordeaux in time for her scheduled flight. She also emailed both her boss and Chief Brian, itemizing her injuries. It was one thing to force herself to ride her bike another couple hundred kilometres, another to report at work in less than prime condition and put others' safety at risk.

Speaking of her remaining distance, she studied the optional routes on Google Maps, paying particular attention to terrain. It would be bad enough making the bike go forward. She wanted to avoid as many hills as possible. That meant taking a longer route, probably highway D936, and the designated bike paths, but with a few extra detours added on to avoid the hard hills. As it was, the trip would probably take her a full two days instead of the seven or eight hours it should have taken. But she would do it.

Awakening early, she began a thorough and intensive series of physiotherapy exercises, assessing each muscle group one by one, spending a long time stretching out the tight and painful areas, and using a roller for massaging them. That was a challenge. She'd had to search all of Didier's house and shop before she found something she could use. She spent extra time on the soles of her feet, and the outsides of her hips, areas she knew got extra tight, and were important for her high intensity cycling. She was in the middle of this when her door creaked open and Didier poked his head in.

"Ah. You're up."

"I've been up for hours. How's it going?"

"Me, I'm great. I thought you and Luc would show up at the night market last night, but I didn't see you."

Luc hadn't gone either? "Oh. Uh, no. Gave it a pass. Did you have fun?"

His face lit up. He came into her room and lowered himself onto her little cot with a creak of its frame. It was a lower bed, and his knees came up to his shoulders. He dwarfed the small guest-room and filled it with his long limbs and bulk.

"I had fun, yes. I went to visit Amélie in the afternoon."

"Oh-ho, did you?"

He nodded. "Yes. I thought to tell her about your accident, and how you were doing. She was very concerned and sends her love to you."

She smiled and nodded her thanks. "Aaaaand?"

His blush was telling. "Nothing. We chatted. I told her about my trip. We had a glass of pastis on her patio. Then she asked if I was staying for night market, and I thought, why put off to tomorrow what you can begin today? So I asked if she would join me, and we talked all evening, and walked the market together, and sat with some of her friends for dinner. Had some wine. It was good."

Her grin stretched wide, and she searched his face for clues. "A date! With Amélie. Good for you, Girafeau. Sounds like you're over your nerves, hey?"

He drew in a big breath, puffing out his chest. "I am still very nervous. But I... I don't know. It doesn't seem so terrifying as before. And most important, I find it easier to think of things to say." He shrugged.

"How is Amélie responding?"

Again with the bashful smile. "I think she likes me."

"Yes she likes you, you goof. That was never in question."

"It was for me. But maybe it was in my head. Now I feel... I don't know... as if, as if I'm not such a bad catch, you know?"

"I do know, as a matter of fact. And I'm glad you know it too, because it's true. You're smart, handsome and talented, you make a good living, which will get better and better. You have a great house. You're sweet and caring, and you make a mean omelette. You're a lovely person, Didier. I'm lucky to be your friend. What else does a woman need?"

His brows flicked up and down suggestively, and they both laughed.

"You're pretty damned good at that, too, for a rookie."

He sobered. "I have so much to thank you for, little monkey."

Her eyes danced around. She studied the pattern on the carpet, the wood grain on the bedside table, and fingered the fringe on her duvet before saying. "Didier."

"Hm?"

"Do you think I was wrong to get so involved in your life? Did I make assumptions, or tread where I shouldn't have?"

He seemed to think about her question for several long moments. "No. Unusual. But perhaps necessary for unusual circumstances. I said before you were a catalyst. After a lifetime of insecurity, maybe I needed it." He shrugged and his face dimpled with a wide smile. "It worked anyway, non?"

"Sure. But do you have regrets? Do you wish you'd saved yourself for Amélie? Your first time?"

"No." He took a deep breath and let it out. "If my wish comes true, I will spend the rest of my days… and nights… with Amélie. If not for you, perhaps I would have always wondered, been curious about other women. Now I don't have to. And also, I feel that I have learned much, and can be better for Amélie because of my little experience. I'm glad of that. I want to be good for her, and confident and courageous, too."

"I'm relieved to hear that. I was feeling like, maybe it was a mistake–"

"No, no. I am very grateful to you, Niki. Never feel regret."

"Good. I won't."

He stood up and stepped to the door. "And if you didn't hang around here for me, you might never have met Luc. That's good, too, right?" He smiled.

She hesitated. It was good. But she'd ruined it. Her response was watery. "Right."

"Come with me to have lunch with Amélie. She invited both you and Luc to join us at her place."

"Oh. I'm not expecting Luc today," she replied, turning and lowering herself to the bed. Why would Amélie want to see Niki? Did she want to see how she was with Didier? Or did she need some reassurance? Niki would just as soon stay out of the village. "You go on, enjoy your time with Amélie."

"Non. She said I must bring you. Even if Luc is not available. She wants to pamper you, and see for herself that you are all right, after hearing the horror stories of your injuries." For a moment he stood awkwardly, his eyes darting around, the old, self-conscious Didier back in the room. "Um. And, there's something I would like to show you." He met her eye again, finally. "I want your opinion on something."

That peaked her curiosity. She had to face Amélie, eventually. Might as well get it over with. Hopefully, they wouldn't run into Luc. That, she wasn't ready for. "Okay. I'll come with you." She could resume her physical therapy when they got home.

Didier drove them to town and parked in his usual spot at the bottom of the hill. Niki welcomed the climb up toward the *Place des Arcades*, though it was challenging for her, putting all kinds of stress on her healing muscles and ligaments, but she insisted on doing it herself, no matter how long it took. She painfully knew of the changed circumstances since the last time she'd been there. How would Amélie react to her fling with Didier? What would Niki say?

Didier grumbled that they would be late, but in moments they reached Amélie's shop. Amélie, as always, was warm and welcoming, ushering them through her shop into the cozy courtyard beyond.

"Is Luc joining us?"

"Um. No. I think he's busy with some house guests of Charles'," Niki said, deflecting. "Thanks for inviting me, though," she said. Now that the moment had come to face Amélie, she was shy.

But Amélie showed no signs of discomfort. They sat down around her little table and she brought out a bottle of rosé and glasses, and then a beautiful salad on a platter. Niki was glad to see cold meat, so she could continue to power load her system with protein.

Amélie had expressed concern for Niki's well-being. After receiving assurance she was on the mend and already focussed on cycling to Bordeaux, the conversation shifted.

"So," said Amélie coyly, "Didier tells me there might be something interesting developing between you and Luc. Is it so?"

Niki hesitated, shooting an accusatory glance at Didier. They talked about her? She wasn't sure how to explain what had happened with Luc, or what had gone wrong.

Seeming to sense her discomfort Didier stood up. "Is it ready?" He asked, reminding Niki of his awkward request earlier. Was what ready?

Amélie's face lit with a bright smile. "*Oui*. It's there," she gestured. "You'll see it."

Didier nodded and excused himself.

In the void that followed Amélie peered closely at her. "So. Luc. What is it Niki? Didier led me to believe that things were hot and heavy between you two. He said the sexual tension was coming off of you in waves." She wiggled her fingers in the air, and Niki clenched her teeth, her eyes wide, tried to picture Didier saying that. Amélie leaned toward her. "I expected it. That's one reason I never worried about Didier and you getting involved."

Niki had trouble meeting her gaze. "I don't know Amélie. Sure, we had a brief thing, while he was staying with me. After the accident."

Amélie frowned. "What do you mean… had?"

"He's very attractive. There was… something." Something so big it scared me to death. Niki's face heated. She shrugged, shifting her gaze to the flowering vines creeping up the stone wall behind Amélie, nibbling on a cuticle with her teeth. "It was delicious but brief and now it's over. I'm focussed on returning home. I need to get back in shape, and I need to get back to work."

At Amélie's expression of concern, she added lightly, "It's fine. I'm not interested in a serious relationship."

"Everyone needs love, Niki. You can't live your life alone."

Niki shrugged. Another one with the lectures. "That's the way I'm made."

Amélie reached out and set a hand on Niki's shoulder. "I'm so sorry to hear that Niki. I've known Luc for many years, and I've never seen him so excited and alive as he has been this past week or two. He saw, as I did, what a special woman you are. The moment you came to town I could sense how important you would be for everyone."

Niki's gaze narrowed, uncertain what she meant. "Do you mean that? I thought maybe you would resent me."

Amélie's mouth pulled into a pensive smile. "No. I could tell that your friendship with Didier was just a passing thing." She bit her lip. "No, that's not fair. What you did for him was important. You freed him. He's so much more confident since he came back from Carcassonne. He's changed. And it's because of you. He's courting me, at last." Amélie paused and dipped her chin, trying to contain the wide smile that stretched her face, without success.

Looking up she said, "I've never felt, well... I always sensed that both of you were more interested in other people than in each other. You and Didier, I mean," she added, a rosy tint rising to her cheeks.

"You don't feel that I... stole something from you?" asked Niki.

"My goodness, not at all," said Amélie, her attention drawn by Didier's return.

Niki glanced up, blinked and let out a squeal of surprise. Didier wore a beautiful dark blue suit, complete with a shirt and tie. He was the most beautiful, biggest gentleman she'd ever set eyes on.

"Oh, my freaking God!" She pressed her hands to her chest. "Is that you, Didier?"

His face and ears were bright pink, but his grin stretched wide. He smoothed his large hands over his chest and down his sides, obviously pleased with his appearance, but shy. "What do you think?"

Niki let her eyes roam over him in wonder, taking in the fine details and excellent fit of the suit. She turned to Amélie. "You did this? When?"

"I had his measurements," Amélie said. "He asked me to make it before he left for Carcassonne, and we did the final fitting when he returned."

Niki shook her head and watched as the two of them peeked shyly at each other and smiled and blushed. They were so adorable. And despite Didier's difficulties, their love was simple and pure. Finally Amélie tore her eyes from Didier's face and looked back at Niki. "Now. What can we do to help you?"

"Oh, don't worry about me. I'm fine. I'm just eager to get home and get back to work."

"*D'accord*," said Didier, but Niki noticed his intense gaze catch Amélie's before he continued. "Then let's talk about tomorrow night. I think we should all dress up and have dinner together. I would very much like to stroll the market with two beautiful ladies on my arms."

"Wow, Didier, you've become an accomplished flirt overnight," Niki said.

"I had many years of practice in my imagination, little monkey," he smirked, tapping his forehead.

"Are you sure that's… uh, what you want?" Niki glanced at Amélie. The whole situation felt weird now. She'd rather fade into the shadows than prance around the village on Didier's arm. But if that's what he wanted, well maybe it made some sense. But Saturday night market! Everyone went. What were the chances she could avoid seeing Luc this time?

"*Absolutement*," Amélie answered for them both, smiling. "In fact, I have a sweet dress that would fit you, if you'd agree to wear it."

"A dress! Well." Niki never wore girly clothes. But she trusted Amélie's good taste and judgement. She wanted to help them mark their new beginning, even though she had little desire to celebrate. "Ok, then. Let's do it."

As they prepared to leave, Didier bent to give Amélie les bises and murmured. "As Niki is my houseguest, I must bring her to town. I hope you don't mind if we meet you here? You understand we are only friends, oui?"

"*Bien sur*, Didier," she replied and kissed him back with feeling. "You're so kind."

And to make sure Niki believed her, too, she gave her a kiss and a tight embrace before they left.

Niki was happy for them. They were both so sweet and loving they deserved to be happy together. But still she felt the weight of her own tragedy press in on her heart. Though she had helped Didier as she'd set out to, there were consequences far worse than her fear of overstepping her role as a helper. Consequences she hadn't foreseen.

How could she know that her brief detour to this little village of Petit Bergeron would leave her a changed woman? But she was. Her eyes were opened to the possibilities of a shared love. Luc, and everyone else she'd met here, had breached the walls around her heart. Though she felt safe and comfortable on her own, and knew she could take care of herself, she also wondered if she'd ever feel joyful again.

CHAPTER 35

The next morning, while Didier went out to meet a client, Niki drove herself hard. After two hours of intensive physiotherapy exercises, she was fatigued, but she pushed on. She had to force her body through these treatments if she would be ready to hit the road in a few days. The demanding regimen was as much about punishing herself and keeping her mind off of Luc as it was about rehabilitation.

Next on her plan was a session of hot-cold contrast therapy. Wearing only her lycra sports underwear, she steeled herself for the shock, marched out to the cold creek behind the forge, and threw herself in.

"Fu-uck!"

It was a good thing nobody was around to hear her shriek. Her heart raced at the shock to her system, and her skin shrunk tight, rigid with gooseflesh, burning from the cold.

But thirty seconds later, she had adjusted, more or less, and sunk down to immerse her entire body in the frigid water. She had to stay for ten minutes, no matter how numb or shivering she was. And shivering she was by then. From there, she went into Didier's shop and stood as near to the hot fire in his forge as she could. She did ten minutes of hot power yoga, until drenched with sweat. She followed this twice more by another ten minutes in the cold creek, another ten minutes of hot yoga.

Limber but limp with exhaustion, she staggered back into the house. But before she could rest, she had to feed her body. She threw what fruit and greens she could find into Didier's blender with two raw eggs and whipped it up. Then she got out the supplements he'd got for her and swallowed pill after pill until she'd bombarded her body with every healing thing she'd ever heard about for rapid injury recovery.

Finally, she got out her magnesium lotion and frankincense oil and rubbed them on every square inch of her skin, from her ears to her toes.

After all that, she expected to fall instantly into a deep sleep. Instead, she lay perfectly still in her bed, stared at the ceiling, and obsessed about Luc.

Luc and his steadfastness, his devotion, and his unrelenting honesty. Luc and his patience, kindness and caring. Luc and his sharp-witted intelligence and self-deprecating humour. Her mind's eye filled with his long, lean limbs, his expert kisses and gentle, sensitive touch that awoke in her a passion unlike any she'd experience before. And especially his intense blue eyes that saw into her soul and spoke to her of truths she was afraid to admit to herself, even in solitude.

What had she done?

She pushed the thought away. She would meditate and add even more power to her rehab with visualizations. She closed her eyes and attempted to empty her mind. Her body was so used up she couldn't even feel it anymore. Instead, a large void opened up inside her, starting under her diaphragm and growing outward, ever larger. The rhythm of her heartbeat sounded in that huge dark space, and she tried to visualize the sound waves of gongs echoing and resonating from her centre outward, like coloured bands. Her heartbeat slowed to a steady march, and she imagined her torn tissues and cells healing.

It was all going well enough, but an image kept intruding of her heart floating in the middle of that darkness, that void. Her heart swelled and bled like an injured muscle or a wound that wouldn't heal. It was the one body part she couldn't fix with intensive physiotherapies. Every time her heart would beat, a little more dark blood would ooze into the darkness of the surrounding emptiness.

Hot tears welled and seeped from her closed eyes, unstoppable. She continued searching in the emptiness, hoping for, waiting for guidance. What she saw were two long-fingered, tanned hands emerge out of the void and rise, embracing and cradling her bleeding heart. They were Luc's healing hands.

But she'd screwed up. Luc was gone.

CHAPTER 36

Once again, Niki partook in a small spectacle in the village of Petit Bergeron. This time, Didier was not only a willing participant, but an instigator. Didier and Amélie so enjoyed themselves, Niki couldn't help but enjoy it with them, despite her apprehensions.

They'd changed clothes at Amélie's and then sauntered into the square at just that point in the evening when people got their food and wine and settled down to dine. Many heads turned, and curious stares and smiles followed their progress across the *Place des Arcade*. Amélie seemed more than pleased to be making an entrance on Didier's arm. And Didier, decked out in his new suit, was for his part so stoked about it his feathers plumped like a rooster.

The tables filled up, yet they still secured Amélie's favourite spot, where some of her friends could find her.

While Didier and Amélie browsed for food and wine, Niki sat alone holding their table, like a neglected wallflower at a ball in the strapless coral sundress Amélie had lent her, with her hair pulled up in a messy bun, and no one to talk to.

She eyed the crowd searching for anyone she knew, but though she recognized a few faces, no one acknowledged her. Despite her acrobatics and her outburst, she was still a stranger, still an outsider. The locals seemed to have forgotten her, whether because of her new dress or her long absence from town after the accident. She supposed every summer was the same for them, their home invaded by thousands of tourists, and then returned to the everyday routines and familiar friends and neighbours the rest of the year

To be honest, she scanned for Luc and his friends. He *would* be here, as summer wound down, and soon, he too would return to normal life in Canada. Yet she didn't see him.

The thought of returning home alone after their brief but blissful connection filled her chest with the weight of all the stone in France that pressed on her poor small heart. She smiled at her bout of self-pity, let out a heavy sigh and shook her head. She was foul company tonight and wished she could slink away and be alone. Alone is how she'd always been and alone is what she excelled at.

That they should both leave here, and arrive home in Vancouver, separate and alone, and never see or speak to each other again felt wrong. So very wrong. The festive spirit she'd donned for Didier and Amélie slipped away, and a mood of melancholy draped over her like a curtain closing on the end of a play.

On the verge of bailing on the whole evening, she jumped when a gnarled hand reached toward her and gripped her arm. Gasping in shock she spun to face the old gypsy woman from the market, whom she had avoided until her accident kept her from town. She'd forgotten how uncomfortable the old woman made her feel.

Tonight, the old woman pressed long stemmed red roses on the crowd, a basket of them looped over her crooked arm. She grabbed both of Niki's hands and held on to prevent her escape.

"Hey!" Niki complained, scowling at her. "I don't want a rose."

"C'est l'heure." With intense occluded eye contact and a steely grip, the old hag held her hands tight. She lifted and shook them, as though with persistence, Niki would get the obscure message delivered. *"Ma petit fille, vos jours de ténèbres se terminent."*

Dark days are ending? Did the old woman predict the end of the world? Niki squirmed and tried to tug loose.

"Écoute!" she hissed, pulling harder. The old woman tilted her head up to the night sky. Niki recoiled from her bugging clouded eyes and the toothless mouth in her shrivelled face. *"L'amour est infini. Sam wishes you to accept all the roses in the garden. He also says, Au revoir et merci pour tout les poisson."*

At last the old woman released her hands and slipped into the crowd like an apparition, leaving Niki stunned and puzzled. Despite her words, the old crone left only a single rose on the paper tablecloth.

Love is infinite. Accept all the roses. And thank you for all the fish? WTF? How the hell did she know to say those things? Was that a weird coincidence or a hallucination? And was Niki dreaming, or did she actually say Sam's name?

∽

The time came to join the evening's celebration with his party at Saturday night's market, his last of the summer. Luc forced himself to dress up and come to town with Charles and Francine. He could not avoid tonight's festivities.

Since a young boy, he'd always celebrated his late summer birthday in France, in Petit Bergeron, with this same group of people. In the beginning his sisters, his parents, Charles and Patrice's parents took part, too. It was the highlight of his summer. His favourite day of the year.

Those glorious times, perhaps this day most of all, made him believe that anything was possible. All he had to do was dream a beautiful dream, and it would one day come true. He deserved it. He could make it happen. The world was a benevolent place.

Not this year. This year, he appreciated how much others suffered. A too happy, idyllic life had coloured his lenses rose.

He'd stood at the mirror in his room in a crisp dress shirt and his favourite linen blazer, donning the persona of an elegant French gentleman. His hair glossy and curling at the edges with its cosmopolitan summer growth, and his *barbe de trois jour* trimmed just so. He frowned.

The image was at odds with the casual but professional west coast teacher image that dominated his day-to-day existence throughout the year–the reliable, relaxed, charming, fun Mr. E. that his students and colleagues knew and loved.

Different again from the helpful, athletic, wry Canadian that spent his summers cycling the back roads of Aquitaine, and lounging around this village posing as a regular likeable guy. He was so busy being what everyone else expected him to be, none of these images fit the man he was inside.

But who was he?

The one guise he couldn't throw off was the heartbroken lonely man to whom melancholy clung like morning dew to ripening sunflowers, their heavy heads hanging in the golden fields, a harbinger of the changing season. Summer was ending. He had to return to his life. The same every year. But this year, different.

Older, wiser, less naïve, less content.

He was still reeling from his brief glimpse of Niki when they arrived. The entire scene was astonishing. Didier sauntering into the market with his two girls, all dressed up and having a grand time. Didier was a new man. He looked so happy. So did Amélie. And Niki, what he could tell from the quick glance he stole before he ducked out of sight behind an arch, looked incredible.

She wore a pretty summer dress the colour of ripe summer peaches- her strong brown shoulders bare, her long shiny dark hair twisted up in a messy knot exposing her beautiful neck. The neck he'd sucked and bitten in the heat of passion. He shuddered as a wave of visceral desire jackknifed through his groin, weakening his legs and his resolve.

She was beautiful and rare, and he wanted her so much. It should be them, smiling, holding hands, planning their future together. He nearly went to her, almost pulled her into his arms and kissed her. Almost told her he loved her and begged her to reconsider. But no.

He had his pride.

She wouldn't welcome him. He would keep his distance tonight, and then, it would be over. With luck, their paths would never cross back home, and life would go on as before.

Then he hurried back to his friends, aware that he was the guest of honour tonight. He put on a good face.

Though he felt like crying.

Niki dropped her face into her hands, overcome with grief and confusion from her encounter with the gypsy. She recoiled as her stomach rolled. Her hands reeked of orange, and she realized the old woman had held her so long, she'd left a slick of orange oils on her skin.

"Aagh!" She lifted her face and grabbed a paper napkin, rubbing her hands and scrubbing her face, but still it lingered like bad stain.

She was about to stand up to go wash her hands when Amélie and Didier returned. They set down wine and plates loaded with food, masking the orange scent and distracting her from her goal.

"Niki, what are you doing? You'll ruin your makeup."

Make up? She'd forgotten that Amélie had put some on her when they dressed at her studio. What a joke. Who was she dressed up for? The only man she'd ever cared about, who'd ever made her feel beautiful and special and loved for who she was, wasn't even here. Why was she?

Amélie pulled the napkin out of her hands, concern on her face. "*Ça va?*"

"Yeah. Yeah, I'm fine. It was just that old gypsy woman pushing her stupid flowers on me." She lifted the rose in illustration.

"*Grand-Mère* Bougie?" Amélie's eyes widened. "What did she say?"

"Nothing I could understand," Niki lied, hoping the old woman's cryptic words were as nonsensical as they seemed on the surface.

"You never know what she will say, but people in this village take her very seriously," said Didier.

"I am one who does," Amélie said. "She has the sight."

Didier pulled a face and filled three glasses with red wine, handing her one. Escape was impossible. She took a big gulp to calm herself.

"Look at this paella, Niki. Doesn't it look delicious?" Amélie pressed a plate toward her. They would get paella. As if she needed another reminder of her time with Luc. This evening would torment her. There was nothing to do but eat and drink, so she did, absorbing herself in the task to avoid conversation.

Suddenly Didier glanced up, reaching across the table. "Ah, Luc. You're here."

Behind her, Luc hesitated, stopping beside them. She could feel the heat of him standing there, his familiar scent sending shivers through her body.

"*Bonjour*." He held his gaze on Didier, nodding hello to Amélie, somehow avoiding looking at Niki. She stared at him sideways like a glassy-eyed rodent about to be eaten, smiling like a fool, unable to draw breath. Was he going to sit down and talk with her? Had he forgiven her for her moment of stupidity?

Dressed in his dinner jacket, like that first night at the festival, before the puppet show, he was so handsome she could taste him. That was the night he'd lasered in on her with those knowing, amused eyes, so blue and kind and wise. He'd made her feel seen, and special, as she'd never felt before. Lighting her on fire. She remembered his teasing, and the intense chemistry that pulled them together like two celestial bodies attracted by powerful unseen forces.

The memory was visceral, and she felt dizzy with it.

He'd changed her, she realized. She'd probably fallen in love with him at that exact moment. Her head felt as light as a helium balloon, and hope bubbled in her chest, her heart dancing to a wild beat. A smile, a real smile, pulled at her cheeks, and she felt warm, having him so near, standing beside her. *He's forgiven me!* He had. It wasn't like Luc to hold a grudge. He was too kind. Too caring.

"*Bonjour,* Luc," said Amélie. "So nice to see you."

"I hear congratulations are in order tonight, *mon ami*. Many happy returns." Didier continued to offer his hand, and Luc finally took it with a weak smile.

"*Merci*, Didier." Luc cleared his throat and threw a glance over his shoulder. "*Desolé*. I must get back to the party."

Niki stiffened. Her smile fell like a *saut-du-fond* from a second-story balcony as a cold chill shook her body. Congratulations? The first horrible thought rushing her mind was that he'd become engaged to Patrice after all. Niki already knew she'd rejected something irreplaceable when she'd pushed Luc away, but she didn't believe, until now, that it was irreversible. Had he turned to another for solace so soon?

"W-what are you celebrating?"

Luc blinked and turned to her, stony-faced. His beautiful blue eyes remained cold and flat as an iced over lake, while he examined her face, but he didn't reply. The only sign he was affected at all was a slight flaring of his nostrils.

Instead, Didier slapped him on the shoulder, jarring him out of his trance, and said, "Today is Luc's thirtieth birthday. Congratulations, old man."

She let out a shaky breath.

Luc nodded in acknowledgment, his jaw ticking with tension. A tight smile flickered on his face and he murmured *excuse me* before he spun on his heel and strode away.

Niki's mouth fell open, her breath hitching, as she watched him retreat into the crowd. She dropped her face into her hands to hide her suddenly trembling chin and stifled the whimper that squeaked out of her tight throat.

Her senses flooded with oranges again. Images of Sam in his bed of orange peels flashed in her mind's eye, unbidden. But now they blurred with memories of Luc, lean and sweaty and smiling, on his bike, offering her a piece of his orange. And her rejection of all he offered. Would the devastation never stop?

She lifted her face to the night sky beyond the white tent overhead and shook her hands as if to put out fire. She grunted. "Ugh! Fuck!"

"Are you ill, Niki?" Amélie turned to her, concerned.

She shook her head to clear the haunting images. Tonight, she was already suffering enough. She didn't need to wallow in her failure as a human being.

"What's going on? I thought he would join us. He's seemed… was he angry?"

Not angry. Hurt. And now she felt it too and knew what she'd done to him.

"What is it, monkey?" Didier's sandy brow furrowed over concerned blue eyes. She'd terrified him. She had to stop acting like a lunatic.

Grabbing the paper napkin she wiped her face again, grimacing. It was a lost cause. "That damned witch stunk me up with oranges!"

Amélie and Didier both sat, dumbfounded, blinking at her incomprehensible outburst. She could well imagine how crazy she appeared.

"I hate oranges," she grumbled, sighing, dropping her head on the paper tablecloth, hands limp at her sides.

What about Luc? That was their silent question. *What about Luc? What about Luc?*

When she couldn't stand them staring at her any longer, she said, "It's no big deal. We… it's over. It didn't work out." She scowled at them, dismissing their concern, putting her hands palm out. "Stop staring at me. Forget about it."

They obliged by peeling their worried gazes from her face, instead making uneasy eye contact with each other, the silent questions flying.

She could pretend it didn't matter, but inside, her heart was breaking.

CHAPTER 37

Cheerful music flowed from the end of the square, drawing their attention as people began to fill the dance floor on the lower terrace.

Niki continued feeling awkward as they watched the locals let loose and have a bit of carefree fun after a hectic tourist season. Of course, not every tourist had left town, but after the festival, it was quieter, and merchants, hosts and business people could relax and party. She recognized a few faces, including Didier's friend, the *maitre'd* of the restaurant they went to, and that British redhead Gisèla from the party, dancing with Charles.

Didier turned toward Niki and touched her hand, his eyes sad. Nonplussed, she stiffened and pulled back. Was he going to ask *her* to dance? "Will you be fine by yourself for a while, little monkey?"

Ah. Thanks for your pity, dude. "You bet, Didier. Knock yourselves out."

The DJ struck up a new, slower, song, and Didier rose. "Dance with me, *cherie*," he said, gazing into Amélie's star-struck eyes. They got up, and he took her hand and led her over to the lower terrace, walking tall and proud through the crowded tables.

Grateful to be alone, Niki rose to find a *toilette* where she could wash her hands and face with soap and water, purging the painful reminder of her losses. Not only Sam, her constant heartache, but now also Luc, who blithely peeled and ate his oranges, and pursued her even though she ignored him and made it as hard for him to love her as possible.

Niki made her way to the arcade to the side of the Place, thinking she could slip into a restaurant to use their facilities. Her route took her past the dance floor, where she could catch a good view of the giant and his lady dancing amid the swirling soft coloured lights, all pink and blue, like a romantic movie.

Niki's eyes filled with happy tears, even though she was never the romantic one. The large difference in their sizes was awkward but cute. It was no big deal, and she hoped Didier realized that now. They were having fun, Didier unselfconscious for once, focused on Amélie, relaxed. And Amélie clearly infatuated with her handsome new beau in his custom tailored suit.

Niki's gaze scanned the other dancers and spectators at the tables to see how everyone else reacted to the new romantic pair. Those that watched smiled, their heads together murmuring comments. From Niki's perspective, it looked like approval rather than mocking amusement.

All was well. She turned to continue when the song ended. But a wave of surprised and delighted exclamations made her pause and look back to see what had caused them.

Oh, wow. Didier had ended the dance by lifting petite Amélie up into his arms and planting a big kiss on her mouth, right there for the entire world to see. A collective sigh swept the crowd, like a big gust of air from Didier's bellows, fanning the flames of romance ever higher. Didier, responding to the attention, deepened the kiss until it was swoon-worthy. There was no stopping him now.

Niki's heart swelled. Bouncing the balls of her feet, she threw herself into a forward handstand, gave her feet a kick of joy and took a step forward, ignoring the fact that Amélie's dress flipped inside out. That was why she wore lycra shorts under it.

Agh! Fucking ouch. Tears sprang to her eyes as pain exploded through her shoulder and ribs. She painfully recalled her injuries. Her therapy was helping enough with agility she'd momentarily forgotten, but it didn't mean torn tissues could go back to work. She'd just aggravated the hell out of them.

Righting herself, she squatted and hugged herself, breathing deeply through the shooting pain. The inconvenient pain didn't diminish her joy, however, for Didier and Amélie.

But her gleeful triumph was short lived when another, more sinister, signal from the crowd brought her to her feet. Picking herself up, she peered across the square to see what had happened this time, her stomach clenching in dread. She couldn't see, so she stepped up onto the ledge of a planter to peer over the heads of the crowd. What she saw tightened her stomach and fists and brought a roar of frustration to her throat. No!

Those assholes. Would they never stop? Would they never learn? Rosaire, with Izar and Sylvan right beside him, always together like the band of small-minded thugs they were, pushed through the crowd, heading for the dance floor.

Even from this distance she could see them sniggering, see the mean glimmer of ill-intent in their beady eyes. What nasty thing did they plan now? What would they do this time?

"No!" She hissed, sagging against a plane tree, defeated. Would he never be free?

A chill ran up her arms and neck as her gaze flicked between Didier and Rosaire, scanning for details. Did Didier see them? Did he realize what was about to happen? The crowd did. The earlier sighs had shifted to murmurs of concern and a hum of low conversation as others speculated, too.

Rosaire called out. At first Niki didn't catch what he'd said, then he repeated it and her heart fell with dread. It was the same old thing. They'd never stop.

"Hey, *Girafeau*! Look at you! Big man about town, aren't you?" He giggled at his own cleverness, and Izar and Sylvan burst out in raucous laughter, jeering. What idiots!

Niki felt a fresh bout of rage at the way everyone just sat there. Any of them could step in and stop Rosaire. What was wrong with them all?

Everyone heard him now. A hush came over the crowd, everyone leaning in to catch the spectacle like a bunch of bloodthirsty ambulance-chasers.

Not now. Please not now. Her arms and legs felt cold, and she rubbed herself with tingling fingers, her heart aching for the waste, the tragedy of it. Just let them be happy! Leave them alone!

"That's a very fine suit, *Girafeau*!" shouted Izar. "Did your girlfriend make it for you special in your extra large size?"

If Didier had been ignoring the pending doom before, the dig at

Amélie made it impossible to pretend. He set Amélie down and set her behind him, turning to squint at Rosaire.

"You think a fancy suit can hide the fact you're a monster, Didier LeGrand?" Rosaire was ramping up his attack now. "I hate to break it to you big guy, but to make a woman love you, you will need to take it off!" That set the three of them laughing hysterically.

"I wish I could see it," piped up Sylvan in his squeaky voice, choking on his laughter, emboldened by his buddy's meanness. "I wish I could be a fly on the wall while the giant naked giraffe tries to *sauter* his little seamstress girl. Try not to crush her, hey *Girafeau*!"

More obnoxious thigh-slapping laughter followed as the trio of bullies closed in on Didier, crowding the dance floor now. Everyone had stopped dancing, and many had stepped back into the crowd. Others stood gawking.

A few others laughed, scattered through the crowd. How dare they? The same people who, moments ago, were relishing the romantic scene unfold. What hypocrites! Niki strode to the edge of the crowd, standing on a vacant chair.

"You will be sorry when she sees your giant *côté de boeuf*, Girafeau!" taunted Izar. "She'll run away screaming."

"How do you know it's *le zob géant*, Izar," said Rosaire, leering. "Maybe the big man has a teeny tiny *zizi*, eh? He is a mutant. Maybe that's why he's kept it hidden in his pants so long. It's useless, eh?"

"Ahahah! That's good, Rosaire. That's good," Izar continued. "You're going to wish you'd run away to join the circus when you were a kid, LeGrand. At least there you could have travel through Europe and make use of your special talent."

"Heehee!" squealed Sylvan, gasping with laughter now. "The bearded lady wouldn't mind his tiny *zizi*."

"Shut up, fool," said Rosaire, pushing the idiot Sylvan away with a hand over his face. "But seriously, LeGrand, *mon ami*. Listen to me. You're ridiculous. You should be ashamed of yourself, making a scene, embarrassing the fair Amélie in public like this."

Didier stood fuming now, his wide shoulders pulled up to his ears, his blue eyes shadowed under his frowning brow as his chin dipped down. Amélie stroked Didier's arm, tugged his hand, looking earnestly up into his face.

But Didier focused on Rosaire and the others, ignoring Amélie. This time he couldn't *shave the walls*. There was no hiding in the shadows when the spotlight, literally, shone onto your face.

Under the slowly spinning strobe lights, he was the proverbial tortured elephant in the circus, conspicuous, heavy and slow, being poked and prodded by the nasty trainers who were oblivious to his intelligence, his kindness, his regal power. And his pain. Niki saw his chest rise and fall in frustration and defeat.

Her heart pounded, and her stomach twisted in sympathy, her aches and pains forgotten. Hot tears pooled in her eyes, blurring the picture before her. But her mental focus was laser sharp, her hands and feet tingling, her muscles bunching, preparing to leap. Niki was no harmless monkey. Niki was the trained tiger in the very same circus, its wild urges barely restrained, her resentment toward the buffoons who ran the show boiling to the surface. She'd tolerated it long enough.

How could Niki let them ruin Didier and Amélie's special moment? It would destroy all of Didier's new confidence and knock him back to the way he was, terrified of his own shadow, lacking the self-esteem to be the man she knew he was, and live his life fully. She couldn't let it happen. She couldn't let them ruin Didier's special night. She jumped down and pushed through the crowd, moving closer to the dance area, her muscles twitching with the urge to rush in there and lay waste to those punks. She had to help!

Lurching forward, she jerked to a sudden stop as two hand grabbed her arms from behind. She gasped.

∽

She let out a squawk of indignation before growling, "Let me go!" She squirmed and fought him, kicking.

That was his Niki, always ready for a fight. "Shh, Niki. Shh. Don't be frightened. It's me," whispered Luc, slipping his arms further around her, gripping her gently but tightly. Whatever she thought to do, he had to stop her.

"Luc?" She tried to spin in his arms, and only managed it half way. The feel of her body sliding against his nearly distracted him from his purpose. Her cool damp skin contrasted with the heat radiating from her face. She was like a coiled spring, filled to bursting with power. It was so delicious to feel her against him, to smell the fresh saltiness of her skin and hair with a hint of oranges. Even though he knew the spectacle stressed her, the blood rushed from his head to his groin, and he felt lightheaded.

She glared at him and their gazes met and held. Her hazel eyes dilated and burned with dark emotion. It was the wrong kind of arousal, but his response was instinctual. His gaze dropped to her mouth, her lips parted with her irritation. She scanned his face, confused.

"What are you doing?" Niki wiggled to escape again.

He tightened his arms, closing his eyes and dipping his chin until his forehead touched hers, releasing a shaky breath. "Don't do it, Niki. Leave him be."

"What are you talking about? Rosaire's eating him alive. There's already an ugly scene. I couldn't make it any worse."

He nodded and softened his voice to a murmur. "I know. But it's not your battle. Let Didier handle it."

"But he can't! He's *not* handling it. He's just standing there! And everyone else just sits and watches. It's cruel to tolerate it and do nothing."

"Shh. Nik. Listen to me. I know you want to help. But Didier is not your brother Sam."

She jerked back, shocked, and blinked at him. "Of course he isn't."

He nodded. "Didier is a grown man, and he's changed. He can learn to defend himself."

She scowled, and he smiled and planted a kiss in the vee between her eyebrows, inhaling the feel of her under his lips. He shifted her to face the crowd, her back to his front, and held onto her. He felt her tension and feared she'd spring from his grasp and throw herself into the fray again.

"Shh. Wait. Watch."

"Stop shushing me. I hate that," she murmured, but she slowly warmed and relaxed into his arms as though she didn't mind the feel of them wrapped around her. It was pure unalloyed torture.

"Sorry." He laughed under his breath. "It's a schoolteacher thing."

They stood there, entwined like lovers, while Luc's heart broke all over again. His heart pounded in his chest, pressed to her lean shoulder blades as her scent rose to meet him. He shook it off. But her slender brown neck, laced with strands of dark hair, drew his attention and he had to tear it away to focus on the scene in the square.

Didier stepped away from Amélie, setting her farther behind him, and moved toward Rosaire. That was novel. He didn't appear angry. Neither was he menacing. He was still Didier, but he didn't cower, or slump into the shadows in resignation. This was his night. You could see the determination on his face, in his jutted jaw and the firm line of his mouth.

The music faded, turned down by the DJ who felt that events in the square deserved everyone's attention. The scene riveted everyone. Despite his insistence that Niki stay out of it, Luc did not know what to expect. He had to admit Niki's intervention, or the sheer impact of her example and her influence, had set things in motion for Didier. Luc believed that Didier was strong enough he would have figured things out on his own. But sometimes a catalyst came along, at just the right time in one's life, to nudge a person into action. That had clearly happened for Didier.

Luc pushed aside the notion that his own situation, though different, was parallel. He'd been searching, but mostly waiting, for something extraordinary to happen to him. And now it had.

Niki helping Didier made him happy. Perhaps not so happy that she'd come into his own life. Or maybe one day he would be glad he knew her. She was a force of nature, like some kind of heavenly body, a wild, spinning meteorite, pushing and pulling on other bodies as it crashed through space, wreaking havoc. But she was as rough as a meteorite, too, as solitary, and as random in her impact, for good or ill. His chest tightened, and his throat felt thick. Perhaps that was unfair. But his heart felt like something had smashed it and left the debris to drift unanchored by gravity.

He knew she was hurting as much as he was, in her own way. Unlike Niki, though, Luc was unwilling to impose himself and be her teacher. Not this time. Niki would have to be find her own center of gravity, and be her own rescuer.

She'd impacted him, changed him too. But she'd also hurt him. He may not have gotten his fantasy happy ending, but he was a stronger, wiser man. And he couldn't spend his life trying to force the universe into a design of his own delusion.

∼

Niki felt Luc's head drop behind her and heard him sigh. For a moment she thought, she wished, he would kiss her neck. Like he had before. A shiver ran through her body in anticipation. But he didn't. He shifted his weight, loosening his arms, and she felt a space open up between them.

She longed to apologize. She needed to tell him how she felt. How much he meant to her. But it would have to wait until the scene in the square had resolved itself. Tension through the square was high as people waited to see what Didier would do next.

He'd stepped slowly toward Rosaire and his friends, leaving Amélie standing alone on the dance floor. Everyone else had scuttled back to their tables, or stood to the sides, watching waiting. Izar and Sylvan, too, fell back, instinctively knowing that whatever was coming was Rosaire's to weather.

The colourful strobe lights that minutes ago created an atmosphere of romance and festivity, now spun eerily, illuminating Amélie's tense expression in flashes of blue, gold and hot pink like the flashing lights of emergency vehicles in the aftermath of a pile-up on the freeway.

Didier stopped in front of Rosaire, peering sternly down at him. The shine had come off Rosaire and his bluster. The obnoxious little man very likely became a bully to draw attention away from his own insecurities and inadequacies. That was backfiring tonight.

As though reluctantly, Didier *tsked*, shook his head, and bent toward Rosaire, reaching forward to take a healthy grip on the front of his shirt and jacket, bunching it tightly in his fist. Didier's hand was so large, there wasn't much left of Rosaire's shirt to accommodate his pudgy form. It came untucked and rode up, exposing his hairy belly.

Then Didier did the unthinkable. He lifted him up off the ground.

A sudden sensation of ice dropped into Niki's stomach like a glacier and permeated her body with cold from the inside out.

"Oh, my God, I've created a monster," she gasped and a collective exclamation from the assembled crowd echoed her. This was uncharacteristic of Didier, and everyone knew it.

He wouldn't hit him. He wouldn't. Didier knew his own strength. Though she wouldn't say Rosaire didn't have it coming. But Didier could crush him.

Rosaire clearly knew it. From his new elevated vantage point, eye level with the glaring Didier, and therefore with his feet dangling a good two feet off of the ground, Rosaire had the time and opportunity to reconsider his beliefs.

Rosaire snivelled. "Hey, hey, my old friend. What's up?"

Didier blinked slowly as if to confirm what everyone thought. "You are, little man."

My God, Rosaire was an idiot. Was that why no one had ever done anything to stop his persistent bullying? The absurdity of it all blazed brightly now, as obvious as a flaming summer sunset across the ripening fields of southern France.

A strangled sound emitted from Rosaire's throat as Didier brought him closer, nose to nose, as though he would take a big bite out of him. Rosaire threw his arms wide, exposing even more of his naked underbelly. "Erm... the view's good from up here, *Girafeau*. I didn't know what I was missing out on. You're a lucky man."

Didier gave him a jerk and let out a terrifying growl, right in his pudgy pinched face. "ARRGGHH!"

"Oh, my God!" Niki flinched, and felt Luc's astonishment as he let out a soft grunt of incredulous laughter.

"Are you enjoying this as much as I am?" Luc said.

"I don't know. It depends what happens ne–oh damn!"

Rosaire flailed and squealed like a piglet and then pissed himself.

A moment passed before the crowd realized it, though, and a low murmur rose in volume as more and more people tittered, chuckled and then outright laughed out loud.

Didier, ever the gentleman, rolled his eyes, let out an exasperated sigh and set the terrified Rosaire back on the ground. He smiled, tilted his head and smoothed the front of Rosaire's severely creased shirt. Then he said in a pleasant conversational tone, "Looks like you could use a new suit yourself, Rosaire. I have an excellent tailor I can recommend." He turned and opened his palm toward Amélie, and she stepped forward and set her hand in his.

The crowd broke into cheers and applause.

"Well. There you go. All is well," said Luc, releasing her and stepping back, leaving her shivering without his arms wrapped around her. Where they ought to be. Where they should always be. She knew that now. Niki'd been a fool to push him away. She needed him.

She loved him.

Niki turned toward him, eager to kiss him, longing to resolve this impasse. She rested her palms on his hard chest. Her body ached for him. She'd missed the feel of him. She'd missed his closeness more than she realized, more than she had been willing to admit. Inhaling, she slid her hands up to curl around his neck, expecting the kiss she craved, and that only Luc could deliver.

But it didn't come. He lifted his own hands, lightly circled her wrists with his fingers, and pulled her arms down as he stepped back.

"I'll be heading home tomorrow." She watched his Adam's apple bob as he swallowed. "So... I'm glad I had this chance to say goodbye, Niki." His kind, intelligent, oh-so-honest blue eyes held sadness as they raked her face, as if trying to memorize her features. He drew a breath and released it on a sigh. "I'm glad I met you."

Her arms fell to her sides and her mouth opened as all her muscles went limp. What was he saying? Her eyes burned and her throat convulsed as if her body were trying to purge the truth it didn't want. That it couldn't accept.

"Luc?" It came out a choked whisper. Cold tightness lodged in her chest like an ice pick, and she wrapped her arms around her middle, reeling from his sudden retreat. What? Was there no hope?

He shook his head haltingly, his own eyes shining, turned on his heel and strode away, disappearing with the dispersing crowd, taking her wrecked heart with him.

CHAPTER 38

She'd half expected Didier to spend the night at Amélie's, but on the drive home he'd said no. It was too soon, and the night had been fraught, so the mood wasn't right. He wanted their first time to be perfect, and she held her tongue.

As for the rest of the evening, they said not a thing about it, both of them stewing in their private thoughts, their nerves frayed. She'd slept, despite going to bed with a heavy heart, and tossing and turning for hours.

When she awoke it was late, and she'd dreamt of Luc, then Didier, then Sam again, one face and fragmented memory blurring into the next. Sam's voice, still familiar, as if they still spoke every day, sounded in her ears, though she saw Luc's face. She opened her eyes expecting to see him in the room with her, that's how real it seemed. He'd said, *"I wanted you to have it. To remember us together. For when you go away."*

She knew the drawing Sam referred to. She carried it with her, taped together, folded and re-folded, dog-eared and frayed at the seams. The vision was some creation of her tortured mind. But why was he giving it to her again and again when in fact, he never had? She'd found it in his wastebin the same morning she'd found him dead in his bed.

What did it mean? What was he trying to tell her? It was Sam that went away. He'd left her. He's the one who'd broken her heart. But he was right in one sense. She had left him alone. She hadn't been there when he'd needed her. She'd let *him* down. Her tired mind was playing tricks on her.

With clenched teeth, she pushed aside thoughts of both Sam and Luc. Time for physio. Trying to get out of bed was another matter altogether. She paid for her intensive exercise the day before. Not to mention her foolish handstand last night. But stiff and painful though she might be, she had to do it all over again.

She groaned with the effort. Lifting herself was impossible, so she rolled to her stomach, inched her legs off the bed onto the floor, and slid to her knees. Easing herself back onto her haunches, she could stretch her tight thigh and calf muscles, and warm up her hip flexors, while hanging off the side of the mattress and slowly lengthening her arms and loosening her tight shoulders.

Despite the expected overall stiffness, her specific injuries felt better. Even her dislocated shoulder, despite her momentary lapse in judgement last night, was less feeble. Maybe in the context of full body pain, they were just less noticeable.

Once she was finally on her feet, she shuffled out to the kitchen, listening for sounds of Didier, but the house was silent. Minou sidled up and rubbed against her ankles as she got out the ingredients for another smoothie and assembled them.

"*Bonjour*, Minou. Did you get fed today?" More ankle rubbing. She checked Minou's dishes and determined that Didier had fed her this morning. She checked the clock. Twelve-thirty! She'd slept so late. Where was Didier?

After her nutrient smoothie and rolling massage, Niki headed outside to see about firing up the forge for her hot yoga session. When she peeked in the open doorway of the forge, there was Didier hammering away on some metal rod, the fire blazing beside him. Instead of disturbing him, she went straight to the creek, fortifying herself for the shock, reminding herself why it was necessary.

She wondered how long Luc would spend in Bordeaux before his flight home to Vancouver. She never asked, and he hadn't said. He must be due back soon to prepare for the start of the new school year. That was the thing about teachers, their schedule was predictable.

It made her ponder what Luc's life was like back home. Where did he live? Who were his friends? What kind of car did he drive? She realized she knew nothing about him. The same was true for him, and yet... and yet they'd connected on a level far above the mundane details of their lives. Those things seemed unimportant when you were with a person who knew you inside and out, who'd seen you at your worst and loved you, anyway.

Her chest squeezed. Or so he'd said. Now he'd gone, the memory of his presence, the look and sound and scent and touch of him, haunted her. Everywhere she looked, every object she touched, reminded her of their week of intimate seclusion. A sound or smell caused a shiver of recognition to snake down her back, images forming in her mind, her body spasming in memory of his skilful lovemaking.

She closed her eyes for a moment, and a small sound vibrated in her throat. Why would she throw that away? What was wrong with her? Maybe she could catch up with him before leaving France, though she suspected her ride to Bordeaux would be long and arduous, and she'd be lucky to have a day to tour around the city before she had to leave for home. Probably he'd be gone by then.

That left hunting him down in Vancouver, which could take a while. Maybe she could find out which school he taught at from Facebook or something. How many French-immersion schools could there be? All it would take was a phone call or two to the school board. But how would she contact him? And how would he react? Would he ever want to see her again after the way she'd treated him? It smacked of desperation.

"Why do you have to make it so damned difficult to love you?"

"You know what you are? You're a liar and a thief."

"You're lying to yourself about us, Niki. What we've started here is not a casual thing. This is life changing, what's happening between us. You can't run from this."

Stupid, stupid woman. She'd thought she could. Closing her eyes she jumped into the creek, the scream that ripped from her throat only partly a response to the shock of the icy water. When she bobbed to the surface and wiped water from her eyes, Didier stood , legs planted wide on the bank, wielding his hammer in one hand and an incredulous expression on his face.

He blinked at her. "*Mais putain, tu fais quoi, là?*"

"Did you just call me a whore?"

His hammer arm dropped slowly and he took another step closer, peering at her. "Heh? No. No, it's an expression."

"I should learn that one, I guess. Sounds useful. What's it mean?"

"It means... what are you doing in the creek you crazy woman? Or something like that."

"I'm doing hot-cold therapy. For my rehab." She splashed around, keeping her limbs moving. She was numb from the cold. Numb from the pain. And she liked it. She'd always been strong and determined. With sheer willpower, she had and would continue to overcome all challenges and obstacles. Not just physical injury, but loss and grief, and even occasional loneliness. She knew she had the ability to live alone and be fine. If she committed to a long term relationship, she'd probably regret it. She'd find herself up to her ears in compromises and she'd end up hating her life.

He shook his head in disbelief. "You're not hurt?"

She climbed out of the water. "Nope. I feel like a fucking Amazon!" She growled in demonstration, raising her fisted hands above her head.

"I'm terrified to ask what is the hot part of this therapy."

"You'll see." She sloshed back to the forge, and he followed.

Then he shared a few more colourful French idioms while she did her sun salutations by the heat of the forge. "How does this help you?" As she repeated the process twice more, and he walked back and forth from forge to stream to forge along with her, she explained how the rapid cold and hot increased blood flow and decreased inflammation.

Afterwards, they went back to the house. On the way, she stopped to examine her bike again, a new thought popping into her head. "Hey Didier. I wonder if you can repair the problems with my bike. I would ask you to take it in to a shop, but when I look at it, it seems the problem is this bent frame here, the front wheel and derailleur. It needs a new wheel and derailleur, which we could get at a shop. But they'll tell me to throw the frame out and, I'm almost done with it, so... it's technical but maybe you could straighten it out? Save me the money?"

"Hmm. Maybe. Let me have a look." He bent to examine her bike, running his large hands over it like a surgeon. "It's a chromoly steel frame, that's good. You're lucky. If it were aluminum or titanium or... well, anyway. I can try." He picked it up and carried it off to the forge.

While Niki slathered herself in healing lotions and oils, Didier researched her bike and took it apart. When she caught up with him an hour later, he was hammering a little part and frowning.

"I don't like that face."

"I could repair the frame by cutting out a section and replacing it with some steel tubing. But..." He frowned at the thing in his blackened fingers, "...some small parts, like this here..."

"The derailleur."

"Yes, it's too fine and I can't straighten out this stainless steel. I had it back together, but I don't think it works properly. It makes noises. You want to try it?" Together they reassembled the bike and tested the wheels, the steering and the gears.

He'd straightened the frame all right, though one tire looked like it would never run true again. She spun the wheels, tried the gears and tested the steering. It was okay, but not great. "I know what's wrong, but I don't have the special equipment or parts to do it."

She straddled the bike and sat in the saddle for the first time since her accident. It felt a little weird, but good. Familiar. She wobbled around the shop messing with the gear shifter. "I think we need to replace a few working parts. Get me a new wheel rim. Do you know of a bike shop in town?"

"Not here, but in Villeneuve-sur-Lot. I can drive there now. Can you specify what you want?"

"Sure." They went over the bike part by part, and she made a list of the parts, with specifications, which were bent or just didn't work properly, but that Didier could replace. The derailleur and one shifter were badly bent, as was the chain guard. One wheel frame had a small but persistent wobble to it. Small things that could make her last ride miserable and dangerous.

Fortunately, Didier could make the repairs. If she had to take the entire bike in, it would cost a lot, and probably take a week or more. "I'll go right now. I can be back in time for dinner."

"You're sure you don't mind?"

"No. I can do some other errands while I'm there. I'll bring something for dinner, and we can have a nice visit this evening. Hey, you don't want to come do you?"

"Mm. Not really. I'd rather finish my therapy and have a nap, if that's okay. We'll catch up later?"

He nodded and was off. After having something to eat, she went back out to the forge to look again at her bike. It wasn't road worthy, but she could practice in the yard to get her backside used to sitting in the saddle again. That would be time well spent. She rolled the bike outside and got on, pushing off. The ride was wobbly at first, as much from her own weakness as the defects of the bike, but as she warmed up, it got better, and the joy of riding, and just plain moving around fuelled her enthusiasm.

While she pedaled slowly up and down the dirt driveway, her mind drifted back to her thoughts just before jumping in the creek. She was being a sentimental fool. Never had she considered changing her plans or chasing after a guy. What had come over her? She had never been so affected by a hookup, one so brief. What had happened this time to affect her so much? No one's leaving had caused her so much pain since… since Sam died. Though her father's abandonment had lingered at home like the scent of onions, she hadn't missed him so much as suffered from the effects of her mother having to work and being stressed all the time.

She'd learned to live without her brother, even though he was the only person she'd ever loved. She was a strong and independent woman, and she'd learn to go on without Luc. But it would be hard. Luc was different. He wasn't arrogant and self-absorbed, like some guys she'd dated, nor weak and child-like. He asked nothing of her, except honesty. He was mature, caring and responsible, and he'd gotten involved in her life and taken care of her.

She'd let him get close. Too close. And this was the price she paid. A piece of her had twisted, ripped, and warped like this bicycle of hers. Every time the wheel went round, there was a click and a whirr, something rubbing where it shouldn't, impossible to balance, reminding her of how it should work, but didn't anymore. Like her heart.

Tears streaming from her eyes blinded her and before she knew it, the bike wobbled out of control. The front tire slid into a rut and jerked to one side, wrenching control out of her hands. Blindly, she careened into Didier's split-rail fence with a shout of frustration, ass over chainstays over front fork, ending in a tangled heap with a scream of pain.

Saddle bags packed, Luc stood on the gravel forecourt with Charles, France, and Patrice, saying his farewells. This was without a doubt the hardest, saddest and most depressing end of summer departure from Petit Bergeron that he remembered. Their time together even eased those years when one of their parents died.

This year was different. He was different.

At this moment he couldn't even say with certainty he'd be back next year. His endless quest to re-create the happy family summers of his youth led to his devotion to spending his summers in the south of France. Worse, he'd pursued his dream of a love, a marriage, and a family like his parents. A dream he finally surrendered. Fate couldn't be forced into a preconceived shape.

Whatever happened now, in his life, would happen because of fate, because he lived with integrity, in the moment and no longer trying to control his own destiny. No more of that.

One last embrace and *les bises* for each of his friends, with only speaking looks from each of them, and a friendly kiss on the lips from Patrice, to comment on his situation, and he pushed off. A brief stop in the village to say goodbye to a few more friends and he'd head west. It would take him two hours on his bike to get to Bordeaux.

Leaving his bike at the *Restaurant l'Entre-cote* by the village gate, he hiked up the avenue to the *Place des Arcade*. On the way he took his leave from any shopkeepers he passed, and any villagers he recognized. In the square he made his way around the arcade stopping in to speak with the people he knew best. It was nearly everyone in the village, and everyone had something to say about the events of the summer.

He stood by the outdoor display of the toy shop on the corner, saying goodbye to Madeleine, his eyes scanning the wooden swords, plastic helmets, and toy Knights Templar, thinking how amazing it would be if he brought his entire class to Petit Bergeron for the Medieval festival. What a learning experience that would be. He could organize a special summer camp. There was a project he could throw himself into so he'd have a reason to look forward to next summer without fixating on this summer, Niki, all he had within his grasp, and lost.

Last night, looking at Niki brought him pain, and yet he'd needed to intervene. It was important for Didier to do this alone. And, Luc, despite his resolution to stay away from her and out of her affairs, was the one to stop her from this one last impulsive gesture. But if she hadn't learned her lesson after this, he could do nothing for her. She wanted to be alone and now she was.

But so was he.

Just then Didier strode purposefully across the *Place*. He said goodbye to Madeleine and went to intercept.

"Hey! Didier!" He shouted, waving.

Didier stopped, scanned him head to toe, his road riding gear and backpack, and said, "*Salut*, Luc." Didier's expression carried layers of meaning. An aura of self-knowledge surrounded him that spoke to the events of last night and everyone's awareness. But it also acknowledged his autonomy, and even the role he'd played in his own oppression. This new wisdom brought a clarity that said: I see you too. Luc shrunk under the implicit judgement in his steady gaze.

"Have you seen Rosaire this morning?" Luc asked.

Didier shook his head.

"Well, I guess he'll show his face when he's good and ready. I'm just saying goodbye to everyone."

Didier lifted a brow. "So, that's it for this year then?"

"Yup."

Didier took a moment to let his gaze wander past Luc and pan across the arcade and its shops. "What a summer, hey?"

If Luc had to hear it again, he'd be ill. Every mention of the special events of the summer pounded home the one variable that changed this year, and like Dominoes, set a series of events into motion that effected everyone. Niki. Their gazes met, Luc squinted at Didier, and a great deal of information passed between them.

"Did you say goodbye to her?"

Luc clenched his fists, gritted his teeth and paused, gathering his patience so he could endure Didier's questions with as much good grace as possible. No one knew what had happened between himself and Niki. Was it blame or pity he saw in Didier's eyes?

"Yes. We spoke last night."

After a moment Didier spoke again. "So that's it then."

Luc nodded with more conviction than he felt. "Yes."

Didier scanned the line of the arcade, his gaze following the path of the villagers traversing the square engaged in their daily business. He seemed to choose his words. He took a large breath, his chest rising, held it while he hesitated, and released in a long sigh.

"You're a fool to walk away."

Luc's head fizzed as he tried to process Didier's sharp words. What did he say? Didier never spoke so forthrightly. He pressed his lips together to control his emotions, and scanned the man's face for clues, dizzy from the blood rushing to his ears and heating his face, torn between shame and indignation. "Oh, so you're an expert on relationships now are you?"

"Believe me, I know you're hurting... but I also have learned some hard lessons. You know I'm right."

"Do I?" *Do I?* Luc found it difficult to hold his steady gaze. Perhaps he did.

"Let me tell you something about what I've learned, *mon ami.*" Didier rested his large hand on Luc's shoulder and squeezed, and though they were the same age, he reminded Luc of his own father, and all the wisdom he'd shared with Luc growing up. "In matters of love, *pride* has nothing to do with it. The question is, do you love the woman? Do you want to spend the rest of your life loving her? And if it is, well..." Didier released him and gave a classic Gallic shrug. "... then you must risk everything. Otherwise you have no one to blame but yourself for your loneliness and your misery."

Luc couldn't speak. His breath stuck in his throat, his chest hardened as though a chunk of Dordogne limestone lodged there and he would never take a breath again. His pulse raced, as though he cycled down a long steep decline, speeding up, the wind in his face, the possibility of losing control and crashing imminent.

"Well. We'll see you next summer," Didier said.

Sweat bloomed on his skin. His mind raced. Luc shook his head, and shook it again, staring at the cobblestones beneath his feet. He wasn't saying no, he wasn't even answering Didier, just trying to process the man's hard won advice, and the unavoidable truth of his words.

Yes she'd hurt him. Yes he was still angry with her. He raked a hand through his hair and clenched his jaw.

Was his pride involved? Or was he being pragmatic? He was trying to act on his principals, trying to be rational. Wasn't he? Pride, hurt feelings, had nothing to do with his determination to leave her. Or did it?

He loved her. Despite her stubbornness. He loved her.

How could he say he wasn't reacting with emotions? Maybe he *was* being a prideful fool.

He knew she was hurting. And lying to herself. If he couldn't break through her defensive barriers, who could? Who would?

He knew how Sam's needs had superceded Niki's. He understood why she'd never learned to rely on anyone. There had *been* no one for her to rely upon. After her father abandoned them when they were young, and her mother had abdicated responsibility for her emotional safety in the overwhelm of dealing with single motherhood and a special needs child she couldn't handle, Sam had been all that anchored Niki in the storm of her young life. How Sam giving up on life meant that he'd given up on her, too.

He glanced up to see Didier's tight-lipped smile and his nod of approval.

Luc thought about his students. Some kids grew up in homes and families as different from his own as could be, without nurturing and support. How would he go about getting through to them if they were hurting, yet unable to reach out and ask for, let alone accept, help? He always found a way. How could he get through to Niki and earn her trust? Was it arrogant of him to think he could?

He had to try.

As soon as the thought called out in his head, his heart answered like an echo. His chest filled with a bubble of hope, lifting his eyes to the horizon and the lifting the corners of his mouth, casting off the stiff clay of regret that weighed him down these past days. He'd go to her. She may refuse his help. That was her choice. The worst could still happen. But he had to try.

This was his choice.

He couldn't be the one who gave up on her. He couldn't abandon her the way everyone else had. Even though she pushed, he wouldn't go away. Whatever happened, he'd be there for her.

His eyes came into focus and he blinked up at Didier. "I have to go!"

Something hurt. Niki's leg throbbed, and sharp arrows of pain darted up and down when she moved. Damn it! But worse than the pain, she couldn't get up. She was tangled, caught between the bike and the broken fence, which had splintered, and poked into her like some kind of crazy torture device. And she was alone.

Damn it. Why had she asked Didier to get parts for her today? Why had she ridden her twisted bike while alone? Her teeth ground. Her stubbornness and reckless independence came back to bite her in the ass.

Every time she wiggled, or even flexed a muscle, the pain intensified. Her thigh burned and throbbed with a pulse of its own. Something was digging into her hamstring. Reaching with her arm around the back, sticky warmth met her touch. A huge splinter protruded from her skin. It was still attached to the fence. Shit! She pulled her hand back to find her fingers covered in a scary amount of dark blood. The metallic tang of iron filled her nose.

Goddam, she better not have punctured an artery. A fresh wave of tears rose to her eyes, this time tears of fear and panic, and she blinked them away. Her breath came in hard gasps and had to tell herself to stay calm. A bark of bitter laughter escaped from her throat into the quiet French countryside. She ripped a sleeve from her shirt, tying it tightly around her upper thigh before she bled out here hanging helpless like a monkey in a cage. How appropriate. For all the times she'd been part of a search and rescue team saving some lonely stranded soul, it had come to this. She'd die alone, slowly, with plenty of time to ponder her foolish mistakes, and regret the choices she'd made in life.

Well, it was what she should expect. If she chose to live alone, she'd better expect to die alone, too.

At least an hour passed. Minou wandered over, nosed around, rubbed against her and then jumped onto her bent back.

"Hello, puss," she said. "What's taking your papa so long, hey?"

The cat began to knead Niki's shoulder with its tiny paws. This provided a strange comfort that brought tears to her eyes. The only sounds beyond the cat's purring were the occasional chirp of birds, and in between, the hypnotic buzz of cicadas in the tall grasses of the surrounding fields. The afternoon sun baked her head, and she went past sweating to uncomfortably dehydrated. Her leg was numb from lack of blood flow. Lethargy overwhelmed her, and her mind filled with fog, drifting in and out of dreamlike places, sometimes joyful memories, others melancholy. At last the distant crunching of tires on the gravel road approached. She jerked, and regretted it, as the pain in her leg reminded her of her predicament. But she was alert again.

Hallelujah! Didier was home. And she wasn't dead yet.

Sitting as motionless as possible, she waited for him. But a few moments later, it wasn't Didier's voice she heard behind her.

"Jesus, woman. Is this going to be a weekly thing with you?"

Her pulse quickened. She squeezed her eyes tight, trying to calm her pounding heart. She kept her voice calm. The last thing she wanted was for him to know she'd been crying for him on her imagined death bed. Or fence.

"Luc. I thought you left town."

"I did. Made it as far as the village square."

She opened her eyes and squinted into the glaring sun. He sauntered into her peripheral vision and stopped a few feet away. She tilted her head. "Can you come around where I can see you? I can't move."

He did so, standing a few yards off, his arms crossed over his chest, a bewildered expression on his handsome face as he studied her. "You can't get up?" He wore lycra bike shorts and a loose tank. Her eyes tripped over the smoothness of his tanned skin, glistening with sweat, and the shadowed lines of his lean muscles.

She shook her head. "I'm tangled, and something's cutting me. I'm bleeding."

He circled around her examining her wreck from every angle. "Fascinating. A spectacular mess." He squatted low and peered at her from ground level. "I see. You're bleeding all right. Nice tourniquet though."

"Is it serious? I can't feel it."

He shrugged. "Hard to say. Why didn't you call the big guy?"

"Uh. Don't have my phone. He drove to Villeneuve-sur-Lot. Bike parts."

"And you had to ride it before he fixed it." He drew a deep breath and let it out in an exasperated sigh. "Niki, Niki, Niki."

Her chest tightened at his implied criticism, and her jaw stiffened.

"Piss off!" Why wasn't he helping her get up? He was mocking her! "Why didn't you leave town?"

He stepped in front of her again, this time with his hands on his hips. He narrowed his eyes. "I stopped to say goodbye to folks in the village. Bumped into Didier, in fact. Before he left, I guess."

She lifted her head. "Why did you come back?"

"I came back because of you. I regret it already."

Her heart did a back flip and leapt off a high parapet, but she kept her voice steady. "Really?"

"Mm-hmm."

"Because?"

"You know why."

Then she registered his last words. "You regret it?"

"Depends on you."

Why was his tone of voice so flip? The things he said made her heart race wildly with happiness, and she didn't care to stop and examine that right now. But his tone was cool, and he hadn't approached her, touched her or made any attempt to release her from her ridiculous deathtrap. He sounded angry. She growled with frustration.

"What was that?"

"What are you doing?" Was this his idea of revenge?

"I don't understand."

"Why are you just standing there? I'm stuck and in pain! Do you want me to bleed to death?" Tears threatened again, but she refused to let him see her cry.

He didn't move. "Do you?"

"What the fuck, Luc!"

CHAPTER 39

"What do you want, Niki?" He had to tread carefully now. His heart twisted to see her there, and he clenched his fists, fighting his instinct to rush to her rescue. He'd made sure her wound wasn't life threatening. It was an ugly gash, made worse because a splinter of fence impaled her thigh, but her tourniquet had effectively stemmed the bleeding. A few more minutes would be okay.

"What do I want? I want to get up! What do you think?"

"And you want to do it all by yourself."

"I don't care! Yes! Just…" Her eyes welled with unshed tears of pain, but also of frustration, and she pressed her lips together to quell the tremors that had begun in her chin. How else could he help her see? She was trapped between two fears, the fear of being alone, and the fear of letting someone in, trusting them, and then losing them.

"But you won't ask for help."

She screamed. "You're being an asshole." Her rage squeezed tears from her eyes, and they ran down her cheeks. She swiped at them angrily and averted her gaze, embarrassed at her perceived weakness.

"I know. I'm sorry, baby. Why would I do that?"

"You're angry at me."

"Am I? Why would I be angry?"

He watched as she fumed. He had to wait. *Did she think he was just playing power games with her? Letting her suffer out of spite?*

"Because I... Stop asking stupid questions! Why are you even here? To torment me?"

He shook his head. She glanced at his face, caught his gaze. He knew his eyes, too, were wet with tears. A muscle in his jaw ticked with tension. But he didn't hide it. He wanted her to know he cared and suffered with her. He wasn't enjoying this any more than she was.

"What the fuck!"

"Do you want my help?"

"I want to get up!"

"But you can't ask for my help."

"Fine! I'll do it myself. I don't need help. And I don't need you!" She was growling at him now.

He had a moment of doubt. Was it cruel to push her to the edge and over it? Was there another way?

Determined to get free without begging, he watched her feel at the wound on her leg again, trying to figure out in which direction the spike of wood entered her flesh.

He sighed. "No one can survive alone, Niki."

"What are you talking about?" She flinched, turning her head away to hide her face. He saw her drag her body back away from the splinter. Her eyes clouded with pain. But she persisted.

"It's not a failure, or a weakness, to rely on others. Love is a two-way street. It's okay to need help, and to take care of each other. Nice actually."

"What do you want?"

"I've got another couple of days, tops, in Bordeaux, before I have to fly home. I have to get back for work." He paused, looking away from her, squinting out at the fields. "I want you to come with me. I want us to be together, Niki. Something happened here. Let's not throw it away. Let's take some time to figure out what we want before we go back. Tell me, Niki. I need to hear you say it."

"Say what?"

He almost lost it then, exhaling through clenched teeth. Sweat trickled down his temples from standing in the hot sun. His brow creased with apprehension, and his jaw ticked from clenching his teeth. Tears continued to flow. Why did she have to be so shut off? Why did he have to fall in love with such a difficult woman?

"That you want me, damn it!" He stepped back. "That you're willing to take the risk to make this real. If you say no, I'll leave right now. If you can't let yourself admit it after all we've shared, it's as good as a no. I need that. I can't stay without that."

Fury and panic filled her and scrambled her thoughts. She couldn't get a grip on what she was feeling. The wild surge of emotions that swirled in her chest confused and immobilized her, even more than the splinter that bound her to the fence. She was so glad he came back but she wanted him to leave her in peace. Her nerves felt raw and exposed, twitching like ripped out electrical wires after a storm.

Her mouth went dry, and her breath caught in her throat.

"Don't leave," she croaked, feeling her chin quiver, and pressed her lips tightly together to stop a full-blown crying jag. There was no hiding the pain in her voice. She couldn't run, had nowhere to hide. And he knew it. That's why he'd left her here, hung up on this broken fence. "What do you want from me?"

His rigid posture softened, and he stepped closer.

"I know you've got… issues to work through. We all do. I want to help you with that, too. But I need clarity, honesty, and openness. Can you do that much? If you say yes, we can make plans together. This can be a beginning for us. Do you trust me, Nik? What'll it be?"

Luc crouched down beside her resting the tips of his fingers on her knee, dragging them back and forth in a minute caress.

"I don't know… I've never…" The tears were flowing again. It was as if he'd punctured her protective armour, and all her fears and needs were pouring out, unstoppable. She wanted to do the right thing. Say the right thing. For him. She was tired of being alone. Of having no one to rely on. No one to go to when she'd had a bad day or yet another of her frequent injuries.

"How did this happen to you?"

"I fell off my bike," she whimpered, swiping a dusty arm across her weeping eyes. "That's all…"

"That's not what I meant." Luc lifted a hand and caressed her cheek with the back of his knuckles, so gentle and loving as his eyes searched hers. Her tears flowed again as she tilted her head, pressing her face into his hand. His touch sent a shiver through her, remembering all their intimate moments, his tender loving.

"I don't want to fight with you, sweetheart. I want to help you and love you. Not just right now, but always. I want to be with you. But I don't think that can happen, Nik, until you realize why you're pushing me away so hard." While he spoke, his hand cupped the back of her head, and gently, slowly slid down her neck and back before wrapping his arm around her hunched shoulders.

"I'm not–"

"What are you afraid of, baby?" Luc's voice was a soft caress, quieting her desire to hit and scream, or run away. Like only he seemed able to do.

No one had ever tended to her so gently and lovingly as Luc had done last week. She craved more of that tenderness. More of his understanding.

"I'm not afraid of anything," she mewled, and knew she was pathetic, and that it was a lie.

Even when she'd been a little girl, there had always been Sam, even littler, so afraid and vulnerable. Needing help. Sam who fell apart at the slightest hardship, sucking all the love and attention out of her parents, until there was nothing left for her, not a father, not a mother. Sam who only she had the ability to calm and explain things to, so much so that her mom came to depend on her to survive, never realizing how she had abandoned her daughter.

Niki was given no choice but to become strong and fiercely independent. Someone everyone relied on, including herself. Especially herself. Someone who didn't need help. But it wasn't what she wanted.

He dragged his thumb under her eyes, clearing away the tears that continued to blind her. "You must fear something, or why else would you put up with this much suffering. It must be bad, whatever it is."

Was she? Niki kept her eyes cast down. He was right. Wasn't this what she'd been thinking about earlier? For all her determination to be strong and independent, she was frightened and lonely. But she didn't want to be an island anymore. She didn't want to die alone. But alone was all she knew how to be.

She focussed on his cycling shoes, grinding into the dry packed dirt of Didier's driveway. She noticed their colour–blue and brown. There was a painted wooden bead threaded onto his laces, purple with handpainted yellow dots.

"What's that?"

"What?" He looked down, puzzled at her turn of attention.

"That." She pointed at his shoe.

"Ah. A present from my niece. A good luck charm. To keep me safe until I get home."

Her world seems to compress and tilt a little, and her head felt tight.

"You have a niece? I never knew that." Some tension eased out of her limbs. Niki felt the fight draining out of her. She wanted this. She wanted him.

The corner of his mouth curled up just a titch. "I have three. There are a lot of things you don't know about me."

"I was thinking about that." She looked up, met his eyes. "What kind of car do you drive?"

He snorted softly. "Nothing very sexy on a teacher's salary."

"It's okay." None of those things mattered to her. She dropped her gaze again. The only thing that mattered was that he stayed close to her. It was time to be truly courageous, and risk everything. "I don't want to die alone." It came out barely louder than a whisper.

"You won't die out here today, no matter what you might be feeling."

"I mean I don't want to die alone… ever. At work, or in my sleep, or in old age. I don't want to be alone anymore, Luc. I've been running away from… from the possibility of more loss for ten years. Avoiding getting close to anyone so I would never have to lose them. But what I have is worse than what I'm running from."

Luc touched her chin gently with his fingertips, lifting her face to meet her gaze, understanding she was giving him what he asked for. "Then open your heart and let me in."

Niki blinked away the wetness in her eyes and peered into his. They were as blue as ever, and yet warm as a summer sky. Luc's eyes were the warmest, safest place she could imagine. She wanted to lose herself in them. She wanted to trust him.

"What if I do something obnoxious and you leave me?"

A sad smile tugged at the corners of his mouth as he gazed into her eyes. "What if I'm so boring you leave me?"

She nodded. He depended on her too. "I've always been alone. Except for Sam, I've always been alone. And I've been okay. But not really, you know."

"I know. Poor baby. But I'm here for you now. It's okay to lean on me." He stood over her, tightening his arm around her back, sliding the other under her legs. "Put your arms around my neck and hang on tight."

She did as he asked.

He pressed his fingers firmly against the back of her thigh, spanning the wound with his fingers, and lifted her up and away from the splintered fence with a small jerk. "Hold on." She felt the splinter catching on her flesh as it pulled out, and it hurt like hell. She sucked breath in through her teeth, but she didn't cry out. Instead she pushed her face into his damp neck and breathed in the familiar scent his comforting, sun-baked skin, his musk and a hint of sunscreen, even a hint of oranges. It took some pain away.

"God, you're a tough little thing," he said, carrying her toward the house, cradling her in his arms, his hand pressed flat and hard against her wound to stem the fresh bleeding.

"Why did you come back, really?"

"I realized I needed you, Niki. My search was over. Having known you, I could never be content with anyone else. I could never forget you." He paused at the door and pressed his lips against her hair. "Are you glad I came back? Do you need me?"

She realized that he needed to hear her say it, as much for himself as for her. For Luc, the caregiver, being needed was his way of loving and being loved. She stroked the back of his soft neck with her fingers, fingering his sweat dampened hair. "I do. Way too much. It doesn't seem like a good deal for you compared to Patrice."

He laughed, looking up at the door frame overhead, exhaling. "Sometimes, we have a very pretty notion of what love should be. As though love can only happen in a... like a made-for-tv movie, with flowers and diamond rings and music playing. And maybe kissing in elevators." He chuckled. "But it's not like that at all. Sometimes love fucking hurts, because you fall in love with someone who doesn't know how to love you back. And all you can do is accept them and hope they figure it out. Even if it means walking away."

He shifted her weight, and she slid down.

"Can you stand?"

She nodded and limped through the door he held open. She could feel fresh blood oozing from her leg. They went together to the bathroom to tend to her wound.

"Is that why you left?"

"I wish I could say I was so noble. No. I left because I was angry, jealous, frustrated. And hurt. And maybe too proud to hang around and get any more abuse from you."

"I'm sorry."

He seemed not to hear her apology. Or perhaps he chose to ignore her. He wet a towel and dabbed at her blood-encrusted leg, sucking air through his teeth when he bent to examine her wound.

"Do I need stitches?"

"Maybe not. It's a small hole. Just deep. A bandage ought to do it. But we ought to take you in, anyway. You might have bits of old wood in there, and need antibiotics. When's Didier due back?"

"I love you, Luc."

He stood up, took her tear and dirt-streaked face between his bloody hands and regarded her in that way that melted her insides and broke down all barriers between them.

"I love you, Niki."

"I love you, so much."

God she loved his eyes. She really loved him. And her heart seemed to puff up and tingle a little, like her ripped and twisted muscles and ligaments, as though it was getting the therapy it needed to heal.

"Thank you for loving me." He covered her mouth softly with his own, caressing her with his lips, conveying all his love with the intensity of his gentle touch. He pulled back. "I hope you're ready to do the hard work of loving me for a long, long, long time, because… I have no intention of letting you go."

She was ready.

CHAPTER 40

The next several hours stretched out as if in slow motion. Luc found someone to come and get them with a car and take them to the clinic in Agen since Didier was still too far away, and Charles and France were both at work. Once they got there, there was the inevitable waiting, x-rays, more waiting, and a minor surgical procedure to clean the wound.

The hours passed quickly. Through it all, they sat together holding hands and talking. They shared stories of their families, both the good and the bad. Niki helped Luc understand her unique bond with Sam, and how it wasn't all about protecting him and worrying about him. When he wasn't under pressure, Sam was remarkable, brilliant and funny. They had a special love that was deep, and in a way her childhood was redeemed by that.

"Tell me about the day he died," prompted Luc. They'd given her some pain medication, and it relaxed her, her muscles gone soft.

"It was the day after," she began. "That incident in the gym washroom, when I'd found him cowering."

He squeezed her hand, encouraging her to go on.

"Mom was working the night shift, not home yet." Niki shifted, rolling from one hip to the other. "I knew he'd had a bad time, but not worse than so many others. I thought maybe we would skip school that day. But I still went to his room to get him up. It's what I did every day."

Luc waited when she went silent, her mind a million miles away, seeing what she saw that day.

Niki swallowed, and swallowed again, and his own throat tightened in sympathy. Her lips trembled, but she pushed through. "He was so pale, the air in the room so still. No breath. I knew right away that something was wrong. There were orange peels all around, on the sheets. He'd had seizures and vomited. And the smell was strong in the morning sun." She shuddered, stiffening.

Luc pulled her head closer and pressed his lips to her temple.

"He loved oranges. We were always eating them." She shook her head. "He must have got up and got himself a snack. His final meal. His favourite thing before… And then he took pills. Mom's diazepam, a pile of acetaminophen, cough syrup, and other stuff. He was smart. I think he knew what he was doing. Probably researched it online."

"He'd had enough," Luc offered.

She nodded. "I didn't see it coming. I was so used to just… coping. I didn't see that he wasn't… he wasn't able to…"

Luc held her while she cried, his thoughts swirling around the events of her life, and how she'd carried on. "What about afterwards?"

Niki explained how she'd already felt responsible, and then when her mother, in her own distress, blamed her, and shut her out, it reinforced her belief, and compounded her own grief. Her relationship with her mother had never been good, but after Sam's death, deteriorated. Her father never even came to his funeral. In time she understood that no one person could compensate for Sam's challenges, and that if anyone could have done more, it was her parents. Or the system, but there never had been much support. Her mother did her best, she supposed, under the circumstances, but her father was a selfish coward and she was glad he'd left.

Luc almost felt guilty sharing how idyllic his own family life had been, and told her something about his remarkable parents, each of his sisters, their husbands and children. The three nieces he'd mentioned, and one nephew. His parents' love for each other was so incredible and true it created a bubble of happiness around them all growing up. He confessed that he'd always felt marginalized, despite the caring companionship of his family, as though he sensed they had something even more special. After they died, seven and eight years ago, tragically young, and both his sisters married, he'd felt so alone. He realized he'd been struggling to recreate a place that made him feel as loved and safe and come up short. Not having found the one person of his own that he could connect with in that special way had left him feeling discontent and lonely.

Until he'd met her.

They also filled each other in about their work, their homes, friends and activities. They didn't live all that far from each other, and had probably crossed paths many times, never knowing that their destiny was within reach.

By that time Didier could meet them and take them back to the farm where, after making Niki comfortable and safe, and slapping Luc on the back in some ambiguous mix of praise and sympathy, he left them alone to go work on her bike in the shop. He said little about her mishap, understanding they needed privacy. And at some point Luc heard his truck rumble out of the drive.

Niki's injuries and the ordeal of the day exhausted her. As much the emotional challenges, Luc suspected, as the physical. They were both drained. She fell asleep, and they lay together. He stayed the night, holding her, watching her, for hours. And luxuriating in his own relief and happiness at having his love in his arms once again.

When later she stirred awake, they talked again in whispers, kissing and caressing that in turn led to tongues, gentle bites, heated bodies and heavy breathing and eventually to intense but low-key lovemaking. They shed a few more tears, and then slept, comfortable knowing that tomorrow would be a better day. The first of many better days as their future together unfurled.

EPILOGUE

The next day, Niki and Luc prepared to depart so they could spend the last days of their summer vacation exploring Bordeaux before flying back to Canada and their respective jobs. Luc had favourite places he was eager to share with her, and Niki wanted to reconnect with Alain, Sabine and Rocco one last time. He was ready to go, and Niki had little to pack. Though her new wound needed time to heal, rather than wait another day, they chose to take their time and cycle slowly, enjoying the countryside, stopping often to rest, excited to be moving toward their future.

In the morning, Didier brought out her repaired bike. He explained what he'd straightened and replaced, and she took it for a test drive up and down the lane, making minor adjustments. Considering all it had suffered, it was in decent working condition. Just like her.

To save time, Luc called Charles, and arranged for his closest friends to rendezvous in the village for a final farewell. Though he'd already said his *au revoirs* yesterday, everything had changed since then, and it seemed improper to leave without acknowledging their new situation.

Didier had beat them to it, spreading the news of Niki's second accident, her reunion with Luc, and their plans to leave together. Everyone stood outside waiting when they arrived. They'd left their bikes and panniers in Didier's truck at the parking lot and hiked up through the main gate to the Place des Arcades. Well, Luc and Didier hiked, while

Niki rode on Didier's shoulders to spare her sore leg. One last hurrah for the monkey and giraffe, they joked. They picked up Amélie at her door, and she joined them.

A cheer rose as they entered the square, so unlike yesterday's sombre mood as Luc had made his rounds. From her elevated position, Niki could scan the smiling faces of the residents. Charles and Luc embraced, with much back-slapping, and Niki imagined that they exchanged teasing and congratulations. Her heart melted to see how welcoming and affectionate they all were, and she felt blessed to be a part of this little community of villagers. The thought of returning next year with Luc, and seeing them all again, had great appeal. She leaned forward, stomach fluttering, wondering what would happen between now and then. Niki had never sat perched on the precipice of such change. In this moment she savoured a new breathless excitement for the thrills to come. Just before Didier lifted her from his shoulders to set her beside Luc, she caught the dark and twinkling eye of *Grand-Mère* Bougie, whose weathered face creased into a broad toothless smile as she winked and turned away.

~

Want to read the First Book in the Having it All Series?
Buy Ebook on Amazon : getbook.at/Enchantment

Want to connect with me?
www.maryannclarkescott.com
maryann@maryannclarkescott.com

If you enjoy reading this book, please rate it and leave a review on Amazon HERE. Your opinion can make or break an author's success, and it means the world to me.
Go here to leave a review: mybook.to/Forged

~

THANK YOU

This time my many thanks must begin with the wonderful supportive people who are part of The Creative Academy. First to Crystal

Stranaghan, Donna Barker and Eileen Cook, each a masterful mentor and teacher in their own right. But equally to all the members of The Creative Academy community who show up every day, share their triumphs, troubles and tears, and keep the process of being a writer stimulating, meaningful and fun, and never lonely or desperate. To my tribe I lift my glass in thanks. Together we write.

    Thank you to my developmental editor Amanda Bidnall for her insightful comments and suggestions, as well as beta and proofreaders Jenny, Natasha, and Leslie for catching errors. Any remaining fall at my feet. Thank you also to my enthusiastic Advance Readers for being the first to read and write reviews for my new book. Without an audience, a writer would soon lose interest in telling stories, so thank you for your continued support. You keep it fun. Finally, thanks again to Gabrielle Prendergast for designing a truly beautiful cover for Niki, Luc and Didier's story that is a happy companion to The Art of Enchantment. As always, to my family, who continue to indulge my passion–Thank you.

XO, MaryAnn

ABOUT THE AUTHOR

 **MaryAnn Clarke** set out to write engaging stories that walk a tight rope between heart-warming Romance and intelligent Women's Fiction, and it's caused her nothing but trouble since, beginning with what to call it. In truth, she writes stories about women healing form past wounds as they define and achieve their own personal happily ever afters.

MaryAnn Clarke Scott is a Chatelaine Grand Prize winner for The Art of Enchantment, first in the Life is a Journey series of romantic women's fiction about young women abroad who discover themselves and fall in love while getting embroiled in other people's problems. Reconcilable Differences is first in the Having It All series about professional women in Vancouver struggling to balance the challenge and fulfillment of career with the search for identity, love, family and home. She also loves to weave dramatic relationships into steampunk and cyberpunk adventures.

She's been an architect, a gerontologist, a telephone operator, a dental hygienist, and an education savings advisor. When not writing, she meditates while hiking wooded mountain trails, does yoga and Pilates to fend off decrepitude, reads eclectically, contemplates wormholes, experiments with painting abstract expressionism, kills plants and tries not to burn dinner. Clarke Scott lives on beautiful Vancouver Island, Canada with her husband and a few small mammals. Although she knows she lives in Paradise, she still loves traveling the world in search of romance, art, good food and new story ideas.

Want to receive a FREE book? Join MaryAnn's mailing list to get all new and exclusive Single Dad in Studio 7D. Stay in touch to hear book news, special deals and updates about next release- Before You Knew Me, Book 3 in the Having it All Series and new projects. Get the book HERE.

You can read more about MaryAnn, her books and ideas that strike her fancy at www.maryannclarkescott.com.
Want to read the First Book in the Life is a Journey Series?

Buy on Amazon ASIN: B07R8LJV14

Want to connect with me?
www.maryannclarkescott.com
maryann@maryannclarkescott.com

If you enjoy reading this book, please rate it and leave a review on Amazon HERE. Your opinion can make or break an author's success, and it means the world to me.
Go here to leave a review: mybook.to/Forged

Subscribe & Follow MACS!
www.maryannclarkescott.com
Question? Fan mail? Sure, you can reach me here.

ALSO BY MARYANN CLARKE

Be Mine This Time

Disruption by Design

The Art of Enchantment

To read a sample of Book 1 a in the Life is a Journey series, turn the page…

THE ART OF ENCHANTMENT ~ SAMPLE

Religion. Rebellion. Sex. It had the makings of a best-seller. Clio hummed and danced her fingers on the steering wheel of her new Fiat 500 as she zoomed along *Strada Provinciale* 88. Everything in her dreary, fettered life was about to change.

A line of twisted cypress trees stood at attention along the crest of a nearby ridge. Like the statues of her beloved Italian saints, they kept watch over the neatly mown fields that rolled down the slope toward her. Maybe they were watching over her, too.

Clio was tortured by doubts that her ideas would gel in time for the critical meeting tonight, at which she must, she *must,* persuade Dr. Jovi that she was ready. If she failed, he would refuse to extend her deadline in the morning - again. If he did that, she would find herself cut loose, without an advisor, without an office or a sponsor, without a Ph.D., and forever without the approval of her patient but demanding academic parents.

Some people would be critical of Clio's need, at twenty-seven years of age, to please her mother and father. Those people had never met her parents.

She was out of time.

Until she'd seen the little statue of Saint Clare of the Cross at the Franciscan Monastery this afternoon, Clio despaired of ever having the clarity of vision to complete her thesis. Oh - she'd come up with a half-baked theory that had sustained her research for the past three years. But Saint Clare had convinced her that she really was onto something, and that would give her the passion and drive to write her final dissertation. Passion. Ecstasy. Bliss.

She laughed out loud. How ironic. She needed passion to complete her thesis about passion.

Long shadows snaked across the green hillside as the early evening sun dipped lower in the Tuscan sky. She would be back in the city within the hour, and still have time to freshen up and go over her notes and sketches before her eight o'clock dinner appointment with Dr. Jovi.

Nevertheless, Clio pressed a little harder on the gas pedal, and leaned into a long curve in the road, thrilled at how smooth and responsive her new car was to her command. The gift from Father was clearly meant as an incentive, and she would make sure he received her long overdue thanks - in the form of graduation, at long last.

Then, free from his prescriptions for her education and her career, she could finally decide how she wanted to live her life.

A pair of headlights flashed over the rise in the dimming light up ahead, and Clio slowed a little, prepared to pass another vehicle on the narrow winding road. The other car took shape suddenly in the gloom, larger than hers. Waves of loud music rolled toward her, punctuated by sharp shouts and laughter. Her pulse kicked. They weren't slowing or pulling to the side, the maniacs. Some young idiots, probably drinking.

Clio gripped the steering wheel tighter, and seconds later they were upon her, hogging the centre of the road. There was no room.

She veered sharply to the right as the car hurtled past with inches to spare. Violent grinding and metallic screeching ripped the air as her wheels slammed into the low barrier at the side of the road. The steering wheel tore from her grip. Her car was hurled up like a stone from a catapult.

Everything blurred. Light and dark flashed. The seatbelt jerked her hard against the seat. Air whooshed from her lungs. Squeals. Crunches. Thuds. The world quaked. Sharp pain shot through her head. Dark and silence enveloped her. Music and shouts echoed in her head, a sickening counterpoint to the terrible drumbeat of her heart.

Guillermo didn't mind riding out to Pia's farm for the weekend, though he was certain he'd have more fun if he'd stayed in Florence and taken Teresa or Patrizia out for wining and dining, followed by a little after-dark gymnastics. Or Teresa *and* Patrizia. Now there was a thought that warmed him. He shimmied on his seat to adjust his suddenly tight bike leathers, the powerful engine of his Ducati Multistrada vibrating between his legs.

A dark car whizzed past him on the empty road, nearly knocking him over with the sheer turbulence of its draft, loud music blaring. *Faccia di merda.*

He was positive he'd have more fun if he were at liberty to ride for the sheer joy of it, with no destination. There was nothing he loved more than a fast ride on his bike through the rolling Tuscan countryside, or failing that, in his Alpha Romeo convertible, the wind in his face, his blood thrumming. Nothing made him feel more free and alive.

But duty called. Bianca was uncharacteristically hysterical when she'd called this afternoon, and he was genuinely concerned about his little sister. She was also nearly incoherent, sobbing and ranting something about their eldest brother Jacopo. His calls to Jacopo went unanswered, not surprisingly, since his big-shot politician of a brother was always in a meeting or press conference.

A phone call to his older sister Pia for answers resulted only in an invitation to join her and Paulo for the weekend. She'd been evasive, and said she'd explain when he arrived. And so he'd dropped everything and raced out of the city after work.

For as much as he loved freedom and speed and good times, he loved his family more. And though the knowledge often felt like a heavy yoke around his neck, he knew he'd do anything for them, even if it killed him.

Buy The Art of Enchantment Now!

Join my VIP Readers list to stay informed about my latest release!

www.ingramcontent.com/pod-product-compliance
Lightning Source LLC
Chambersburg PA
CBHW020519080526
44583CB00013B/657